TRADE LIBERALISATION: GLOBAL ECONOMIC IMPLICATIONS

By
Ian Goldin, Odin Knudsen and Dominique van der Mensbrugghe

ORGANISATION FOR ECONOMIC CO-OPERATION AND DEVELOPMENT
THE WORLD BANK

ORGANISATION FOR ECONOMIC CO-OPERATION AND DEVELOPMENT

Pursuant to Article 1 of the Convention signed in Paris on 14th December 1960, and which came into force on 30th September 1961, the Organisation for Economic Co-operation and Development (OECD) shall promote policies designed:

— to achieve the highest sustainable economic growth and employment and a rising standard of living in Member countries, while maintaining financial stability, and thus to contribute to the development of the world economy;
— to contribute to sound economic expansion in Member as well as non-member countries in the process of economic development; and
— to contribute to the expansion of world trade on a multilateral, non-discriminatory basis in accordance with international obligations.

The original Member countries of the OECD are Austria, Belgium, Canada, Denmark, France, Germany, Greece, Iceland, Ireland, Italy, Luxembourg, the Netherlands, Norway, Portugal, Spain, Sweden, Switzerland, Turkey, the United Kingdom and the United States. The following countries became Members subsequently through accession at the dates indicated hereafter: Japan (28th April 1964), Finland (28th January 1969), Australia (7th June 1971) and New Zealand (29th May 1973). The Commission of the European Communities takes part in the work of the OECD (Article 13 of the OECD Convention).

24

The Development Centre of the Organisation for Economic Co-operation and Development was established by decision of the OECD Council on 23rd October 1962.

The purpose of the Centre is to bring together the knowledge and experience available in Member countries of both economic development and the formulation and execution of general economic policies; to adapt such knowledge and experience to the actual needs of countries or regions in the process of development and to put the results at the disposal of the countries by appropriate means.

The Centre has a special and autonomous position within the OECD which enables it to enjoy scientific independence in the execution of its task. Nevertheless, the Centre can draw upon the experience and knowledge available in the OECD in the development field.

The World Bank is a multilateral development institution whose purpose is to assist its developing member countries further their economic and social progress so that their people may live better and fuller lives. It does so through three related functions: lending funds, providing economic advice and technical assistance, and serving as a catalyst for investment by others.

Publié en français sous le titre :
LIBÉRALISATION DES ÉCHANGES :
CONSÉQUENCES POUR L'ÉCONOMIE MONDIALE

Reprinted, 1993

Foreword

This book is the result of a research collaboration, begun in 1989, between the World Bank and the OECD Development Centre as part of each institution's research on agricultural policy, developing country trade, and international economic trends.

ALSO AVAILABLE

Agricultural Trade Liberalization. Implications for Developing Countries *edited by Ian Goldin, Odin Knudsen.* Series Development Centre Seminars (1990)
(41 90 04 1) ISBN 92-64-13366-6 FF180 £18.00 US$32.95 DM60

Biotechnology and Developing Country Agriculture: The Case of Maize *by Carliene Brenner.* Series Development Centre Studies (1991)
(41 91 14 1) ISBN 92-64-13595-2 FF100 £13.00 US$24.00 DM39

The Future of Agriculture: Developing Country Implications *by Martin Brown, Ian Goldin.* Series Development Centre Studies (1992)
(41 92 02 1) ISBN 92-64-13628-2 FF160 £20.00 US$38.00 DM62

Prices charged at the OECD Bookshop.

THE OECD CATALOGUE OF PUBLICATIONS and supplements will be sent free of charge on request addressed either to OECD Publications Service, or to the OECD Distributor in your country.

Table of Contents

List of Tables and Figures

Preface *

In their research activities, the OECD Development Centre and the World Bank try to identify and analyse the policies which may contribute to sustainable and equitable growth. In 1989, the two institutions joined hands to review the state of the existing knowledge concerning analysis of agricultural trade liberalisation and its impact, particularly on developing countries. The resulting best-seller, "Agricultural Trade Liberalisation: Implications for Developing Countries", edited by Ian Goldin and Odin Knudsen, highlighted the value of agricultural trade modelling. Significant shortcomings in the modelling of the effects of global reforms were nevertheless identified, not least with respect to the incorporation of developing countries in a global, economy-wide perspective.

In 1990, the OECD Development Centre and the World Bank decided to develop the Rural/Urban-North/South (RUNS) global general equilibrium model and simultaneously to commission a series of country models, with a view to gaining insights into international, regional and national impacts of trade liberalisation on agricultural development and food security. A complementary volume entitled "Modelling Economy-Wide Reforms" provides a synthesis of the country modelling work, while this joint volume provides the international perspective and examines the global implications of the economic reforms currently underway in developing and formerly centrally planned economies. It provides estimates of the income and other gains from trade liberalisation and evaluates the costs of protectionism.

The RUNS model is "general equilibrium" and aims to capture both the national and international dimensions to economic reforms. The entire world economy is modeled and disaggregated into 22 regions and 20 economic sectors. This book represents the "state of the art" in the modelling of global economic interactions. Simulations using the RUNS model provide insights into the implications of alternative reform scenarios and a quantitative basis for evaluating economic policy options.

---

* Ian Goldin is senior economist at the World Bank and formerly Head of Programme at the OECD Development Centre, Odin Knudsen is Division Chief at the World Bank. Dominique van der Mensbrugghe is an economist at the OECD Development Centre.

The conclusions are striking. For example, full multilateral trade reform yields over $450 billion per year. While the highly protected OECD countries benefit most from opening their economies, developing countries and formerly centrally planned economies also enjoy gains of over $200 billion, equivalent to four times the level of official development assistance. In the case of multilateral trade reform, the potential losers are mainly food-importing countries which suffer from higher world prices. Their legitimate concerns need to be addressed in order to ensure that the gains from liberalisation and from a levelling of the economic playing field accrue to those whose livelihoods are most threatened by existing protectionist policies, notably poor people in poor countries.

Jean Bonvin
Director
Development Centre
OECD
Paris

Michel Petit
Director
Agriculture and Rural Development
World Bank
Washington

May 1993

Acknowledgements

The authors are indebted to a large number of individuals who have contributed to the OECD Development Centre-World Bank trade liberalisation project. Among those who have assisted in this collaborative activity, the results of which are evident in this volume and in the companion volume which analyses trade liberalisation at the country level, we would particularly like to thank the following individuals: Kym Anderson, Paul Armington, Malcolm Bale, Hans Binswanger, Gillian Blakeley, Richard Blackhurst, David Blandford, Jean Bonvin, François Bourguignon, Colin Bradford, António Brandão, Arishay Braverman, Carliene Brenner, Martin Brown, Mary Burfisher, Jean-Marc Burniaux, Csaba Csaki, Alain de Janvry, Jaime de Melo, Sébastien Dessus, Shanta Devarajan, Joe Dewbre, Ron Duncan, Louis Emmerij, David Evans, Gershon Feder, Colm Foy, Tom Hertel, Bob King, Sandra Lloyd, Ramón Lopez, Steven Mageira, John Martin, Will Martin, Knud Munk, Catherine Nallet, David Naudé, Sheila Page, Arvind Panagariya, Michel Petit, Sherman Robinson, David Roland-Holst, Vernon Roningen, Elisabeth Sadoulet, Albert Simantov, Karen Thierfelder, Marino Rsigas, Alberto Valdés, Jean Waelbroeck, Frank Wolter.

The financial support of the OECD Development Centre, the World Bank Research Committee, the Finnish and Swiss Governments and the Rockefeller Foundation is gratefully acknowledged. The opinions expressed in this volume are the sole responsibility of the authors and do not necessarily reflect those of any institution or government.

List of Abbreviations

AGE	applied general equilibrium (model)
CAP	Common Agricultural Policy (of the European Community)
CES	constant elasticity of substitution
CET	constant elasticity of transformation
CGE	computable general equilibrium (model)
CSE	consumer subsidy equivalent
CV	compensating variation
EC	European Community
EFTA	European Free Trade Area
ELES	extended linear expenditure system
EP	export promotion
EV	equivalent variation
FAO	Food and Agriculture Organization of the United Nations
FCPE	former centrally planned economies
FSU	former Soviet Union
GATT	General Agreement on Tariffs and Trade
IFPRI	International Food Policy Research Institute
IIASA	International Institute for Applied Systems Analysis (model)
IMF	International Monetary Fund
IS	import substitution
LES	linear expenditure system
NIE	newly industrialising economies
OECD	Organisation for Economic Co-operation and Development
PSE	producer subsidy equivalent
RUNS	Rural/Urban-North/South (model)
SAM	social accounting matrix
USDA	United States Department of Agriculture
WALRAS	World Agriculture Liberalisation Study (model)

Executive Summary

The purpose of this book is to use model simulations to explore the implications of further trade liberalisation as envisaged under the Uruguay Round and to examine other dominant issues in world trade, including the effects of the opening up of the Soviet Union and China and technological change.

Outline of the book

In Chapter 1 we provide an introduction to the issues of trade liberalisation and to the background of the modelling project. The following chapters develop the simulations that form the basis for assessing the implications of trade liberalisation. Chapter 2 describes the main elements of the Rural/Urban-North/South (RUNS) model as well as presenting the levels of protection, both agricultural and non-agricultural, across the world. Chapter 3 provides the core simulations of the volume. The RUNS model is used to assess the impact of partial trade reform, similar to what is likely to occur at a successful conclusion of the Uruguay Round. A second simulation is performed to assess the impact of complete global trade reform, which indicates the maximum potential benefit for the world from a distortion free global economy. The effects of agricultural and non-agricultural trade reform are assessed separately in order to decompose the role of protection in each of the two sectors separately.

The quantitative analysis using the RUNS model clearly demonstrates the effects of protectionism. World prices, trade patterns, trade volumes, and the global distribution of production are all distorted, and lead to an inefficient allocation of resources, both within and across countries. The aggregate measure of these distortions could be $450 billion (in 1992 dollars) or more per annum, or roughly half the income of the less developed countries having a population of three billion people. Partial trade reform, as envisaged by the Uruguay Round, would add around $213 billion (1992 dollars) per annum to world income, or about 50 per cent of the income of China.

The probable increase in the world price for cereals and other main temperate products may stimulate production of developing countries **only if** a range of policy measures are taken. These include: *(i)* passing on the rise in world agricultural prices to domestic farmers and *(ii)* improving yields through enhancing technologies, storage facilities, distribution, and other related infrastructure. In such a situation, the negative impact of higher world price on food-deficit countries could be dampened and could even lead to a reduction in food imports because of expanded domestic production. Chapter 3 also deals with some of the specific problems of the developing countries. Chapter 3 introduces some of the issues and presents the global results of several simulations common to all of the regions. In addition, Chapter 3 introduces unemployment into the RUNS model. This is seen as a key aspect of the distributional problems between the rural and urban sectors. The real wage, relative to the price of the urban food budget, has proven to be a key factor in the success or failure of internal structural reform, as demonstrated by the numerous food riots in different developing countries. A rise in the world price of food can be detrimental to countries if this implies a rise in urban unemployment. In many countries, this can be alleviated by higher rural incomes which lead to less rural-to-urban migration and higher rural consumption of both urban consumer and investment goods.

Following Chapter 3, five chapters explore the specific regional effects of liberalisation on the developing country regions. Chapter 4 concentrates on Latin America which is divided into three components in the RUNS model. Agriculture has played a significant role in Latin American development and has been an economic stabilizer in bad times. Latin America is also significantly industrialised, though traditionally with high rates of protection. Latin America has been a major producer of tropical products such as coffee, cocoa, and fruits, as well as temperate products such as cereals. It has a vital stake in the outcome of the Uruguay Round and many of the larger countries have joined the influential Cairns Group of agricultural exporting nations. The simulations show that Latin America has much to gain from trade reform, but that partial trade reform will lead to only mixed results across nations and across sectors. Brazil is in a precarious position because it has had significant protection of its urban sector, high protection of cereals, and taxes tropical crops and livestock. Partial reform leads to a drop in both rural and urban incomes. Full reform, multilateral or unilateral, leads to significant improvement in real incomes in all of Latin America. In all reform scenarios, the rural-to-urban income disparities decrease, leading to an improvement in income distribution. Higher growth of OECD countries, though having a positive effect on Latin American growth, has only a weak impact, implying a small transmission effect. Finally, an increase in foreign transfers to Latin America provide a boost to Latin American growth.

Chapter 5 continues the regional exploration of consequences but focusing on Africa. Africa is of special concern because of its inability to attain significantly positive per capita growth rates, its dependence on a few key primary commodity exports and its reliance on food imports. The consensus is that prospects for Africa for the next 10 years will not change this picture very much. In the chapter, simulations which might modify this pessimistic prognosis for Africa are discussed. Trade reform, while beneficial, helps the urban sector most. Under full liberalisation, Africa can expect to gain at least 6 per cent in real income, but the consequences on income distribution are uneven. An increase in net transfers of $12 billion per year would provide a greater boost, with real income improving by over 7 per cent. Higher OECD growth provides only marginal benefit to Africa.

Chapter 6 examines one of the principal concerns of some of the African and Latin American food-importing countries. These countries fear that their reform efforts will be associated with a deterioration in their terms of trade. Countries which rely significantly on the export of a single commodity crop, such as coffee or cocoa, need to evaluate the extent to which reductions in taxes and other reform measures may lead to increased export volumes, and whether these will, in turn, be translated into higher total export revenues. Where the price of the exports declines as a result of the improved performance, a so-called fallacy of composition in policy advice may exist. Chapter 6 provides a quantitative assessment of this issue and through modelling experiments examines the dimensions of the problems facing tropical product exporters in Latin America and Africa.

Chapter 7 is devoted to Asia and focuses on China and India. Together these countries represent over 40 per cent of the world's population. While their potential as agricultural producers is of course significant, their comparative advantage may lie more in manufacturing. However, given the size of their populations, they will play a greater role in agricultural markets as consumers. The RUNS' projections show, for example, that China's self-sufficiency rate in crops is expected to drop from 100 per cent in 1985, to 87 per cent in 2002, though it will be greater than 100 per cent in livestock. Reform would modify this picture. As rural taxation is diminished, incentives to produce would increase. In all trade reform scenarios, there is a large increase in the rural-to-urban income parity in China, which leads to a significant improvement in income distribution. Trade reform does not have tremendous impact on the Indian economy. Agricultural production is diversified, so that some farmers benefit from higher world prices while others, particularly rice farmers, lose from a reduction in the world price of rice. However, the direct and indirect taxation of the rural sector is significant, and trade reform leads to a significant improvement in income distribution.

The profound changes taking place in the former Soviet Union are examined in Chapter 8. This final regional analysis considers the specific role of the former Soviet Union in world trade and considers the impact of alternative scenarios regarding the reform of the regional economy on world markets. Internal reform could lead to a substantial boost to agricultural output, and a decline in the demand for agricultural products in the former Soviet Union. While this will reduce agricultural export markets for the rest of the world, it will relax the former Soviet Union's balance-of-payments constraint, enabling it to purchase much higher levels of manufactured goods from the OECD countries and elsewhere. These reforms would lead to higher world income as each country reveals its comparative advantages.

These regional chapters show the importance of the global effects of trade reform as changes in world prices are transmitted to individual countries. They also show the importance of the links between the rural and urban economies. While higher food prices can be detrimental to the urban sector, they benefit the rural sector. The negative effects on the urban sector can be mitigated by several factors: stronger rural demand for manufactured goods, a reduction in rural-to-urban migration, a reduction in manufactured goods' prices due to lower import tariffs, and a relative shift to urban goods as the price of food increases relative to the price of urban goods.

Chapter 9 relaxes the assumption of exogenous agricultural productivity. Agricultural productivity is linked directly to agricultural profitability. Compared to exogenous technological change, induced technological change will have a different effect on world food prices resulting from trade liberalisation. In general, developing countries will benefit more from trade reform with induced technological change, as farmers respond even more strongly to higher world food prices, than in the situation with exogenous productivity. This chapter attempts to show the importance of introducing a link between profitability and changes in productivity. However, it is recognised that this link cannot simply be reduced to a price transmission mechanism, but that it requires substantial investment in research, infrastructure, and education.

Policy Conclusions

The concluding chapter draws together the results of the simulations and analysis and points to an agenda for further research and policy analysis. The contrast between trade liberalisation theory and practice in the industrialised countries is striking. Whereas OECD Member countries unanimously endorse liberalisation as an economic ideology, their trade practices point in the opposite direction. Formerly centrally planned economies and developing countries, which in the past have been seen as more protectionist, have been making major reform efforts. Their remarkable courage in undertaking economic adjustments is now threatened by the failure of the industrialised countries to undertake reciprocal measures. The industrialised countries are expected to gain most from a liberalisation agreement because their economies are currently most distorted by protectionism. However, from a development and poverty-alleviation perspective, the former centrally planned and developing countries stand to suffer most from a continuation or, worse still, intensification of protectionism.

Food importers, as we have noted, stand to lose the most from the higher world prices which are expected to result from trade liberalisation. These countries have nevertheless remained resolute in their support for the Uruguay Round, concentrating their efforts on securing concessions which will insulate their consumers from the possible negative consequences of higher prices. Their legitimate fears should be recognised and appropriate mechanisms be developed to alleviate the temporary hardships resulting from liberalisation.

It is noteworthy that both the wealthiest and the poorest participating countries are food importers. However, the wealthiest countries, which cannot conceivably suffer a risk of famine, have shielded themselves from liberalisation and defended protectionism behind food security arguments. Developing country food importers, which are most threatened by higher prices, have in contrast embraced trade liberalisation. Their concern has been to ensure a comprehensive approach, so that their potential losses in terms of their food import bills are compensated for by gains in other areas, for example, in textiles.

Growing concern regarding the environment has introduced new issues in the trade debate. It is necessary to consider the effects of trade policies on the environment, and environmental policies on trade. It has been suggested that whichever the starting point, protection of the environment is incompatible with liberalisation. The association of trade liberalisation with environmental degradation is, however, unfortunate and is likely to prove counterproductive not only to economic welfare but also to the environment. What is necessary is to ensure that countries implement policies which improve the environment and that the benefits of trade liberalisation accrue through the development of comparative advantages based on environmentally appropriate patterns of production. In industrialised countries, producers have joined with the increasingly powerful environmental lobbies to frustrate liberalisation. This has negative implications for developing countries since their environmental problems are essentially poverty related;

the eradication of poverty is facilitated by growth and access to industrialised markets. In industrialised countries, environmental degradation is often the result of protectionist distortions. This is particularly notable in agriculture, where, for example, the combination of set-asides and subsidies have served to raise land prices and encourage excessive use of chemicals. Trade policies, *per se*, are not a direct cause of environmental problems. Trade instruments are an extremely blunt tool with which to tackle environmental issues, but trade liberalisation does provide the economic base upon which sustainable environmental policies may be constructed.

The potential gains from freer trade has been one of the factors that has motivated the international community to seek more liberalised trade and to broaden the coverage of the GATT. The simulations from the RUNS model have shown that the gains from even the liberalisation of a relatively minor contributor to most countries' GDP — agriculture — can produce benefits on the order of hundreds of billions of dollars. Full agricultural trade liberalisation, meaning the elimination of all interventions from tariffs to subsidies, could add $430 billion to global annual income. Of this sum, $250 billion would accrue to OECD countries and $180 billion to the rest of the world. Expanding the liberalisation to products where tariffs are already low, such as manufactured products, can produce even more gains. These are conservatively estimated as over $10 billion by the RUNS simulations. Manufacturing liberalisation — defined as the removal of only manufactured good tariffs — would add about $20 billion to the gains from agricultural liberalisation.

Partial liberalization, such as that negotiated in the Uruguay Round, would produce significant gains. The removal of 30 per cent of the tariffs and subsidies for agriculture could yield gains of $190 billion, with the OECD countries accounting for $120 billion of the net gains and developing and formerly centrally planned countries benefiting by $70 billion. An additional 30 per cent liberalisation of manufactured products produces $23 billion more income, with the OECD countries gaining about 64 per cent of the extra benefit derived from manufacturing liberalisation.

There would be losers as well as the gainers from trade liberalisation. Those producers that have been sheltered from competition by trade barriers and have received input subsidies would lose from their elimination, although indirectly there would be compensatory gains from reform elsewhere. Food importers would also suffer as a result of the higher prices projected for a number of cereals. However, improvement of internal and external terms of trade would benefit even those producers no longer benefiting from direct protection and subsidies.

For the losers, the aggregate level of losses are small compared to the gains. For example, the total losses from full agricultural liberalisation would be $21 billion, with most of this impact falling on farmers in OECD countries, although even they, as a result of productivity and overall economic growth, are expected to be better off in 2002 than currently. From partial liberalisation, the losses are small — $2 billion — which is a small fraction of the current $300 billion subsidy given to producers in the OECD countries. Domestic direct income support could easily compensate for these relatively minor losses. Moreover, in some regions, adding the liberalisation of manufactured trade could fully compensate rural producers from the losses of agricultural trade liberalisation. For example, global agricultural trade liberalisation would reduce African rural incomes even though the countries as a whole would gain. The loss of subsidies and the fall of export prices of tree crops would contribute to lower rural income. The beneficiaries would be urban consumers who find lower food prices as domestic protection is reduced. However, full liberalisation of both agricultural and non-agricultural trade results in aggregate real income increases of about 6 per cent compared to the base run and gains in rural value added (except in South Africa, where the (white) farmers have benefited from subsidies) as the secondary effects of improved terms of trade benefit rural producers.

Another potentially important outcome of agricultural trade liberalisation captured by the RUNS model is the impact of endogenous technological change on developing countries. Adding price-induced technological change benefits rural producers in developing countries — increasing the gains from agricultural trade liberalisation by about 40 per cent. However, since producer prices in the OECD countries are lower, the effect of agricultural trade liberalisation is to lower technological progress in these countries, in effect, transferring the productivity gains to developing countries. Despite increased losses in some of the OECD countries from the movement of technological gains from developed to developing countries, the world as a whole is better off, with the losses of rural households in the OECD countries more than offset by the gains elsewhere.

Besides demonstrating the enormous gains from freer trade, the RUNS model has also shown the substantial impact that liberalisation in the former Soviet Union could have on agricultural markets. Unilateral full-price liberalisation and removal of input subsidies in the FSU would cause a fall in most world agricultural prices. The removal of the large consumer subsidies results, in particular, in a decline of meat and dairy product consumption while the elimination of producer distortion leads to only minor changes in domestic production. From the base run, imports into the FSU fall by about $24 billion as a result of domestic liberalisation. When the elimination of processing and distribution losses is added to the initial liberalisation exercise, imports decline further, to about $3 billion. Conceivably, therefore, with domestic productivity increases the former Soviet Union could become an exporter. However, these scenarios would change dramatically if the reforms result in a recovery of overall income growth and hence in food consumption. OECD and developing country exporters of food products for this reason alone have a strong interest in the recovery of income growth in the FSU. Foreign assistance to the FSU is, in essence, an excellent policy for promoting farm product exports for OECD countries.

Many developing countries have learned from hard experience that they cannot afford subsidies and distortions. Trade liberalisation, especially in the reduction of the coverage of quantitative restrictions, has been widespread in developing countries, with 60 countries lowering barriers to imports. Their future depends on a standardized system of international trade like that being offered by the Uruguay Round of the GATT. This book shows that industrial countries could make a substantial contribution to their own development, and also to developing country and global development by following through on their Punta del Este commitment to "halt and reverse protectionism and to remove distortions to trade". The dismal alternative is to leave in place a world trading system that is contrary to the principles of the market system which they profess and under which the OECD economies have prospered. This would deprive their citizens and those of non-OECD countries of potential higher employment and income — in reality, the prospects for enhancing economic development, and with it, greater social harmony.

Chapter 1

Introduction

In 1986, the world trading system reached a critical juncture. After four decades of expanding world trade and reductions in protection, the member nations of The General Agreement on Tariffs and Trade (GATT) met in Punta Del Este, Uruguay and agreed to expand substantially the coverage of the rules that had governed and sustained the expansion of manufactured goods in trade. The agreed scope of trade negotiations that launched the Uruguay Round included sectors with substantial restrictions to trade — such as agriculture and textiles — and attempted to address troublesome but important new areas such as services and intellectual property rights. The goals of the Uruguay Round went well beyond those of previous trade negotiations, thus involving the most complex multilateral negotiations ever undertaken. This was a situation in which the potential for major gains increased the risk of failure.

The purpose of this book is to use model simulations to explore the implications of further trade liberalisation as envisaged under the Uruguay Round and to examine other leading issues in world trade, including the effects of the opening up of the Soviet Union and China and technological change. To provide the background for this examination of trade issues, this introductory chapter will present the institutional framework governing international trade and introduce several issues important for understanding the context of the simulations. The chapter will also present the modelling approach selected and the limitations involved in using simulations to quantify effects of major policy and structural changes.

The GATT

GATT is the basis for a global rule-based trading system. Members agree to treat each other equally and to reduce barriers to trade. The tariff concessions are linked to **non-discrimination** through the principle of **most-favoured nation** (MFN) treatment. Through tariff concessions, contracting countries reduce the tariffs imposed on imports from other GATT signatories, while the MFN rule obliges contracting states to extend to other GATT signatories the most favourable trade treatment accorded to an individual country[1]. These non-discriminatory rules are critical to the developing countries and those with formerly centrally planned economies whose future growth depends on access to industrialised markets[2]. The non-discriminatory policies which are at the heart of the GATT, provide a basis for equal treatment with well-established traders. Moreover, the multilateral nature of the GATT, including its procedures for resolving disputes, prevents large countries from exerting undue pressure on smaller countries; the latter can and do use the rules to win equal status with larger countries.

Tariff concessions have been periodically negotiated by the contracting parties through a series of Rounds conducted under the auspices of the GATT. The Uruguay Round is the eighth since the General Agreement came into being. The latest negotiations include areas that previously had been largely or completely excluded, such as services, intellectual property rights and agriculture.

The Uruguay Round has taken place in a difficult economic and political environment. Many participating countries, both developed and developing, are facing a slowdown in growth, rising unemployment, and large domestic and/or international debts. Moreover, in many countries, excess capacity in traditional industries, and intense competitive pressures in these and more modern sectors, such as electronics, from emerging industrial competitors, have provided an impetus for strengthening protectionism. Politically, governments in the industrialised countries appear insecure, with the governing parties or coalitions vulnerable to small swings in support. Meanwhile, the democratic tide sweeping developing and formerly centrally planned economies has meant that competing political claims have imposed added constraints on their governments' ability to negotiate.

Against the background of growing protectionism and politicisation, it is not surprising that, while the previous seven Rounds concentrated on tariff structures for industrial products, the Uruguay Round has also devoted attention to domestic subsidies for agriculture, non-tariff barriers, services, textiles, trade-related investment measures (TRIMs) and trade-related intellectual property rights (TRIPs). Whereas developing countries have much, and perhaps even most, to gain from the negotiations on services, TRIPs, TRIMs, and textiles, the negotiations concerning agriculture have occupied the centre stage[3]. They have also proved to be the major sticking point and source of friction among the industrialised countries.

The Uruguay Round and Agriculture

Successive GATT Rounds have treated agriculture as an exception and it has not been subject to the same discipline as industrial products. Its special treatment from the outset reflected the post-World War II position of the United States not to accept international treaty obligations that would constrain domestic agricultural policy. Despite the heightening of trade frictions, as reflected in the "chicken war" of 1960-61[4], the Dillon Round (1961-1962) failed to address agricultural issues. By the time of the Kennedy Round (1963-1967), the United States regarded the emerging European Community (EC) Common Agricultural Policy (CAP) as a major threat. The current conflict over the CAP was already underway at that time, but the EC only agreed to accept industrial and not agricultural trade liberalisation. The Tokyo Round (1973-1979) involved an intensification of the skirmishes of the Kennedy Round, although the transatlantic conflict continued to be fought through limited bilateral accommodations.

Against a backdrop of growing trade friction, accentuated by balance-of-trade pressures within the United States, and growing budgetary pressures within the EC, and in light of the constellation of major leaders — Reagan, Thatcher, Kohl and Chirac — committed to economic liberalism, pressure mounted for the ending of agriculture's exceptional treatment in the Uruguay Round[5]. Between the 1982 GATT Ministerial meeting and the signing of the Punta del Este Declaration in November 1986, agriculture remained the major source of contention, with the dispute focusing then as now on the transatlantic conflict between the European Community and the United States.

The broadening of the GATT Contracting Parties' ambitions in the Uruguay Round may be understood in the context of the growing international concerns regarding the adverse effects of existing trade practices[6]. In agriculture, rising protectionism in the EC, United States and Japan, has seen a growing juxtaposition between falling world prices and high and rising domestic prices, implying both an increase in costs to consumers and a rise in public expenditures on agricultural subsidies. These and other problems convinced the GATT's contracting countries of the need to "bring more discipline and predictability to world agricultural trade by correcting and preventing restrictions and distortions including those related to structural surpluses so as to reduce the uncertainty, imbalances, and instability in world agricultural markets"[7].

The instability is partly due to increasing domestic subsidies and unfair trade practices. During the 1980s, industrial countries have greatly increased subsidies to agriculture[8] while agricultural trade has been shifting towards bilateral agreements and market-sharing provisions. Moreover, the increasing use of non-tariff barriers (NTBs) has reduced the effectiveness of negotiated tariff reductions. Since the end of the Tokyo Round in 1979, the average level of industrial tariffs in developed countries has fallen by nearly a half to 6.4 per cent and the value of total world merchandise trade has grown by a remarkable 4.8 per cent per year. This growth is mainly confined to the industrialised countries; in the 1980s, developing countries' exports grew by only 1.6 per cent, and their share of world trade fell from 28 to 21 per cent[9].

In part, the explanation for these trends is to be found in the protectionist policies of developed countries, but developing countries have also discriminated against their own agriculture. In these countries, the situation tends to be the mirror image of that in the richer countries, with distortionary policies discriminating against, rather than favouring, agriculture. Many developing countries followed "infant industry" policies in order to promote industrialisation by protecting manufacturing from competitive imports and taxing agricultural producers. In part, this penalisation has occurred through "direct" taxation of agriculture, through tariffs and other means, but "indirect" taxation by overvaluation of exchange rates and other macroeconomic distortions has also served to penalise agriculture[10].

Developing Countries' Concerns

There is increasing divergence between trade liberalisation theory and the practices of the industrialised countries. OECD Member countries unanimously endorse liberalisation as an economic ideology, but their trade practices point in the opposite direction. Formerly centrally planned economies and developing countries, who in the past have been seen as more protectionist, have been making major reform efforts. Their remarkable courage in undertaking economic adjustments are now threatened by the failure of the industrialised countries to undertake reciprocal measures. Since the Uruguay Round was launched in 1986, over 60 developing countries and former centrally planned economies have unilaterally liberalised their trade, but only 12 industrialised nations have responded similarly and only one has undertaken full liberalisation[11]. (N Z)

The industrialised countries are expected to gain most from a liberalisation agreement, because their economies are currently most distorted by protectionism. However, from the perspective of development and alleviating poverty, the former centrally planned and developing countries stand to suffer most from a continuation of or, worse still, increasing protectionism.

At the heart of the GATT, is the principle of non-discrimination, by which all signatory countries commit themselves to provide all other members with most favoured nation (MFN) treatment. Nevertheless, an increasing share of international trade in agricultural products has been conducted on a discriminatory basis. Moreover, in recent years there has been a growing use of non-tariff barriers (NTBs)[12], with these increasingly taking the place of border tariffs. Some 18 per cent of the manufactured imports and 38 per cent of agricultural imports are currently subject to NTBs[13].

In the developed countries NTBs protect domestic producers and processors through a wide assortment of policies restricting trade. Trade is limited directly by quantitative restrictions such as import quotas and voluntary export restraints, while variable levies, minimum entry prices and technical standards have an indirect effect on the volume and price of imports. In developing countries and formerly centrally planned economies, tariffs in the past were combined with import quotas and foreign-exchange rationing to insulate the domestic economy.

Developing countries' particular problems have been acknowledged by the GATT signatory countries since the mid-1950s. Under the "Special and Differential treatment", exports from developing to developed countries under the Generalised System of Preferences (GSP) have been exempted from GATT's MFN requirements. Under the GATT rules, developing countries have been allowed preferential access to developed countries' markets while keeping their own markets relatively closed.

Despite this "special" dispensation, developing countries have in practice been most exposed to discriminatory export restraint agreements and other trade-distorting measures, with the incidence of this discrimination being greatest in those sectors in which they have a comparative advantage, such as agriculture, and textiles. Increasingly, it is developing countries which have engaged in liberalisation, and who are required to liberalise their trade before applying for GATT membership. In this sense, it is the developed countries, not the developing countries, who enjoy exceptional treatment.

The exemption accorded to developing countries from reciprocity, as well as the effective exclusion from earlier negotiations of agricultural products[14], has meant that until the current Round developing countries have tended to be on the sidelines of the GATT. They have tended to concentrate attention on the MFN prerogatives as GATT signatories, rather than on multilateral bargaining, and on bilateral concessions granted by major developed countries or groupings, such as the EC. Previous GATT Rounds have focused on industrial products and have not involved developing countries.

Traditionally, negotiations on agricultural trade have been carried out mainly between the larger developed countries — including the United States, the EC and Japan — and resulted in major trade concessions. During the Uruguay Round, however, other countries, in particular the Cairns Group countries, have taken an active part in GATT discussions[15].

These countries have a large stake in Uruguay Round, with agriculture at the centre stage of the GATT and the increased commitment by developing countries to trade liberalisation. Even the poorest countries have invested large amounts in their participation in the negotiations[16] because of their dependence on agriculture[17], their concerns about growing developed country protectionism, and the threat of regionalisation.

Since 1968, developing countries have mainly relied on the GSP to facilitate trade on a non-reciprocal and non-discriminatory basis. The GSP, however, has come to be regarded by many developing countries as less preferable to preferential arrangements, such as those embodied in the Lomé Convention and the Caribbean Basin Initiative. The poorest countries are particularly sceptical about the GSP as they derive the least benefit from it. In the case of the EC, in 1988 GSP countries saved a total of $1.2 billion on import duties to the EC on exports worth $18.8 billion, but the poorest countries only derived 1 per cent of the benefit. The scheme mainly benefited the exporters of manufactured goods, notably the member countries of the Association of Southeast Asian Nations (ASEAN) and Hong Kong.

Agricultural imports covered by GSP rules account for only 20 per cent of total value of GSP trade of major industrial countries. Furthermore, major consumer countries normally impose import tariff levies which increase according to the degree of processing and value added[18]. Moreover, GSP provisions do not include NTBs, but since the 1980s, developed countries increasingly have used these border measures to insulate domestic agricultural markets. Nevertheless, in previous Rounds negotiated concessions to developing countries have exclusively affected nominal tariff reductions.

Besides the GSP, major developed countries accord preferential entry to most agricultural exports from certain groups of developing countries, for example, under EC agreements with African, Caribbean and Pacific (ACP) countries and Mediterranean countries or US agreements with Caribbean countries and Israel. However, since tropical and other agricultural products are poorly covered by most GSP schemes, GSP preferential tariffs cover only a minor share (40-45 per cent) of agricultural MFN-dutiable exports from least developed countries to industrial countries. Trade in unprocessed tropical products is subject to GATT regulations and these products face relatively low levels of import barriers in OECD countries, with tariffs rising with the degree of processing, in order to protect the industries which process cocoa in the developed countries[19].

Individual developing countries do not all have the same objectives. For example, given existing preferential agreements between the EC and ACP countries, a reduction of EC's MFN or GSP tariffs on tropical products could have a negative impact on the export revenues of most ACP countries[20]. Consequently, the original EC Uruguay Round proposal to reduce both MFN and GSP tariffs has been opposed by ACP countries because they view this as narrowing ACP preferences compared to GSPs.

Developing countries have not adopted a united position, and the objectives of individual developing countries have been quite varied. Two main approaches may nevertheless be identified in recent trade negotiations. The first, supported by Brazil and other exporter countries in the 14-nation Cairns Group, is favourable to agricultural liberalisation but demands reciprocity from industrialised countries and exemptions for developing countries. The second approach, taken by net agricultural importers, such as Egypt, Mexico, Nigeria, Jamaica and Peru, while remaining committed to liberalisation, emphasizes the need for mechanisms to ensure that they do not suffer from budgetary crises or food shortages. The overall approach of developing countries in the Uruguay Round has been to defend the Special and Differential treatment where possible and to extend its rules to the whole final agreement[21].

Instability, Stocks, Food Aid and Food Importers

Whereas border and other interventions may have served to reduce the price instability faced by individual farmers and consumers, these same protectionist policies have served to increase instability in world markets. The effects have been particularly devastating for poorer consumers and producers whose governments have been unable to insulate their countries from global markets in the longer term. Farmers' income and consumers' food security have thus fluctuated over a wider range, forcing them to adopt risk-averse strategies in which savings are higher and investment lower than might be expected in a world of more stable prices. For developing country governments, the effects have been equally severe; sharp variations in the revenues derived from agricultural exports or the costs of food imports have destabilized domestic economies and undermined investment[22].

Price instability on world markets cannot be attributed solely to protectionist policies. In agriculture, climatic variations and speculative activities by large traders and stockholders are also important. Nevertheless, wider and more equitable participation in markets should narrow the range of these activities. In the first place, a wider distribution of production will bring more players into the market, which in itself suggests more stability[23], especially as production will be distributed over a wider climatic range, with Southern and Eastern Hemisphere producers increasing their market shares. Greater participation and more transparency are expected to reduce speculation and lower transaction costs.

Those who argue that existing protectionist policies contribute to food security assert that high stock levels could help meet emergency demands, such as may arise from natural disasters. It should be noted, however, that strategic stocks can be accommodated within free markets through hedging operations, or through non-distortionary international accords, which could be managed through multilateral institutions like the World Food Programme. Stockpiles created by programmes subsidising industrialised country farmers cannot be justified on the basis of their potential use in overcoming emergencies. The link between these stockpiles and the willingness of industrialised donor countries to grant food aid is, however, a matter of concern, because circumstantial evidence suggests that food aid has been seen as a politically acceptable means of disposing of "food mountains".

The long-running debate concerning the effectiveness of food aid involves its possible negative implications for farmer incentives in the recipient countries. Food aid provides a vital function in reducing famine, but the long-run solution to food security lies in improving domestic incomes and food supplies. This calls for policies, including trade policies which promote developing country growth, and particularly the position of farmers in the food-deficit countries. Food aid is a necessary short-term response to famine, but to avert dependence, longer-term policies for sustainable development are necessary. These include reductions in protectionism, improving the competitive position of the developing countries. Industrialised countries should play a greater role in averting starvation by purchases of grains on international markets and in markets neighbouring the countries in need, lowering transport costs and improving incentives for farmers. Linking food aid to farm subsidies in industrialised countries may be politically convenient, but it is not a solution for the world's hungry people.

Food-importing countries, as noted above, stand to lose the most from the higher world prices which are expected to result from a successful completion of the Uruguay Round[24]. These countries have nevertheless remained resolute in their support for the Round, concentrating their efforts on securing concessions which will insulate their consumers from the possible negative consequences of higher prices.

The Net Food Importers' Group[25] have requested special treatment to alleviate the burden of increased prices on the balance of payments of food-importing countries and assistance for enhancing the productive capacity of their own farmers. Their legitimate fears should be recognised and appropriate mechanisms be developed to alleviate the temporary hardships resulting from liberalisation. In particular, the potential for the International Monetary Fund's Compensatory and Contingency Financing Facility to provide balance-of-payments support, the World Bank to provide other financial assistance and the World Food Programme to co-ordinate direct food aid, should be examined as possible elements of a package to deal with adverse effects of liberalisation in vulnerable developing countries.

It is noteworthy that while both the wealthiest and the poorest participants in the Uruguay Round tend to be food importers, it is the wealthiest countries, who cannot conceivably suffer a risk of famine, who use food-security arguments to shield themselves from liberalisation and defend protectionism. In contrast, developing country food importers, who are most threatened by higher prices, have embraced the Round and supported its speedy resolution. Their concern has been to ensure a comprehensive outcome, so that their potential losses in terms of their food import bills are compensated for by gains in other areas, for example, in textiles[26]. This attitude, is indicative of the wider shift in developing countries' views on trade liberalisation.

Trade and the Environment

Growing concern regarding the environment has introduced new issues in the trade debate[27]. It is necessary to consider the effects of trade policies on the environment, and environmental policies on trade. It has been argued that whatever the starting point, protection of the environment is incompatible with liberalisation. Firstly, it is claimed that trade liberalisation, by expanding production and accelerating growth, inevitably has a negative effect on the environment. Secondly, domestic pressures to protect the environment and increasing discrimination against trade in products which are seen to be produced at a lower environmental threshold are likely to be associated with a heightening of non-tariff barriers and "green" conditionalities on trade.

However, policies based on an assumption that trade liberalisation, *per se*, is responsible for environmental degradation are likely to be counterproductive not only for economic welfare but also for the environment. The answer is ensuring that countries implement policies which improve the environment and that the benefits of trade liberalisation accrue through the development of comparative advantages based on environmentally appropriate patterns of production. In industrialised countries, producers have allied with the increasingly powerful environmental lobbies to frustrate liberalisation. This has negative implications for developing countries, as their environmental problems are essentially poverty related; the eradication of poverty is facilitated by growth and access to industrialised markets.

The distortions in domestic resource use resulting from protectionism in the industrialised countries may also have negative environmental implications. This is particularly true in agriculture where, for example, the combination of set-asides and subsidies have served to raise land prices and encourage excessive chemical application. In the EC this situation has already had disastrous consequences on the quality of water, making agriculture a greater polluter of water than industry, even though accounting for less than one-tenth of the economic activity[28].

The environment is a critical concern at the local, national and international levels. Trade policies, like any other economic policies, can have environmental implications. Trade policies, *per se*, are not a direct cause of environmental problems. The resolution of environmental problems depends on the development of effective **environmental** policies. In developing countries and formerly centrally planned economies, environmental problems tend to be the result of domestic policy failures and/or poverty-related factors. Their resolution demands the development of appropriate environmental policies and growth, which is facilitated by trade, as well as international assistance. In industrialised countries, both protectionism and liberalisation may be associated with environmental degradation. Trade instruments are an extremely blunt tool for tackling environmental issues, but trade liberalisation can provide the economic base upon which sustainable environmental policies may be constructed.

The World Bank and OECD Collaboration

During October 1989, in a unique collaboration between the World Bank and the OECD Development Centre, the two institutions attempted to address the potential impact of solutions to the most pressing issue in world trade: agricultural trade reform and, in particular, its implications for developing countries. An international symposium in Paris organised by the two institutions brought together leading researchers on agricultural policy and trade to address the central issue of the Uruguay Round — agricultural trade liberalisation. Using state-of-the-art modelling techniques, these researchers attempted to measure the effects of possible outcomes of the trade negotiations on agriculture. The results of this symposium were published in a volume edited by Ian Goldin and Odin Knudsen, *Agricultural Trade Liberalisation:*

Implications for Developing Countries. The broad conclusion was that developing countries will be among the most seriously affected — positively or negatively — by the outcome of the GATT negotiations.

Although in qualitative terms, this is not a surprising result, given developing countries' dependence on agriculture for income and employment and their heavy reliance on agricultural trade, the magnitudes of these effects were unanticipated, ranging in the hundreds of billions of dollars. The results collected in the volume provided forecasts of the potential effects on prices, production, consumption, trade and welfare from various simulation models developed at that time. While most developing countries were expected to gain from global and full liberalisation of trade, some developing countries — those heavily dependent on imports were expected to loose.

Despite this conclusion, disparities in results existed. Many of the models used for the forecasts were partial and based on old data. Developing countries were not fully modeled and technological change was neglected. Even more important, the models were incomplete; they did not take into account the manufacturing sectors and the possible liberalisation of their traded commodities. As was stated earlier, the Uruguay Round is not just focused on agricultural trade but has important components involving manufacturing and services. These questions are linked in the negotiations, and thus it would be impossible to conceive of an agreement only in agriculture, manufacturing or services. Global trade reform will succeed or fail as a "package". A country which loses in the context of one of the set of reforms might be compensated by gains in another area of trade liberalisation.

The need for addressing agricultural liberalisation in a multi-sector or macroeconomic framework required using general equilibrium models. However, the existing general equilibrium models had several deficiencies. The IIASA model developed by the institute of the same name is based on a series of linked national models, many of which would require extensive updating and modification by the individual country modelers. Although it contains a relatively detailed specification of agriculture, it has a highly aggregated representation of other sectors. The IIASA model has become dated and because of its complexity, size and decentralised structure, is not easily adaptable or modifiable. The WALRAS model developed by the OECD focuses on the OECD countries, not developing countries, and its representation of the agricultural sector and non-OECD countries is also too highly aggregated. Since one of the book's main purposes was to explore the impact of trade liberalisation — in particular, in agricultural products — on developing countries, the WALRAS model was inappropriate.

The RUNS Model

Another model, the RUNS model, originally developed under World Bank sponsorship, was promising. The model had many of the important characteristics needed to explore the impact of agricultural trade liberalisation. It treated the agricultural sector in detail with 13 commodity groups and was fairly disaggregated with, in its original form, eight developing and two developed regions or countries represented. Furthermore, the RUNS model was compact and transparent. It could be developed with less technical and management resources than the other models and appeared more suited to modification and use for policy simulations. In the RUNS model, each country or region was modeled under the same structural framework with the same policy instruments and variables; only the base data were different. In other words, each country had exactly the same sectoral and commodity breakdown and was governed by the same behavioral equations. Once the model of one country or region was understood, the entire world model structure could be known. The major deficiencies were its outdated database and structural relationships that needed to be strengthened and elaborated. Further disaggregation was also required to describe other important countries and regions in agricultural trade and to elaborate the non-agricultural sectors. In addition, it was unable to evaluate some important impacts, including a means of assessing welfare gains or losses under full and partial liberalisation scenarios.

In a subsequent collaborative effort, the OECD Development Centre and the World Bank began the task of updating the RUNS model and further disaggregating it into 16 developing (including the formerly centrally planned economies) and six developed countries or regions. Other structural changes were also made to enrich the model further. As the Uruguay Round continued, the model as it was being refined was used for policy scenarios, resulting in several papers that received wide attention. Furthermore, a parallel research effort attempted to probe deeper into the implications of trade liberalisation through specific and more elaborate country models. The results of this country-based research are reported in the companion volume to this book, *Modelling Economy-Wide Reforms*.

The Limitations of Modelling

In order to place the results of the simulations of the RUNS model in the proper context, it is important to understand the limitations of modelling and how we regard this research effort. Researchers cannot remain mute about the implications of the fundamental structural reforms taking place in developing countries and formerly centrally planned economies and on the interaction between these and OECD country policy changes. In analysing the complex economy-wide and global dimensions of macroeconomic and trade reforms, and not least, the multilateral reforms sought in the Uruguay Round of the GATT, analysts are presented with several options.

One approach is to focus on relatively simple truths that provide insight into the results of various interventions by mathematically tracing the flow of their effect, measuring their impact or testing their mathematical logic econometrically. Much of the literature on agricultural policy follows this path and is valuable in illuminating, in a stylised manner, the effects of individual interventions such as the United States acreage set-aside programme.

Another approach is to measure the amount of distortion by, for example, using coefficients of nominal or effective protection or producer subsidy equivalents. These measures, which have been produced by the OECD, the World Bank, and other institutions, are indicators of the status quo — the degree of distortion caused by existing government policy; they do not give policy makers much information about how the impact of reformed policies would change these coefficients or measure the concurrent welfare impact. Many international organisations, including the OECD and the World Bank, have reported such measures.

A step forward from the measurement of distortions is to use them in rather simple models that simulate the interactions of commodity markets. With this step the demand for information becomes more severe as the operation, responsiveness and interaction of markets need to be determined and modeled. This is usually stylised through sets of own and cross price and income elasticities. The advantage of this partial equilibrium approach is that the theory is well understood and that many of the parameters — the elasticities of price and income — have been measured statistically for many agricultural commodities and over a large set of countries. Its disadvantage is that it misses the full impact and complexity of policy impacts that affect other sectors or the macroeconomy in general. Nevertheless, it has proven to be a valuable tool, not too demanding empirically, and based on a well accepted body of economic theory. Many of the modelling efforts for measuring the potential impact of the Uruguay Round have used this approach.

A further and more demanding step is to close the representation of the agricultural markets with the inclusion of other sectors, resource constraints and other aspects constituting the macroeconomy. Large data sets that stretch resources and the representation of economic structures are now demanded. However, a choice must be made: remaining within the framework of partial equilibrium with its clear limitations or making the more demanding step to full economic representation. If it is believed that the interaction with other sectors or with the general macroeconomic relations is not important then one could well be satisfied with the partial approach. However, if the expected effects of policy change are large, as would be the case with agricultural trade reform, then for credibility and rigor, the next step to general equilibrium becomes necessary. And with this step, the role and art of the modeler becomes more prominent and determinant.

Besides demanding a large body of data describing not only agriculture but other sectors, general equilibrium modelling also requires a solid theoretical base (unless it is done purely econometrically using reduced form equations). The data demand is more or less solvable with enough effort and resources (except for a set of largely behavioral variables that must be chosen and tested later through simulations that attempt to match model results with actual time series of production or macroeconomic variables such as GNP changes). The theoretical requirement tests the veracity of macroeconomic theory, especially with regard to investment behaviour and the capital flows.

General equilibrium models are sensitive to the closure adopted, that is, whether investment drives the model or whether net capital flows (net trade) close it. The driving identity in these models is the relationship that requires investment to be equal to domestic savings plus foreign savings or net capital flows. Domestic savings are usually specified through a consumption function directly relating income and prices to consumption and hence savings. Once domestic savings are determined by income levels and prices, the modeler can specify investment by a functional relationship, exogenously, or set net trade (the mirror image of net capital flows or foreign savings) by a functional form or also exogenously.

Other complications arise, depending on how detailed sectors or macroeconomic relationships are represented. Furthermore, in some models imperfect competition is introduced so that oligopolistic behaviour becomes important. In other words, in concept and practice one can take the general equilibrium model as far as allowed by the theory and/or the data and/or the willingness of the modelers to make assumptions about data or economic relationships.

The RUNS model falls somewhere between the relative simplicity of a partial equilibrium model and a full-blown general equilibrium model that demands extraordinary discretion or assumptions by the modeler. While the agricultural sector is specified in some detail through well-accepted supply and demand relationships rooted in resource constraints and expenditure functions, the other sectors are specified relatively simply and straightforwardly. Furthermore, several variables that would require elaborate modelling or relationships outside of the direct interest of studying agricultural trade are left exogenous, with estimates taken from the results of other models designed to forecast these variables or from World Bank and OECD projections. Macroeconomic results such as economic growth and net trade flows are taken from more powerful macroeconomic models designed to give these variables as outputs. Furthermore, expert opinion and the projections of specific commodity models are used, for example, to drive productivity gains in the base case (the simulation where policy changes are not introduced). Although the RUNS model includes trends derived from other models, these exogenous inputs are checked for consistency in the base simulations. For example, the agricultural productivity projections are examined in the light of competing claims for land and other resources and in the context of the macroeconomic, investment and economic growth constraints. The base line model therefore takes into account the best available knowledge and data. The judgement of the modelers determines consistency. This artistry in building the model rests upon a theoretical base — in the case of this book, that the capital flow results are invariant to the simulations.

The entire procedure is a process best described as empirically based logic. That is, it takes all the available information and data and frames it with mathematical relationships derived from and consistent with economic theory. The particular choice of variables and how they are structurally related are very much the decisions of the modelers.

The resulting model is a product of the judgement and ingenuity of its constructors and the available database — in this case, the available and (in some cases) unpublished data of the World Bank, OECD, FAO, United Nations and other sources. The results of this book reflect the data assumptions and the choices made by the modelers. To emphasize this creative side to the model, we have been transparent in specifying the underlying equations and the data that support the model.

This Book

In this book, we offer the results of the modelling simulations to a wide audience of policy makers and applied economists. A companion volume provides a full technical specification of the model, and includes a full listing of the equations, discussion of the model's properties, and analysis of the sensitivity of the model to the underlying assumptions.

The following chapters develop the simulations that form the basis for assessing the implications of trade liberalisation. Chapter 2 of this volume describes the main elements of the RUNS model as well as presenting the levels of protection, both agricultural and non-agricultural, across the world. While the levels of protection used in the RUNS model may differ somewhat from the levels of 1992, they do represent the broad picture, as it exists today.

Chapter 3 provides the core simulations of the volume. The RUNS model is used to assess the impact of partial trade reform, similar to what is likely to occur at a successful conclusion of the Uruguay Round. A second simulation is performed to assess the impact of complete global trade reform, which indicates the maximum potential benefit for the world from a distortion-free global economy. The effects of agricultural versus non-agricultural trade reform are assessed separately in order to decompose the role of protection in each of the two sectors separately.

The quantitative analysis using the RUNS model clearly demonstrates the effects of protectionism. World prices, trade patterns, trade volumes, and the global distribution of production are all distorted, and lead to an inefficient allocation of resources, both within and across countries. The aggregate measure of these distortions could be $355 billion[29] ($450 billion in 1992 dollars) or more per annum, or roughly half the income of the less developed economies representing a population of 3 billion. Partial trade reform, as envisaged by the Uruguay Round, would add around $165 billion ($213 billion in 1992 dollars) per annum to world income, or about 50 per cent of the income of China.

The probable increase in the world price for cereals and other main temperate products may stimulate production of developing countries **only if** a range of policy measures are taken. These include: (i) passing on the rise in world agricultural prices to domestic farmers and; (ii) improving yields through enhancing technologies, storage facilities, distribution, and other related infrastructure. In such a situation, the negative impact of higher world price on food deficit countries could be dampened and may even lead to a reduction in food imports because of expanded domestic production. Chapter 3 also deals with some of the specific problems of the developing countries. Chapter 3 introduces some of the issues and presents the global results of several simulations common to all of the regions. In addition, Chapter 3 introduces unemployment into the RUNS model. This is seen as a key aspect of the distributional problems between the rural and urban sectors. The real wage, relative to the price of the urban food budget, has proven to be a key factor in the success or failure of internal structural reform, as demonstrated by the numerous food riots in a variety of developing countries. A rise in the world prices of food can be detrimental to countries if this implies a rise in urban unemployment. In many countries, this can be alleviated by higher rural incomes which lead to less rural-to-urban migration and higher rural consumption of both urban consumer and investment goods.

Following Chapter 3, five chapters explore the specific regional effects of liberalisation on the developing country regions. Chapter 4 concentrates on Latin America which is divided into three components in the RUNS model. Agriculture has played an important role in Latin American development, and as an economic stabilizer in bad times. Latin America is also significantly industrialised, though traditionally with high rates of protection. Latin America is a major producer of tropical products such as coffee, cocoa, and fruits, as well as temperate products such as cereals. It has a vital stake in the outcome of the Uruguay Round and many of the larger countries have joined the influential Cairns Group of agricultural exporting nations. The simulations show that Latin America has much to gain from significant trade reform, but that partial trade reform will lead to only mixed results across nations and across sectors. Brazil is in a precarious position because it has had significant protection of its urban sector, high protection of cereals, and taxes tropical crops and livestock. Partial reform leads to a drop in both rural and urban incomes. Full reform, be it multilateral or unilateral, leads to significant improvement in real incomes in all of Latin America. In all reform scenarios, the rural-to-urban income disparities decrease, leading to an improvement in income distribution. Higher growth of OECD countries, though having a positive effect on Latin American growth, has only a weak impact, implying a small transmission effect. Finally, an increase in foreign transfers to Latin America provides an important boost to Latin American growth.

Chapter 5 continues the exploration of regional consequences but focusing on Africa. Africa is of special concern because of its inability to attain significantly positive per capita growth rates, its reliance on a few key primary commodity exports and its reliance on food imports. The consensus is that prospects for Africa for the next 10 years will not change this picture very much. In the chapter, simulations were performed which might modify this pessimistic prognosis for Africa. Trade reform, while beneficial, helps the urban sector most. Under full liberalisation, Africa can expect to gain at least 6 per cent in real income, but the consequences on income distribution are uneven. An increase in net transfers of $12 billion per year would provide a greater boost with real income improving by over 7 per cent. Higher growth in the OECD countries provides only marginal benefit to Africa.

Chapter 6 examines one of the principal concerns of some of the African and Latin American food importing countries. They fear that their reform efforts will be associated with a deterioration in their terms of trade. Countries which rely significantly on the export of a single commodity crop, such as coffee or cocoa, need to evaluate the extent to which reductions in taxes and other reform measures may lead to increased export volumes, and whether these in turn will be translated into higher total export revenues. When the price of the exports declines as a result of the improved performance, a so-called fallacy of composition in policy advice may exist. Chapter 6 provides a quantitative assessment of this issue and uses modelling experiments to examine the dimensions of the problems facing tropical product exporters in Latin America and Africa.

Chapter 7 is devoted to Asia and focuses on China and India. Together these countries represent over 40 per cent of the world's population. While their potential as agricultural producers is of course significant, their comparative advantage may lie more in manufacturing. However, given the size of their populations, they will play a greater role in agricultural markets as consumers. The RUNS' projections show, for example, that China's self-sufficiency rate in crops is expected to drop from 100 per cent in 1985, to 87 per cent in 2002, though it will be greater than 100 per cent in livestock. Reform would modify this picture. As rural taxation is diminished, incentives to produce would increase. In all trade reform scenarios, there is a large increase in the rural-to-urban income ratio in China, which leads to a significant improvement in income distribution. Trade reform does not have a tremendous impact on the Indian economy. Agricultural production is diversified on the one hand, so that some farmers benefit from higher world prices, while others, particularly rice farmers, lose from a reduction in the world price of rice. However, the direct and indirect taxation of the rural sector is significant, and trade reform leads to a significant improvement in income distribution.

The profound changes taking place in the former Soviet Union are examined in Chapter 8. This final regional analysis considers the specific role of the former Soviet Union in world trade and considers the impact of alternative scenarios regarding the reform of the regional economy on world markets. Internal reform could lead to a significant boost in agricultural output and a decline in the demand for agricultural imports in the former Soviet Union. While this will reduce agricultural export markets for the rest of the world, it will relax significantly the former Soviet Union's balance-of-payments constraint, enabling it to purchase much higher levels of manufactured goods from the OECD countries and elsewhere. These reforms would lead to higher world income as each country uses its comparative advantages.

These regional chapters show the importance of the global effects of trade reform as changes in world prices are transmitted to individual countries. They also show the importance of the links between the rural and urban economies. While higher food prices can be detrimental to the urban sector, they benefit the rural sector. The negative effects on the urban sector can be mitigated by several factors: stronger rural demand for manufactured goods, a reduction in rural-to-urban migration, a reduction in manufactured goods prices due to lower import tariffs, and a relative shift to urban goods as the price of food increases relative to the price of urban goods.

Chapter 9 relaxes the assumption of exogenous agricultural productivity. Agricultural productivity is linked directly to agricultural profitability. Compared to exogenous technological change, induced technological change will have a different effect on world food prices resulting from trade liberalisation. In general, developing countries will benefit more from trade reform with induced technological change, as farmers respond even more strongly to higher world food prices, than in the situation with exogenous productivity. This chapter attempts to show the importance of introducing a link between profitability and changes in productivity. However, it is recognised that this link cannot simply be reduced to a price transmission mechanism, but that it requires significant investment in research, infrastructure, and education. The final chapter draws together the results of the simulations and analyses and points to an agenda for further research and policy analysis.

Notes

1. The only exceptions relate to customs unions and other free-trade arrangements, and to special and differential treatment for developing countries, as discussed below.
2. Czechoslovakia, Hungary, Poland and Romania although long-time members of the GATT, failed to undertake their GATT obligations and were never entitled to the full MFN benefits. However, these countries are renegotiating their membership and have been given MFN status. Meanwhile, other countries with formerly centrally planned economies are in the process of joining the GATT. China's application to resume membership in the GATT, which it left in 1950, stalled in 1989 because of political disturbances, ambiguity regarding its commitment to liberalisation, and the question of the status of Taiwan, which has also applied for membership.
3. Trela and Whalley, p. 2, estimate the gains from removing textile and apparel trade restrictions to be $31 billion for developing countries and $22 billion for developed countries.
4. In which the United States was accused of subsidising its chicken exports to West Germany.
5. Other areas, such as services, intellectual property rights and investment were also brought into the GATT negotiations for the first time. The significance of developing country markets is indicated by the fact that they now offer the biggest hope for reducing the US deficit; more than two-thirds of the growth in US exports in 1991 was accounted for by developing countries. Exports grew by an average 7.2 per cent in 1991, helped by a growth in demand of 31 per cent from China, 22 per cent from Brazil, and 18 per cent from Mexico.
6. An indication of the trade friction is the increase in the number of anti-dumping cases initiated by major trading partners; in mid-1991, 209 anti-dumping measures were in effect in the United States, 143 in the EC and 71 in Canada. The surge in anti-dumping measures in the 1980s meant that within that decade 1 456 cases were registered with the GATT, placing the institution in the position of intermediary in bilateral conflicts involving controversial national laws restricting trade, rather than enforcing international rules accepted on a multilateral basis.
7. GATT (1986), Part D, para. 7.
8. Between the beginning of the 1980s and 1990, assistance to agricultural producers in OECD countries, as measured by the total producer subsidy equivalent (PSE), has increased from $99 billion to $176 billion, i.e. 7.5 per cent per annum on average (and 78 per cent over the decade), see OECD (1991), p. 115. In particular, average assistance per farmer (on a full-time farmer equivalent basis) rose to $15 000, while assistance per hectare farmed increased to $171.
9. GATT (1990) and UNCTAD (1991).

10. The difference between direct and indirect transfers is discussed in Chapter 2.

11. GATT (1992a). The measures undertaken include tariff reductions, elimination of quotas, abolition of licensing restrictions and removal of other non-tariff barriers. The rules governing accession to the GATT have become much stricter in recent years, so that countries are now forced to liberalise their trade policies **before** applying for membership. New Zealand is the only OECD country to have undertaken a full set of structural adjustment measures.

12. NTB instruments include quantitative restrictions or quotas, voluntary export restraints, government procurement policies, technical barriers to trade (regulations on health, sanitary requirements, packaging, labelling, etc.), customs valuations and nomenclature.

13. UNCTAD (1991), p. 59; OECD (1990a), p. 75. The estimates are our own calculations based on value shares.

14. Due, in particular, to the waiver from GATT provisions granted to the United States from 1954 and the tacit acceptance of the Common Agricultural Policy of the EC from the late 1960s.

15. The Cairns Group, named after the town in Australia where they first met, includes 14 so-called non-subsidising agricultural exporters (also called fair traders). Members are both developed and developing net-exporter countries, namely Argentina, Australia, Brazil, Canada, Chile, Colombia, Fiji, Hungary, Indonesia, Malaysia, New Zealand, Philippines, Thailand and Uruguay.

16. The cost of participating in the Uruguay Round is extremely burdensome. In order to participate in the committees which meet simultaneously and provide support to the delegates, a large staff is required, but this is often beyond the financial or human resources of the poorest countries, who cannot afford to have a large number of senior staff in Geneva for long periods of time.

17. In developing countries, on average, agriculture accounts for 15 per cent of GDP, 57 per cent of employment and a significant part of their merchandise exports.

18. The notion of effective protection is able to capture the degree to which tariff escalation reflects higher protection, since the effective protection is measured by comparing tariff levy to value added rather than gross output.

19. All major consumer countries charge import tariff levies which rise according to the degree of processing and to the value added. Normally, unprocessed cocoa is imported duty free by these countries, but because it favours ACP suppliers, the EC charges a 3 per cent *ad valorem* tariff for cocoa bean imports from non-ACP countries. Tariffs levied on cocoa products vary with countries and final products, but generally higher tariffs are levied on sweetened cocoa powder and chocolate products, both to protect the local cocoa processing industry and as a consequence of the domestic sugar support regime.

20. ACP countries have better preferential tariff entry than other developing countries in some important sectors, such as processed and unprocessed cocoa in which Africa competes with Brazil, Malaysia and Indonesia; processed and unprocessed coffee in which Africa competes with Colombia and Brazil; bananas in which the Caribbean countries compete with other Latin American countries; pineapples in which Africa competes with the Philippines; tobacco in which Zimbabwe and Malawi compete with Brazil, India and the Republic of Korea; palm oil in which West Africa competes with Malaysia; and beef meat in which Africa competes with Argentina.

21. During the Uruguay Round, however, the approach of many developing countries has been different, especially with regard to the principle of special and differential treatment. In fact, because of specific structural adjustment accords negotiated directly with the IMF and World Bank, many developing countries have reduced import tariff levies without any reciprocal concessions from developed countries.

22. See Siamwalla.

23. The central limit theorem shows that as the sample size increases, the variance declines by 1/n. The implication is that increased participation in a market may be expected to lead to a decline in variance. See Goldin and Knudsen, pp. 466-486.

24. As noted in Goldin and Knudsen pp. 476-480, the projected increase in prices resulting from liberalisation is a relatively short-run phenomenon. Since the Second World War, the real price of most agricultural commodities has declined. This downward trend is expected to continue, and to more than offset short-run price rises which may associated with liberalisation. In the longer term, food importers are expected to face lower prices, irrespective of the outcome of the Uruguay Round.

25. The group has a core membership consisting of Jamaica, Mexico, Morocco, Peru, Nigeria and Egypt, and associate membership made up of South Korea, China and India.

26. The Multi-Fibre Arrangement (MFA) which controls world trade in textiles and garments expired in December 1992, by which time textiles were expected to be incorporated within a GATT Agreement. Failure to conclude the Uruguay Round successfully would require renewal and renegotiation of the MFA, but given the strength of the vested interests in the MFA, this is likely to be less favourable to developing countries than the inclusion of textiles within the GATT.

27. See Anderson and Blackhurst for a summary of the debate, and GATT (1992b).

28. RIVM.

29. All numbers are in 1985 US dollars, unless otherwise stated.

Chapter 2

The Rural/Urban-North/South (RUNS) Model

Introduction

The first version of the Rural/Urban-North/South (RUNS) model stemmed from a long tradition of World Bank global modelling and forecasting, undertaken at the initiative of Hollis Chenery, Senior Vice President in charge of research at the World Bank in the 1970s. The first such model was the experimental GEM[1] model of Ginsburgh and Waelbroeck, on which work began in 1971, a little after the start of Klein and Hickman's Project Link[2]. GEM was conceived as a linear programming model. The authors were soon aware of the limitations of linear programming as a tool for global modelling and, using ideas developed by Negishi, solved the model as a general equilibrium system in 1973[3]. In 1973 Wouter Tims, Director of the Economic Analysis and Projections Department of the Bank, directed the first of what came to be called "the aggregations", numerical exercises in which so-called "Minimum Standard Models" (MSMs), that were available in the World Bank for a large number of developing countries, were solved separately and the results added up, providing a forecast for the developing world as a whole. No sooner was that lengthy piece of econometric work completed than oil prices exploded, making the results obtained obsolete. In response, Chenery and Tims initiated the construction of SIMLINK, built very swiftly by Norman Hicks[4]. SIMLINK was the first operational global macroeconomic model where, in contrast with the Project Link strategy of combining models for individual countries, models are developed for major regions of the world[5]. Models based on regions are far easier to build and manage than systems of country models. The results were incorporated into the first of a series of "Prospects Papers", which were formally confidential but were distributed in thousands of copies to governments of member countries, and were widely discussed by development economists.

This set a lasting pattern. Each year, "aggregation" exercises were run, providing useful summaries and consistency checks of the projections of the Bank's country economists. The computer technology used was gradually improved so that the calculations could be made more quickly and cheaply. However, it was impossible to run variants of the aggregations. The basic "minimum standard models" used by country economists were too primitive for that; also, the country economists who ran those models were too busy with operational duties to participate in lengthy global modelling work. The implications for the developing world of alternative assumptions about aid, oil prices and growth of OECD countries were explored by a more manageable global model based on regions, which was both easier to build and manage than the aggregations, and based on a more sophisticated theoretical structure than the MSMs[6]; thanks to suitable calibration, the base run of those models reproduced the results obtained by the aggregation exercises. The supposedly confidential Prospects Papers were replaced by the better known and public World Development Reports. Used for several years, SIMLINK was replaced by Syama Gupta's very different "World Development Report Model", a linear programming description of the world economy[7].

Hollis Chenery, the initiator with Wouter Tims of the global modelling program, was aware of the short life span of models. This led him to contract out to the Université Libre de Bruxelles in 1978 the construction of a third world general equilibrium model, in a project directed by Jean Waelbroeck. The results were to be available in time for use two years later in the third World Development Report.

Two models were developed[8]. Construction of the first, **Varuna**, was directed by Jan Gunning[9]; in this version, all agricultural goods were aggregated into a single good. The impact of the first oil shock was fading when the work started and it was thought that the world would return to a steady pattern of general equilibrium growth. In 1979, as the outbreak of war between Iran and Iraq triggered a renewed jump of world oil prices, it was decided at the suggestion of Gunning to embed into Varuna a disequilibrium theory of markets under rationing of the type developed by Barro and Grossman[10] and others. This suggestion complemented work done in the 1920s by the Soviet economist Preobrazhensky, whose "scissors theory" of a conflict of interests between town and country[11] emphasizes the crucial development problems that originate in the relationship between the rural and urban sectors. These ideas led to the development by Jean-Marc Burniaux of the Rural/Urban-North/South Model, otherwise known as RUNS. RUNS took over the urban model structure of Varuna but, in the Preobrazhensky mode, set up distinct general equilibrium systems for the rural and urban sectors. The single agricultural commodity of Varuna was disaggregated into twelve commodities, sold by the various regions in perfect competition with each other[12]. Other influences were the highly original **MOIRA** model of Linneman and Keyzer[13], from which stems the use of pass through equations describing domestic agricultural prices as a weighted average of domestic consumption and of world market prices[14]. Results from RUNS were used for several World Development Reports in the 1980s and a thorough description of the model and its properties was published by Burniaux in 1987.

After a short period of dormancy, the RUNS model was revived in 1989, in part, because of the significance of agriculture in the ongoing Uruguay Round discussions. The first new developments included modelling Japan and the dairy sector. It was decided to make a complete overhaul of the model in 1990, when RUNS was integrated into the OECD Development Centre's research programme. A fundamental feature of the model's overhaul was the changing of its base from 1978 to 1985, with a further disaggregation of the regions and commodities. Given the global nature of the model (and therefore its underlying database), the development of a new database required significant resources. The current version of the model includes 22 regions, and 20 commodities, of which 15 are agricultural, and covers the period 1985-2002.

The Model Structure

Introduction

The RUNS model has three dimensions: regions, commodities, and time. At present, the model has 22 regions; the breakdown is given in Table 2.1. As mentioned above, the original model had 10 regions. Some of the larger countries are now modeled separately. For example, India was extracted from the South Asia region, and the China component was developed and extracted from the rest of the world aggregate. Two of the former regions were based on their roles as petroleum exporters. These two regions were abolished and the new regions represent more clearly geographic distribution. Asia now includes five regions: the above-mentioned South Asia, India, and China, as well as Indonesia, and East Asia and the Pacific (or simply East Asia). Africa and the Middle East have been reconfigured, with Nigeria and South Africa modeled as country components, and then a large sub-Saharan African aggregate (designated as Sub-Saharan Africa though it excludes Nigeria and South Africa), the Maghreb, a Mediterranean Basin Aggregate, and a Gulf Region aggregate. Latin America has been split into three regions with Brazil and Mexico modeled individually, followed by a rest of Latin America aggregate. Previously, several Latin American countries were included in the oil exporting regions. The developing world has been transformed from seven regions to fourteen, with more emphasis on location rather than as a function of exports.

The OECD regions were also transformed. From two regions, the model now has six OECD-country regions. Europe was split into two components, the EEC and EFTA. The EEC was also expanded from EEC-9 to EEC-12 to reflect the dynamics of the European Community. (More recently, the former German Democratic Republic was added to the Federal Republic of Germany.) The food-exporting countries, the United States, Canada, Australia, and New Zealand, have been split into three, with the United States and Canada modeled individually, and Australia and New Zealand forming one region. The remaining OECD region is Japan, which initially was part of the rest of the world aggregate.

Finally, the rest of the world aggregate, which in the original model included China, Japan, the Soviet Union and most of the other centrally planned economies, was eliminated. The poorer centrally planned economies of Indochina were aggregated into South Asia. The former centrally planned economies of central and eastern Europe and the former Soviet Union have been developed into two regions. One region, designated as the Eastern European Economies in Transition (EET) include the former centrally planned economies of Eastern and Central Europe. The final region is known as the former Soviet Union (FSU), and includes all 15 republics of the former Soviet Union (including the Baltic republics)[15].

In the text, reference will be made to separate regions and to aggregated regions. **Low Income Asia** refers to a four-region aggregate: South Asia, India, China, and Indonesia. The aggregate **Africa** consists of three regions: Nigeria, South Africa, and sub-Saharan Africa (it excludes the Maghreb). The **Middle East** designates a three-region aggregate: Maghreb, Mediterranean, and the Gulf Region. **Latin America** refers to Brazil, Mexico, and other Latin America. The **Developed Food Exporters** are the United States, Canada, and Australia/New Zealand. **Europe** refers to EC and EFTA combined. The **OECD** refers to all six OECD regions: the United States, Canada,

Australia/New Zealand, Japan, the EC, and EFTA[16]. The **formerly Centrally Planned Economies** (FCPE) designates the European Economies in Transition and the former Soviet Union.

The commodity space has 20 sectors. Given the agricultural focus of RUNS, 15 of the 20 sectors are agricultural. Table 2.2 provides a complete list of the commodities. Many of the agricultural commodities are relatively homogeneous including wheat, rice, coarse grains, sugar, coffee, cocoa, and tea. There are two large aggregates referred to as other food and other non-food. Other food includes fruits, vegetables, and beverages. Dairy was originally part of the other food aggregate but was separated from the aggregate in large part due to the high levels of protection in the dairy sector within the OECD regions. The meat sector was also split into two components. One includes beef, veal, and sheep meat, i.e. ruminants; the other meat sector includes pork, poultry, and other meats. There has been no change in the non-agricultural sectors. The **Food Crops** aggregate refers to wheat, rice, coarse grains, sugar, vegetable oils, and other foods. The **Tree Crops** aggregate refers to coffee, cocoa, and tea. The **Crops** aggregate, in addition to Food and Tree Crops, includes cotton, and other non-food. The **Food Livestock** aggregate designates Beef, Veal, and Sheep Meat, Other Meats, and Dairy products. Finally, **Livestock** refers to the latter three sectors plus wool.

The time range covers the period 1985-2002, i.e. a total of 17 years. Table 2.3 presents the solution years for the model. After 1987, the model jumps in increments of three years. All the factor accumulation functions and growth parameters reflect the three-year gap. The 1985-1990 period is used to validate the model to observable data.

The mechanisms of the model are easier to comprehend by separating the static relations and the dynamic relations. This also helps explain the impacts from reform which often include static gains, the efficiency gains, and the dynamic gains which are realised from higher levels of investment and cumulative income gains.

The Static Model

In each year, the model simulates the world economy, given a fixed level of resources: land, labour, and capital. Supply and demand relations are specified for each good and for each region. These in turn define trade relations across countries. In agriculture, we assume goods are perfectly homogenous across the world. Therefore, any country which produces more than it consumes of a particular good will export that good, otherwise it will import. For manufactured goods, trade relations are more complex. In the case of manufacturing, goods are distinguished by region of origin. Therefore, a domestic consumer is not indifferent to buying a local car or a foreign car. A domestic producer is not indifferent to selling domestically or abroad (for example, quality control may be more important for exports). As a result, countries can both export and import the same class of goods since they are differentiated by place of origin.

Supply is driven by the underlying technology and resource endowments: labour, land, and capital. In addition, government policies affect supply directly via input subsidies, and export subsidies or taxes. Demand is mainly driven by household incomes. Government plays a role in demand via import tariffs or subsidies which affect the relative price of goods. For example, an import tax on beef may induce consumers to buy more poultry or pork.

In a static framework, we can analyse how changes in government policies affect the supply and demand relations in each region, and how changes in supply and demand modify the trade balance. Within each region, certain sectors will contract, while others are likely to expand. In the absence of all trade distortions, each region will exhibit its comparative advantage. Economic theory suggests that the world economy will be larger in the absence of all trade distortions. While this is true in aggregate, economic theory does not tell us that everyone will necessarily be better off. In any given region, there might be some groups that are better off, and some that are worse off. For example, a rise in food prices may hurt the urban poor, but improve the incomes of the rural poor. Regions as a whole may be negatively affected if the gains to the winners do not outweigh the losses of the others. However, if the world economy is larger, it is always possible to compensate the losers (through income transfers, for example), so that everyone is better off.

While the level of detail is greater in the agricultural sector than in the urban sector, one of the key features of the RUNS model is that it captures the links between the two. These links work in a variety of ways. Income growth in the rural sector increases demand for urban goods. In China, for example, over the last 10-15 years, as rural incomes have grown dramatically, demand for urban goods — refrigerators, televisions, etc. — has increased, leading to an expansion of the urban economy. Improvement in farming technologies is another key rural-urban linkage via investment in irrigation systems (pumps and dams), tractors and other types of farm equipment. The links go in the other direction as well. Abundant supplies and varieties of food lead to the development of the food processing sector. Food prices can also influence wages and employment in the urban sector. Obviously, there is also the potential for conflict. Government provision of subsidised food to urban consumers is a tax on farmers if farmers are forced to sell their produce at lower prices. This will directly influence income distribution between the rural and urban sectors.

The RUNS model also captures the links between the world markets and the domestic markets. This is one of the key mechanisms which explains the winners and losers from trade liberalisation. If trade liberalisation leads to increases in the world price of food, countries which import food will need to pay more, in other words, they will suffer from a deterioration of their terms of trade. There are factors which may partially, or even totally, mitigate the loss in the terms of trade. As it turns out, some regions would lose from multilateral trade liberalisation.

Rural Production

Production data for separate agricultural products are limited. For this reason, RUNS imposes input-output separability and uses multi-input/multi-output production functions to characterise agricultural production. Composite input is formed from individual inputs. Individual outputs compete for this aggregate input. The choice of outputs depends on the price of the output and the average input price. Supply functions for individual output are based on modified Cobb-Douglas production functions and have the general form:

$$S_{it} = (1 + \gamma_i)^t \, \alpha_i \left(\frac{PP_{it}}{P_{it}} - c_i \right)^{\beta_i} \qquad (2.1)$$

where S is supply, PP is the producer price, P is the composite input price, γ is a supply trend, and α, c, and β are parameters[17]. Optimisation requires that marginal revenue product equals marginal cost, and inversion of the supply function leads to the optimal level of the aggregate input for use in output i. In general, we have $R_i = f(PP_i/P_i, S_i)$ where R is demand for the aggregate input. Due to the nature of the base data, it is not possible to identify the production structure for each agricultural commodity. Agricultural production is characterised by two distinct types of farming: crop production and livestock production. The crop production sector produces 11 of the 15 agricultural commodities[18]. The livestock production sector produces the other four[19]. The aggregate input for the crop sector is simply the sum over the aggregate input for each of the crop subsectors: $R_{cr} = \Sigma R_i$[20].

The input structure of the crop sector is a mixture of Leontief fixed coefficient functions and a nested constant elasticity of substitution (CES) function. The Leontief components include seed inputs, feed input for draught cattle, and manufacturing, energy, and services[21]. The residual input is modeled using a CES aggregation function. This function captures the degree of substitutability among land, labour, and fertilizers. The three factors in the CES function are a composite factor of land+tractors, a composite factor of labour + irrigated land + draught cattle, and fertilizers. The mix of factors will depend on their relative prices.

The treatment of the livestock sector is similar, but the production structure is different. The CES aggregation function is characterised by the substitutability between range-fed livestock and ranch-fed livestock. There are four factors in the CES function: wheat, coarse grains, oils (meal), and the land + tractor composite. The intensity of use of all these factors will depend on their relative prices. All other inputs are used in fixed proportions.

Urban Production

Urban production is modeled along the classical lines of many AGE models. Intermediate inputs are modeled using a Leontief-fixed coefficients structure. Substitution is possible between imports and domestic intermediates. The residual aggregate, value added, is modeled using a CES aggregation function which implies imperfect substitutability between capital and labour. Most models use sector-specific value added functions, in RUNS there is only one value added function. The urban technology implies constant returns to scale, and therefore producer prices can be calculated through unit input costs.

Income Distribution

The RUNS model incorporates two types of households, rural and urban. It is assumed that all rural income is derived from rural production. In other words, rural income is generated by payments to rural factors and rural surplus. Urban income is generated by urban value added.

Household Consumption

Each household type, rural and urban, has its own specific consumption function, though both are modeled using the extended linear expenditure system (ELES). The ELES is similar to the LES but is extended to incorporate future consumption in the form of savings[22]. The ELES leads to the following consumption function:

$$C_i = \theta_i + \mu_i \frac{Yd - \sum pc_j \theta_j}{pc_i} \qquad (2.2)$$

where C is consumption (by commodity), Yd is disposable income, pc is the consumer price, and μ and θ, are parameters[23]. Consumption is the sum of two components, a constant θ which is often interpreted as the subsistence minimum, and a variable part which is a share of disposable income minus total expenditures on the subsistence minimum[24]. The income and price elasticities are household specific[25].

Government

The government plays its usual role as tax collector, buyer of goods and services, and manager over a wide variety of economic instruments. The main tax is a direct tax on household incomes. Expenditures on goods and services are modeled as fixed shares of a real aggregate expenditure level. The economic instruments include agricultural input subsidies, agricultural price wedges (described below), import tariffs/subsidies, export taxes/subsidies, agricultural stocks, and income transfers. All these instruments generate additional revenues or expenditures which are allocated between the two households and the government using fixed shares. In the base scenario, the government's budget surplus/deficit is endogenous. In the liberalisation scenarios, the real budget surplus/deficit is assumed to be fixed (at the base simulation level), and the direct household tax rates are endogenous. This may be a strong assumption in certain regions of the world where taxation of labour and capital income are difficult to implement. However, these regions rely to a large extent on import and export taxes to finance the government. Reduction and or elimination of trade taxes will require these countries to switch to another system of taxation if they are to achieve fiscal sustainability. Recent evidence suggests that countries undertaking trade reform also make serious attempts to improve the administration of income taxes.

Savings/Investment

Household savings are determined by the ELES, but they can also be derived as a residual from income minus expenditures. Government saving is determined as the residual between government revenues and expenditures. The final component of savings is foreign savings, which is fixed for each region (the sum over all regions is obviously zero). This latter assumption is further discussed below. The sum of savings is therefore:

$$S = S_r + S_u + S_g + S_f \qquad (2.3)$$

where S_r is rural saving, S_u is urban household saving, S_g is the government surplus/deficit, and S_f is foreign savings (capital flow). Total savings are allocated to the investment sector. The investment sector splits total savings into investment in the rural sector (land, tractors, etc.), and investment in urban capital. The division of total investment is usually determined by household saving rates. For example, aggregate investment in rural factors is given by:

$$I_r = S_r + \chi_r S_f \tag{2.4}$$

In other words, rural investment equals rural savings plus a share of foreign savings. In certain simulations, we will allow for a different allocation of aggregate savings. The allocation of investment between rural and urban investment is a strong assumption. In the long run, theory suggests that investment should be allocated in order to equalise rates of return in the two sectors. Aggregate investment generates a demand for goods which is determined using fixed value shares.

Trade

Agricultural trade is simply determined as the difference between domestic production and domestic demand (including changes in stocks). Each agricultural commodity is modeled as a perfect substitute globally, and therefore there is no matrix of agricultural trade among countries.

Non-agricultural trade is more complex. Goods are differentiated by region of origin and this in turn requires a trade matrix for each good. This assumption is known as the Armington assumption and is an assumption often used in trade models. One of the consequences of the Armington assumption is that the law of one price does not hold. The world price facing country *i*, is not the same as the world price of country *j*, unless the each country purchases exactly the same shares of commodities from all the regions[26].

In practical terms, the Armington assumption can be seen as a multi-nested decision process by each domestic agent. For example, consumer demand for a particular good, say automobiles, is determined by the ELES. This is the top level of the nest. At the second level of the nest, consumers allocate purchases of automobiles between domestic purchases and imports. At the third and final level, consumers allocate expenditures on automobile imports across all regions of the world. In other words, even though at the top level consumer demand appears to be for one commodity, it is an aggregate commodity which generates demand for twenty-two commodities in all. The Armington assumption is motivated by several reasons. The level of aggregation, in terms of commodity aggregation leads to trade statistics where two-way trade is observed. At the atomistic level, we do not observe two-way trade. For example, the United States does not both export and import a particular model of Toyota, but it both exports automobiles to Japan and imports automobiles from Japan. The level of aggregation in RUNS in the non-agricultural sectors is very high. Another reason for adopting the Armington specification is that it avoids corner solutions, i.e. perfect specialisation, which is rarely observed in practice.

The Armington assumption by itself is not a strong assumption, but its implementation can have strong implications. In the RUNS model, we use the CES formulation of the Armington assumption. In order for a region to increase its share of a market, it must lower its price, relative to the aggregate import price[27]. A symmetric assumption is used on the export side. Domestic producers differentiate between goods sold for domestic use and exports. There are two reasons why. Aggregation of goods implies that the mix of goods sold domestically is not the same as the mix of goods sold for exports. Also, even the same good may be differentiated. For example, the quality of exports may be different from the quality of the same good sold domestically. Domestic production is therefore modeled using a transformation frontier which is a constant elasticity of transformation function (CET).

Domestic Agricultural Prices

Because agricultural commodities are homogeneous across the world, generally the world price determines the domestic price. In the RUNS model, the government (and parastatal institutions) may intervene, in which case a wedge is generated between the domestic agricultural price and world price. In all cases, international trade occurs at the world price. In the most general form, the domestic price is set according to the following formula:

$$pp = [\varphi pw + (1 - \varphi)\, \pi]\, (1 + \tau) \qquad (2.5)$$

where pp is the domestic agricultural price, pw is the world agricultural price, π is a domestic price index, and τ is a scale variable which may be thought of as a tariff equivalent. The parameter φ is a critical parameter, it is a pass-through coefficient. If there are no market distortions, φ is 1, and τ is 0, in which case the domestic price is simply the world price. The simplest form of market distortion is perfect price pass through and a constant tariff, i.e. φ is set to 1, and τ is set at some level. The other extreme is zero pass through, in which case the domestic price is independent of the world price, and farmers are insulated from changes in world prices. This latter situation has been prevalent in many sectors under the EC's CAP, in Japan, and in most centrally planned economies, as well as in some developing economies. Amongst the industrialised countries, the justification for price insulation is to protect farmers' income. Changes in domestic agricultural prices simply rise with the price index, albeit with occasional adjustments of the τ factor. In developing economies, the justification has been more geared to protecting urban real wages by keeping the price of food relatively low. In the base version of the model, it has been assumed that φ is 1 in all regions (i.e. perfect price pass-through). The factor τ has been varied in each period through 1990 so that the price wedge is consistent with observed data. From 1991 onwards, perfect price transmission is also assumed, and τ is set at the 1990 level through the year 2002. Given the current changes in the EC's CAP and in many of the former centrally planned economies, and the structural adjustment programmes undertaken by many developing countries, this characterisation is not improbable.

The revenue consequence of a domestic to world price wedge depends on the trade position of the region. Table 2.4 describes the income effects of the price wedges. Trade revenues are positive if the domestic price is higher than the world price and the country is a net importer (beef imports in Japan for example), and they are positive if the world price is higher than the domestic price and the country is a net exporter (typical of many coffee exporters). Revenues are negative if the domestic price is lower than the world price and the country is a net importer (typical of certain developing countries with heavy food subsidies), or if the country exports and the world price is lower than the domestic price (the EC's export restitution programme for example). The revenues (or expenditures) generated by the agricultural price wedges are shared across households and the government.

Equilibrium

Most factors are predetermined in any given period, i.e. current investment is only reflected in future factor stocks. While total labour supply is also predetermined, RUNS incorporates a rural-to-urban labour migration function. One of the key factors in the migration function is the ratio of per capita incomes between the rural and urban sectors[28]. In the urban sector, the basic version of the model solves for the nominal wage which clears the urban labour market. In some simulations, the model implements a semi-rigid real wage which generates unemployment. This is discussed in later chapters. Urban capital is assumed to be fully utilised at all times.

In the rural sector, aggregation functions are used to create the two composite rural factors, i.e. labour + irrigated land + draught cattle, and land + tractors. Both these composite factors are assumed to be fully utilised and these markets generate two equilibrium prices. (Note, this implies full employment in the rural sector.)

For each region, there are therefore four equilibrating variables. Two in the urban sector, wages and capital rental rate, and two in the rural sectors. The only other equilibrium prices in the model are world agricultural prices. World agricultural prices are determined by equilibrium between world supply and demand. World supply and demand are calculated by adding up supply and demand in all regions (this is the same as setting the sum of all regions' net trade to zero).

All equilibrium prices, the four domestic factor prices, and the fifteen world agricultural prices are determined via a tâtonnement procedure. Supply and demand for each market are calculated. If demand is greater than supply, the price in that market is too low. The tâtonnement procedure calculates a new higher price. The tâtonnement step is:

$$p_{t+1} = p_t \, (D/S) \qquad (2.6)$$

where t is the iteration counter, D is demand, and S supply[29]. The choice of the distance factor δ proves to be crucial, but is more art than science, particularly in a model such as RUNS with 103 (4×22+15) equilibrium prices per period. If the δ factor is too low, the model may take a long time to converge. If it is too high, the markets may be unstable leading to huge swings and potential model crashes. The final problem is one of lengthy cycles around the equilibrium path. In general, a period solution takes about 100 iterations. While this may seem a lot, the tâtonnement procedure has several positive features. It is parsimonious on memory and function calls since there is no need to store or calculate the Jacobian matrix, and it turns out to be quite robust.

Closure

The final section on the static description of the RUNS model concerns closure. There are three key macro relations — fiscal closure, investment-savings closure, and trade closure. Fiscal and investment-savings closure were described above. The fiscal balance in the base model is endogenous, and investment is savings driven. The RUNS model has a fixed-trade balance closure rule. In any given period, and in all regions, the net trade balance (in value) must sum to the capital flow. This is a strong assumption with significant consequences. Any disequilibrium in the trade balance calls for a real exchange rate adjustment, in essence, an adjustment in the domestic factor prices. For example, an agricultural trade liberalisation scenario typically implies a reduction in the

EC's agricultural exports. In order to maintain a fixed trade balance, this requires an increase in exports of other commodities which is accomplished by lowering the price of manufactured goods. Alternative trade closure rules are feasible. Country models, for example, may fix the exchange rate and let the trade balance be endogenous. In a global model, endogenous trade balances are possible, however, consistency requires that the sum of the trade balances equals zero. The key to consistency is to introduce a global investment model which allocates total savings in a consistent fashion[30].

Finally, the RUNS model is a barter model, therefore only relative prices matter. Any price can be used as an anchor (the numeraire). The base version of the model uses an export price index as the numeraire. It is the export price index of manufacturing exports of OECD countries and is comparable to the World Bank's manufacturing unit value (MUV) index. The index is set to 1 in 1985 and in all subsequent years. All monetary values in the RUNS model are in millions of 1985 dollars in all years. Unless otherwise indicated, all monetary values are in 1985 dollars.

The Dynamic Model

The RUNS model captures some of the dynamic growth processes that are inherent in the world economy. The key elements are factor accumulation — growth in the labour force, and growth in capital via savings and investment — and productivity improvements. Productivity gains are exogenous (though variable over time)[31]. Changes in trade policies, therefore, mainly affect growth via their effect on savings, investment, and government revenues. For example, agricultural protectionism in the OECD countries may be inducing higher investment in the rural sectors than necessary, even though in the absence of protection certain OECD countries may have a comparative advantage in industry. This inefficient allocation of investment leads to a reduction in the long-term growth rate.

Factor Accumulation

The total labour force grows at an exogenously given rate. The division of the total labour force between the rural and urban sectors will depend to some extent on the labour migration function. Population plays no direct role in the model except to calculate per capita statistics in the post-simulation analyses. The population and labour force growth rates are quite similar.

The urban capital stock grows via urban investment and a depreciation factor. In the simple variant we have:[32]

$$K_t = (1 - \delta)\, K_{t-1} + I_{u,t-1} \qquad (2.7)$$

Rural capital is more complex since there are four rural factors (other than labour), irrigated and non-irrigated land, farm equipment, and draught cattle. The allocation of rural investment across these four factors occurs via a transformation function which incorporates each factor's relative rate of return, i.e. the factor's rental rate versus its investment cost. However, the model does not incorporate forward-looking behaviour in any of the investment decisions. The investment in land is constrained by a total land maximum in each region. As a region approaches this maximum, the rental price of the land factor increases.

Productivity

Each agricultural sector and the urban aggregate output contain a productivity factor which is exogenous, i.e. not related to any other variable in the model. The factors may vary over time, but are fixed in any given time period. All the productivity factors are in fact initially generated by the model. Calibration of the model parameters is done in two phases. In the first phase (and in a pre-simulation program), the basic parameters of the model are calibrated so that the model is able to reproduce the 1985 base data set. In a second phase of the calibration process, the model is solved forward through the year 2002 with output fixed and the productivity factors endogenous. This yields a set of productivity factors which are model-consistent and consistent with a consensus view of the future of the world economy. Sensitivity analysis can be undertaken to see how robust the liberalisation scenarios are to changes in this basic view of the future.

In formal terms, the single period model is:

$$F(y, x, z;\ \theta_i, \theta_2, \gamma) = 0 \qquad (2.8)$$

where y is the set of endogenous variables, x is the set of exogenous and predetermined variables, z is the set of policy instruments, θ_1 and θ_2 are two sets of parameters, and γ are the productivity coefficients. In the first phase of the calibration, y, x, and z are known, they are all given by the base year social accounting matrix (SAM) for each region. The productivity coefficients are all zero in the base year. The base parameter set is partitioned into two sets. The first set contains a set of **key** parameters about which the modeler has *a priori* knowledge, θ_1 in the equation above. These are typically elasticities which the modeler has estimated, or the estimates have been gleaned from a literature search, other studies, or from experts. The second set of parameters is calculated so that the model is able to reproduce the base data set. In other words, equation (2.8) is inverted, using the 1985 base data set, to solve for θ_2, rather than for the endogenous variables y[33]. Typically, these parameters are share parameters, and intercept terms.

The second phase of calibration determines the productivity coefficients endogenously. In this case, the model can be written as:

$$F_t(y_t, x_t, z_t;\ \theta, \gamma_t) = 0 \qquad (2.9)$$

where the set x_t contains the variables y_{t-1}. In the base simulation, x_t and z_t are assumed to be known, and the model solves for y_t, conditional on θ and γ. In a policy simulation, z_t is perturbed, leading to a different y_t which is compared with the base y_t. In the phase 2 calibration, y_t is assumed to be known. Generally, we assume we know the growth rate of y_t, i.e. $y_t = (1+r)\ y_{t-1}$ with r, the growth rate, given. In this case, we invert the function F_t to solve for the values of γ_t These productivity trends are stored and used for the base simulation and all subsequent policy simulations.

Some Statistics

In each period, the model solves for roughly 400 variables in each region, plus it solves for the trade matrices, i.e. somewhere around 11 000 variables in all. The model is dynamically recursive, so each period can be solved individually, but in total, the model solves for approximately 77 000 variables (if we ignore the base year). The model is coded in FORTRAN and is portable across different platforms and operating systems. Running on a 80486-based PC, the base model is solved in about 10 minutes. Needless to say, the output can be voluminous. There is a post-simulation analysis program which can generate reams of summary listings. Typically, in the interest of saving forests the information in the listings is read directly off the computer screen.

Welfare Measurement[34]

Introduction

The RUNS policy simulations produce vast quantities of statistics — changes in GDP, both urban and rural, price movements, changes in income distribution, structural changes both across sectors in a region, and across the world via changes in prices and trade. The list is quite exhaustive, since in each region there are over 400 variables in each time period, and other statistics are generated from these base variables such as price indices. One of the elegant features of most AGE models is that they are based on solid microeconomic theory with optimising behaviour by economic agents. The theory of the consumer allows us to develop several different measures of consumer welfare.

To measure the overall implications of trade liberalisation, some precise and well-defined means of providing money measures of welfare outcomes is needed. In particular, it is essential to have a measure of welfare change which will accurately measure the welfare consequences of partial reforms in the presence of a number of distortions.

There is an extensive literature on the evaluation of welfare changes in partial equilibrium models and the equivalent variation (EV) and compensating variation (CV) measures are widely used and well understood in this context. General agreement exists that the appropriate money-metric welfare measures are the Hicksian equivalent variation or compensating variation even though there has been considerable discussion about specific approaches for their actual evaluation[35].

Some AGE models utilise EV or CV measures of welfare changes which are well defined even if somewhat difficult to explain to a general audience. Most models, however, tend to use various measures of **real** GDP or absorption as a general indicator of changes in welfare or potential welfare[36]. Even studies which explicitly use EV or CV measures have a range of different approaches to evaluation which may yield slightly different results. Since conventionally measured welfare changes are typically small relative to total income, even an apparently minor difference in methodology may have a large effect on measures of welfare change as a proportion of income. A recent re-examination of estimates of the marginal welfare costs of taxation[37] found that major discrepancies in the estimated marginal welfare cost per dollar of revenue collected resulted from seemingly minor differences in the measurement approaches used by different authors.

A modification of the welfare indices for distorted open economies proposed by Lloyd and Schweinberger (1988, 1990) is used as a basis for obtaining monetary measures of welfare changes. These measures have a number of advantages over other approaches currently applied. Firstly, they can provide exact measures of the welfare consequences of liberalisation. Secondly, they can be shown to be consistent with the popular and intuitively appealing partial equilibrium concepts of consumer and producer surplus[38], with the major advantage of allowing for generalisation to the multiple distortion case. Finally, the welfare measures obtained in this way have a simple, intuitive interpretation in terms of the change in capital inflow or outflow required to achieve a given level of utility.

Theoretical Basis

The approach to welfare evaluation proposed in this paper is based on a modification of the **economy trade expenditure function** for a distorted economy utilised by Lloyd and Schweinberger, and by Anderson and Neary. This function is defined as:

$$B(p,p^*,w,v,u) = e(p,w,u) - g(p,w,v) - (p - p^*)m(p,v) \qquad (2.10)$$

where p is a vector of (distorted) domestic commodity prices, p^* is a vector of world commodity prices, w is a vector of factor prices, v is a vector of the economy's resource endowments, u is the level of consumer utility, e is the expenditure required to achieve utility level u at price p, g is the revenue at domestic prices attainable with the given resource vector, and $m(p,v,w,u) = d(p,w,v) - g_P(p,w,v)$ is the vector of (uncompensated) net imports/exports, where $d(p,w,v)$ is the actual demand vector given the model closure assumptions and g_P denotes the first derivative of the GDP function with respect to price. Both e and g are evaluated consistent with the model specification.

The vector $(p - p^*)$ in equation (2.10) can be interpreted as the tariffs or tariff equivalents of the prevailing trade distortions in the economy. The last term in equation (2.10) therefore refers to the actual tariff revenues, or quota rents, accruing to residents of the country under consideration. While these revenues impose a cost on domestic consumers, they typically accrue as revenues to the government or domestic holders of quotas and hence must be added to the revenue obtained from production when evaluating the country's net expenditure position.

The modification made to the trade expenditure function proposed by Lloyd and Schweinberger is the use of actual as distinct from compensated demands in the third (tariff revenue) term of equation (2.10). This respecification reflects the recent emergence of a consensus in the public finance literature that the appropriate revenue base for evaluating the welfare costs of taxation is the actual revenue rather than the compensated revenues used in most of the earlier literature[39]. The actual import demands used in this specification are general equilibrium import demand functions, rather than simple Marshallian demand functions, and depend upon the prices of goods and factors, the vector of resource endowments, and on the means by which tax revenues are redistributed.

The value of the function B in equation (2.10) can be interpreted as the net transfer from abroad required for households to achieve a particular level of utility. It provides a useful means for obtaining exact money measures of the welfare consequences of changes in world prices or domestic distortions. Furthermore, it has a powerfully simple intuitive interpretation: any change which requires an increase in transfers from the rest of the world to maintain current living standards causes a reduction in welfare. Loo and Tower (1989) used this equivalence to compare gains from developing country trade liberalisation with foreign aid flows.

The economy-wide counterpart for the Hicksian *EV* measure of welfare change resulting from a change in world prices from p_0^* to p_1^* is given by the change in *B*, at the initial utility level u_1, between the initial world price p_0^* and the final world price p_1^*:

$$B_1 - B_0 = B(p_1, w_1, p_1^*, v, u_1) - B(p_0, w_0, p_0^*, v, u_1) \quad (2.11)$$

The measure defined above is a generalisation of conventional partial equilibrium definitions of EV defined using only consumer expenditure functions. The major differences arise from the move to general equilibrium reflected in the inclusion of the revenue (or GDP) function and from the incorporation of existing distortions reflected in the inclusion of the $(p - p^*).m(p,v)$ terms.

The approach to evaluation represented by equation (2.11) has the desirable feature of allowing for welfare changes resulting from multiple, and multi-level, price distortions. In the case of a single price distortion, these measures can be shown to relate to conventional graphical measures which allow useful insights into the interpretation of the measures and of the marginal effects of changes in distortions. The specification of (2.10) can be readily generalised to incorporate domestic consumption and production taxes.

Model variants

The RUNS model has a wide variety of options which include changes in functional specification, policy assumptions, parameter values, and changes in trends. In this section, we will describe the more important model variations.

Macro Closure

As described above, the base model has three closure rules: exogenous government balance[40], savings driven investment, and a fixed trade balance for each region. The motivation for fixed government balances is that many developing economies rely on import tariffs for a significant part of their public revenues. Since liberalisation often eliminates this source of revenue, the choice was between allowing the government to run unsustainable deficits or rebalancing the taxing mechanism towards direct household taxes. This latter option has been pursued. The effect in some of the industrialised countries will be the reverse. The elimination of the costly agricultural programmes will lead to a reduction of household taxes. In terms of the model, the real government deficit/surplus is fixed at its base simulation level, and the household tax rates are calculated endogenously in order to meet the government's budget constraint.

In another variant of the model, the savings driven investment and the fixed trade balance closure are both modified simultaneously. Since the ELES explicitly incorporates savings, it also can explicitly incorporate the price of savings, i.e. the relative price of a future consumption bundle. The counterpart to the future consumption bundle is current investment. The two can be linked. Investment today will depend on the relative cost of one unit of investment versus the potential return which is the price of providing a unit of future consumption. In the first and simple variant of this closure, each region is endowed with a simple investment function which is an increasing function of the price of savings. Regional savings are determined as previously, except that foreign savings is endogenous. The equilibrating variable becomes the world price of savings. Total world savings are summed as well as total national investment (from the individual investment functions). A world savings price is calculated which clears the savings-investment balance at the global level. Foreign savings is then the difference between domestic savings and domestic investment. Given the world market clearing mechanism, we have insured that the sum of foreign savings is zero, and from Walras' law, the sum of the trade balances is also zero. While this is a simple implementation of the global investment function, it does rely on some strong assumptions. The closure assumes perfect interest rate transmission, i.e. each region's domestic interest rate is equal to the world interest rate. Second, investment is myopic, i.e. economic agents base their decisions on contemporaneous variables only, there is no forward-looking behaviour. Third, this closure rule ignores the significant literature on portfolio choice and risk.

Price behaviour

The base version of the model is completely neo-classical. There is market-clearing behaviour in all markets in all regions, albeit with price-distorting policies. At its inception, one of the key features of the RUNS model was some of the built-in non-market mechanisms, particularly with respect to agricultural prices, and urban employment. The arguments for this non-market clearing behaviour were two-fold. It is clear that in many countries, governments attempt to control the rural-to-urban terms of trade, either to protect farm incomes as in the case of many rich countries, or to maintain low food prices in the urban area. In either case, domestic prices are decoupled from world prices. In the case of the EC, for example, this has led to large and increasing budgetary costs since world prices have been decreasing while the internal price has been kept high. Since productivity has been increasing as well, the EC's surplus has been increasing, which has led to dumping on world markets (further decreasing world prices), or to a large increase in stocks. In the case of developing countries it has led to inefficient allocation of resources and increasing rural poverty. There have been several attempts to measure the degree of pass-through, and the estimation procedures are difficult both because of data difficulties and problems with model specification[41]. Given the availability of PSE data, both over time and for many regions between 1985 and 1990, it was decided to run the base model using perfect pass-through, while calibrating the price wedges using observed data. Imperfect price transmission as modeled in RUNS is a reduced-form version of all the instruments that a government (or parallel institutions) has at its disposal to affect domestic prices: marketing boards, variable levies, stocking policies, loan rates, deficiency payments, procurement practices, food aid, etc.

The second reason for implementing market imperfection is the realisation that urban labour markets often do not clear, and that unemployment (or underemployment) is a persistent feature of many urban economies. It may also be linked to attempts by certain countries to define the rural-to-urban terms of trade. If the aim is to maintain a certain living standard for the urban working class, governments will attempt to maintain low food prices. This can be linked with a real wage policy which fails to achieve labour market clearing prices. Attempts to liberalise food prices in such regimes, where food prices need to rise to match world prices, may be difficult to achieve, depending on the rigidity of the real wage. In RUNS, unemployment is generated via semi-rigid real wages, where the degree of rigidity is under user control. The basic wage equation has the real wage defined by a weighted average of a rigid reference wage and the equilibrium real wage.

Modelling of the price of energy deviates from the standard market clearing mechanism. Rather than assume a perfectly competitive market, and without a detailed description of alternative specifications, the RUNS model assumes an exogenous path for the internationally traded price of energy. The exogenous path is determined outside the model using projections from the World Bank and the International Energy Agency. The exogenous energy price is relative to the price of manufacturing exports of the OECD countries (i.e. the model's numeraire), since all price's in a real AGE model are relative[42]. The basis for this specification is an assumption that the main oil-exporting countries attempt to maintain a stable relation between their main export, oil, and their main import, OECD countries' manufactured goods. This specification has two consequences. It leads to a revenue flow (as do all price wedges). If the exogenous world price of energy is greater than the unit production cost, oil-exporting countries will benefit from additional profits. On the other hand, if world energy prices fall below unit production costs, oil exporting countries will suffer reductions in their mineral rents. The second consequence relates to liberalisation scenarios in which the OECD countries must lower the price of the manufacturing exports due to the trade balance constraint. This induces a *de facto* devaluation of the OECD countries' export manufacturing prices, which results in a devaluation of the world energy price. Since oil-exporting countries do not only purchase manufactured goods from the OECD countries, this can lead to a deterioration in the terms of trade.

Government Policies

Other than the policies affecting domestic agricultural prices and agricultural input subsidies, RUNS incorporates several other policy instruments: consumer subsidies, stockholding policies, tariffs on non-agricultural commodities.

Consumer subsidies have not been used frequently in the RUNS model, which implies that domestic agricultural consumer prices are the same as domestic producer prices. Due to the importance of consumer food subsidies in the former Soviet Union (FSU), these were incorporated as part of the base model, only in the FSU. Unless otherwise mentioned, changes in consumer subsidies are not part of the liberalisation scenarios, including the full reform scenarios. The consumer subsidies have been modeled in one of two ways. Either a wedge is introduced between the producer price and the consumer price, or a wedge is introduced between the consumer price and the world price (clearly the latter will also likely introduce a wedge between the consumer price and the producer price as well)[43]. The choice of which relationship prevails will partly depend on the available data, and partly on the historical relationship between consumer prices and the other prices. In the case of the FSU, it was decided to implement the consumer-to-world price wedge since it corresponds to the available consumer subsidy equivalent (CSE) data.

Stockholding policies, whether voluntary or mandated, play a significant role in world agricultural markets. Beyond their influence on world prices, they also have budgetary impacts which can be non-negligible. RUNS does not adequately model stockholding behaviour. Several different strategies have been implemented, though given the medium-term focus of RUNS, most have involved constant stocking policies for the projections. The different strategies have included constant policies (i.e. a constant volume level in the change in stocks), a gradual reduction in the stock change policy to zero in the year 2002, and variations in stocks based on current production ($\Delta St = \alpha S$). All of these strategies ignore the sustainability of the stock policy, or in other words, they only model the flow of stocks, and not the level of stocks. Time series data are available for many commodities and many regions on the supply-demand balance including stock flows. Where available, these data are used in the 1985-1990 period to track stocking policies to the observed data. This has the additional benefit of permitting changes in world prices to be tracked more accurately since these will be sensitive to changes in stocks. After 1990, the base simulation assumes that all stocking policies are removed since stocking is largely a cyclical phenomenon and not easily modeled by RUNS. The only exception is the FSU, where it is assumed that the significant loss of production in waste will continue throughout the 1990s[44]. Reduction of losses in the FSU will constitute one of the liberalisation scenarios for the FSU.

While distortions in the agricultural sectors are significant, there are also significant distortions in the non-agricultural sectors. These have been modeled exclusively through the use of import and export price wedges, which are specific to both region of origin and destination. In other words, for each sector, a full matrix of trade instruments is required. While these distortions are known to be significant, the data are poor, spotty, and often difficult to interpret. The wedge data are presented further in this chapter. It suffices to say that the RUNS data on export trade wedges in non-agricultural commodities are nonexistent. The tariff price data largely consists of statutory import tariffs, ignoring the significant effects of NTBs. The tariff data is also based on 1985 data and ignores more recent moves by many developing countries to liberalise trade. The trade instruments not only affect the relative price of tradables and non-tradables, but also affect government revenues, particularly in certain developing countries.

Base Trends

The model covers a time period from 1985 to 2002. There are many exogenous elements which are needed to close the model. Amongst them are:

- Population and labour force growth rates
- Agricultural and non-agricultural productivity trends
- Net foreign resource transfers (in the base model with fixed trade balances)
- Energy price trends
- Policy instruments

Population and Labour

Table 2.5 reproduces the base 1990-2002 projections for population and total labour force. The percentages are the annual average growth rates. The global rate of growth is 1.6 per cent, which will make the world population roughly 6.4 billion people by the year 2002. The growth rates are uneven. African population growth rates are among the highest with a 3.1 per cent average. In the rest of the developing economies the growth rate ranges from 1.4 per cent (in China) to 3.3 per cent in the Gulf region, and the average is roughly 2 per cent. The OECD regions and the FCPE have the lowest population growth rates with respectively a 0.5 per cent and 0.6 per cent average. The growth rate differentials will necessarily affect population distribution. While 23 per cent of the population in 1990 reside in the OECD countries and the FCPE, in the year 2002, this will fall to 20 per cent.

The global labour force growth is slightly greater than that of the population, with an average per annum growth rate of 1.8 per cent. In some regions, the gap between the labour force growth rate and the population growth rate is high, reflecting variations in the age pyramid across countries. For example, the growth rate of China's labour force is 2.2 per cent, while the population growth rate is 1.4 per cent. This reflects a relatively young population, i.e. many young people entering the labour force, while the low population growth rate reflects the success of the birth control programme and rapid income growth. Some of the gaps, particularly in the OECD regions, are most likely too large since many of the growth rates reflect historical trends and are not based on a more thorough examination of the demographic and economic determinants of the growth in the labour force.

Productivity Trends

A dynamic model requires assumptions on the rates of productivity growth. In the case of RUNS, technological progress (as opposed to growth in the capital stock), is exogenous. There is a separate productivity trend for each one of the 15 agricultural commodities. In urban manufacturing, there is a single productivity trend which is applied to the value added aggregate. Thus there are 16 productivity parameters (per period, and per region).

There are two ways to introduce the productivity trends. The direct method simply requires a percentage growth rate in productivity for each of the 15 agricultural commodities and for urban value added. This requires a set of 16×22×7 productivity parameters. Most of the parameters would be provided by specialists, but there would presumably be some gaps for certain countries and/or commodities. There could also be a measurement problem, since the technical trend used in RUNS may not correspond exactly to the trend used by the specialists. Instead, an alternative method is used which has been described above. In the dynamic calibration phase of the model the supply trends and the GDP trends are assumed to be known, and the model calculates the technical trends consistent with these exogenous trends and with the model. These trends are saved and become exogenous for all future simulations, including the base run.

Table 2.5 provides the average annual growth rates of agricultural supply for all commodities and for all regions for the period 1990-2002. The total GDP trend is also given. (The world totals are provided in the final column.) Most of the trends have been provided by the World Bank, supplemented by data from the FAO and the OECD. Global food supply is expected to grow faster than population, with an aggregate food crop growth rate of 2.6 per cent, and a food livestock growth rate of 2.3 per cent. This in principle allows the world to have a more than adequate food supply and allows for per capita growth in food consumption in line with increases in income[45]. As income grows and demand for meat rises relative to grain demand, some of the growth in the crop food supply will be diverted to livestock feed, particularly if land becomes a relatively scarce commodity. There may also be severe distributional impacts as the growth in supply is far from uniform across the regions. The region with the most to worry about is Africa where agricultural supply lags behind population growth, thereby increasing Africa's dependency on food imports. Higher agricultural growth rates in Africa would allow it to allocate more of its scarce foreign exchange resources to the import of other commodities. The Maghreb is in a similar, though less extreme, situation. The OECD countries in general will see an increase in their self-sufficiency rates, although livestock growth in North America appears to lag behind population growth.

Figures 2.1 and 2.2 present the food crop and the livestock self-sufficiency ratios for all regions in the base simulation. In the case of crops, Figure 2.1 clearly indicates a growing self-sufficiency in the OECD countries as supply outstrips population growth, and demand for food is relatively income inelastic at the higher income levels. This leads to a sizable increase in the marketable surplus of the OECD countries. Amongst developing economies, several regions increase their crop self-sufficiency ratios (between 1993 and 2002) including Indonesia, the Maghreb, other Latin America, Brazil, and East Asia. Despite this increase in self-sufficiency amongst certain developing countries, many of them will import food crops, with Brazil and other Latin America as key exceptions, and India, Indonesia, and East Asia also with marketable surpluses. The FSU, despite a small improvement in self-sufficiency, is projected to remain a large importer of food crops.

(While we use the term self-sufficiency, we attach no special importance to achieving and/or maintaining self-sufficiency. Trade and growth in trade is generally perceived as a desirable phenomenon. One of the aims of trade reform, which we are trying to illustrate in this volume, is that there are significant gains from trade reform, and many of these gains come from allowing each region to benefit from its comparative advantage. The main reason we use the self-sufficiency statistic in this volume is that it is a relatively stable index of trade performance, whereas net trade is extremely volatile since it is the difference between two numbers.)

In livestock, the picture is somewhat different as may be seen from Figure 2.2. Many developing regions attain self-sufficiency by 2002, with the exception of Africa, the Middle East, and East Asia, while in 1985, most regions were at best self-sufficient. The trends in the OECD countries are not uniform. North America experiences a decline in self-sufficiency with the United States becoming a net importer of livestock products. However, Japan and the EC experience an increase. The FSU experiences a sharp drop in its self-sufficiency ratio which could make it as influential on world livestock markets as it is in the cereals market.

Figure 2.1. **Food Crop Self-Sufficiency Ratio**

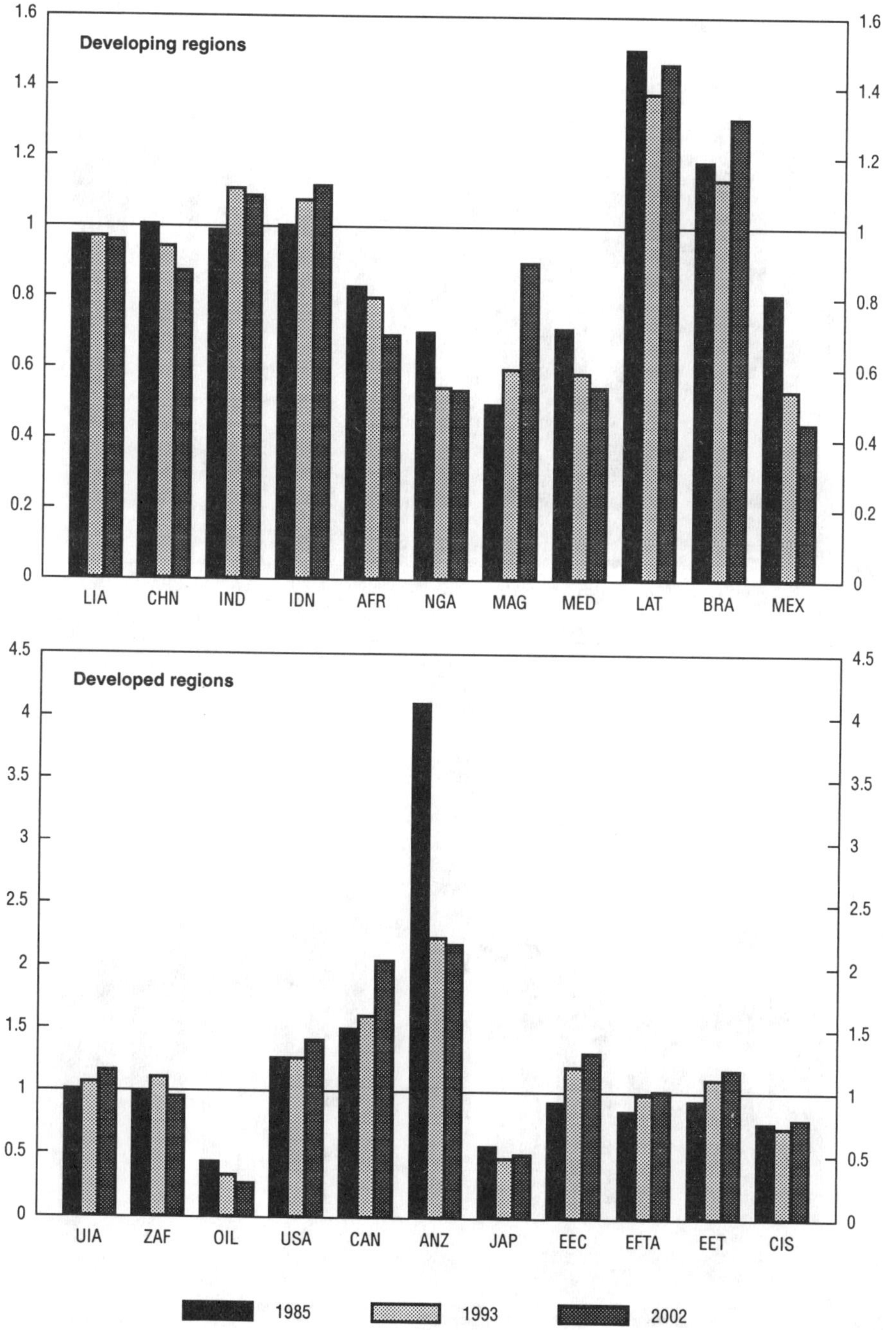

Figure 2.2. **Livestock Self-Sufficiency Ratio**

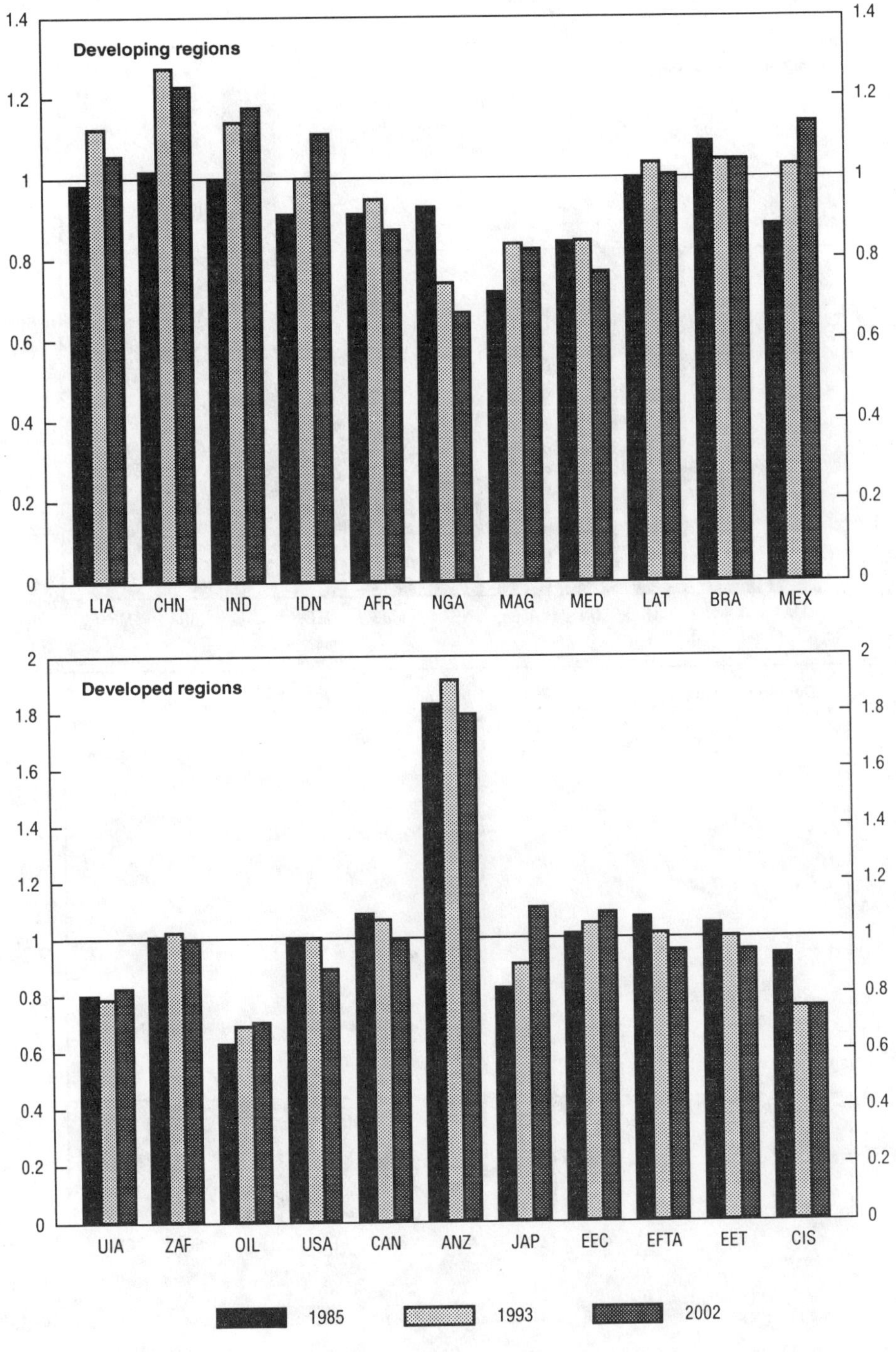

The remaining productivity trend in the model is the total productivity trend for urban GDP. This number is calibrated in the dynamic calibration phase, assuming an exogenous growth rate for total GDP. The total GDP growth rate assumptions are also provided in Table 2.5.

Real world growth is assumed to be 3.3 per cent per annum through 2002, or roughly twice the growth rate of population, i.e. real per capita GDP will increase about 1.7 per cent per annum. There are of course significant variations across regions. Some of the largest per capita increases are in East Asia and China, with per capita rates of growth greater than 4.0 per cent. Latin America and most of the OECD countries are projected to have per capita growth rates of between 2.4 per cent and 3.3 per cent. The slowest growth rates occur in Africa, North America, and in the Gulf region, the latter with potentially negative growth. These growth rates are meant to be indicative and should be interpreted with prudence. As in most exercises of this sort, it would be preferable to report the results of a range of growth rates, for example, low, best guess, and high. However, the purpose of the study is not to forecast the future, but to see how policy changes may affect the direction of change of the future. To a large extent, the analysis of the direction of change is independent of the base assumptions on growth rates.

Financial Flows and Energy Price Trends

Table 2.6 presents the financial flow projections for the base simulation[46]. The numbers in Table 2.6 are based on World Bank projections, with some minor modifications. To reiterate the point stressed above, these numbers should be seen as indicative, and further, their levels in the base run are unlikely to affect the interpretations of the subsequent policy shock simulations. The numbers do not take into account the sustainability of the flows (i.e. the level of indebtedness is ignored). The reform simulation results in general will not be dependent on the base level of the capital flows, though the closure rule itself strongly influences the results. Other models have used alternative hypotheses concerning capital flows. One option is to let capital flows drop to zero by the final period. In a time-consistent dynamic long-term model, this would of course be a necessary stability condition.

The energy price assumption is that energy prices will progress in real terms by 2 per cent on average from 1990 to 2002. For example, if the price of a barrel of oil is $20 in 1992, in real terms it will be $24.4 in 2002, or $34.4 in nominal terms (assuming a world inflation rate of 3.5 per cent per annum).

The next section introduces and discusses the trade wedges, both agricultural and non-agricultural, and the agricultural input subsidies.

Trade distortions and trade instruments

Many domestic policies, and the distortions they generate, may be evaluated with reference to their implications for trade. Subsidies which reduce the costs of domestic production serve to enhance the competitiveness of the beneficiaries, enabling them to enjoy more favourable terms than others who are not subsidised. In international trade, subsidies may offset higher costs or lower quality, reducing competitive threats. In domestic trade, subsidies serve to increase the effectiveness of one sector in defending its position, allowing it to bid resources from other sectors in the economy. Taxes have an effect opposite to subsidies and tend to penalise producers or consumers. These taxes, as we show below, may be direct or indirect.

Trade measures are among the most common and effective means of protecting or penalising different economic groups. Tariffs and quotas are widely used to discriminate against imports, while levies, taxes and licences serve a similar purpose of deriving revenue from exporters and increasing their costs. Attention in the past has tended to focus on tariffs. However, the growth of non-tariff barriers and more comprehensive technical standards concerning health, safety and the environment have broadened the range of trade-distorting instruments.

Historically, tariffs have been the most widely used form of intervention in international markets. The widespread significance of these and other barriers, and the resulting changes in the direction and volume of trade have led to a number of attempts at measurement. The different concepts and measurement methods share in common their desire to measure the difference between domestic and world market incentives.

In this chapter, we discuss the major instruments and their measurement. The economy-wide perspective adopted has called for the introduction of measures which cover different economic sectors. Thus, the following discussion is divided into an analysis of agriculture and non-agriculture.

Agriculture

Distortions in agricultural markets may be traced to those induced by domestic food and agricultural policies, on the one hand, and those which have their origin in macroeconomic policies. In OECD countries, which are not generally characterised by exchange rate distortions, macroeconomic distortions are not as significant as specific trade and sectoral policies. In developing countries, by contrast, exchange rate, interest rate and other macroeconomic distortions have tended to be pervasive. Krueger, Schiff and Valdés have shown that these "indirect" effects are often more significant than "direct" distortions arising from pricing or tariff policies.

Much effort has gone into the development of analytic measures which provide a basis for international comparisons of levels of intervention. The formulation of summary methods has been seen as an important means of heightening awareness of the extent of the interventions and providing a common basis for negotiations aimed at their reduction.

The simplest and the most widely used measure is the nominal rate of protection (NRP), which only takes account of trade barriers and measures the wedge between domestic and world prices. It is defined as the percentage difference between the domestic market price and the world price of a given commodity, measured in a common currency.

The nominal rate of assistance (NRA) is wider in its coverage. It takes into account all policies which raise the price to domestic producers. The NRA is defined as the percentage difference between the gross returns to producers — which is the market price received by producers, plus any other subsidies or taxes on output, including deficiency payments — and the world price of a given commodity.

The more that assistance is provided through domestic market price support and trade measures, the closer the NRP will be to the NRA. However, neither the NRA nor the NRP includes any border protection measures or subsidies on inputs. The effective rate of protection (ERP) takes account of policies that effect both outputs and inputs, and is the difference between the value added per unit of output at domestic prices and the value added at world prices.

The ERP only takes into account policies which affect inputs and outputs through trade barriers. The effective rate of assistance (ERA) is a more comprehensive measure and includes both the assistance to domestic production and the inputs used, and also measures this assistance in terms of the activity, rather than the product itself.

The producer subsidy equivalent (PSE) and consumer subsidy equivalent (CSE) include all the information represented in the ERA. It has been endorsed by the Ministers of the 24 Member nations of the OECD[47] and is also used, in a slightly modified form, by the United States Department of Agriculture (USDA). The OECD collects data and provides calculations for the industrialised countries. The USDA has extended this coverage and has estimates for over 22 developing countries and formerly centrally planned economies. In many cases, these cover only the key traded crops, and are based on estimates from the mid-1980s. Despite its shortcomings, the PSE remains the most consistent and widespread measure of agricultural support. Accordingly, we have adopted this measure as our starting point for the analysis of agricultural distortions.

Producer Subsidy Equivalents (PSE)

The producer and consumer subsidy equivalent (PSE/CSE) method to estimate assistance to agriculture provides in a single, all-inclusive value the sum of the transfers to farmers arising from agricultural policies, even though these may be implemented through a variety of complex policy instruments. Specifically, the PSE goes beyond simply evaluating trade measures, and also captures the role of domestic policies in distorting trade.

The PSE/CSE methodology provides the basis for creating statistics which are comparable across countries, commodities and through time and which can be easily understood by policy makers who are not economists.

The PSE is an indicator of the monetary value of the transfers from domestic consumers and taxpayers to producers resulting from a given set of agricultural policies, at a given time. It includes six forms of policy intervention: market price supports, direct payments, input subsidies, general services, and regional incentives, and tax concessions. The PSE can be expressed in different ways. For example, as a total value of transfer by commodity, by hectare, by farmer, or by ton. The choice of measurement depends on the purpose to which the statistics will be put.

The value of the PSE can be expressed in domestic prices or at world prices. World prices allow comparisons across countries, but conversion to world prices raises the difficult issue of choice of exchange rates. Where exchange rates are relatively stable, annual averages may prove accurate, but in countries experiencing rapid inflation and exchange rate fluctuation, as has been the recent experience of many developing and Eastern European countries, annual averages may mask large differences, and not be indicative of the actual price wedges facing farmers.

Exchange rate distortions are important, but difficult to measure. Exchange rate overvaluation in many developing countries penalises agriculture more than other direct measures, and these distortions need to be taken into account in measurement and comparison. To the extent that official exchange rate comparisons fail to take into account the extent of currency disequilibrium, they are unlikely to reflect accurately the translation of domestic into foreign or world prices. In general, exchange rate comparisons in the RUNS modelling system are based on the orthodox conventions of the International Financial Statistics. In OECD countries, these do not pose problems, as the official and the shadow exchange rates tend to coincide. For developing and Eastern European countries, where differentials exist, we have followed the approach developed by the United States Department of Agriculture and adjusted the official exchange rates to reflect more accurately the equilibrium position. We also use sensitivity analysis, which provides a means of evaluating the significance of the different exchange rate assumptions. This is particularly important in the analysis of the countries of the former Soviet Union.

The PSE statistics included in the modelling exercise are based on those of the OECD and the USDA. For countries where the statistics are not available, we have made estimates based on FAO producer price data. The PSE statistics are made compatible with our modelling of policy instruments, as illustrated in Table 2.7, based on a sample of published OECD data (note that the data is always presented in local currencies).

Line (1) is total production in thousands of metric tons. Line (2) is the producer price per metric ton. Line (3) is the total value in millions of local currency units, i.e. Line (1) multiplied by line (2) (and divided by 1000). Line (4) is the level of direct payments. Line (5) is the adjusted value of production, i.e. line (3) plus line (4). Lines (6)-(11) are the government outlays for sectoral support. Line (12) is the gross total PSE, which is the sum of lines (6)-(11). Line (13) represents the level of support per metric ton (in local currency units per ton), i.e. line (12) divided by line (1) (times 1 000 to get the units correct). Finally, line (14) is the gross percentage PSE, i.e. line (12) divided by line (5).

RUNS uses two policy instruments, the domestic to world price wedge, and an input subsidy which is applied to all inputs uniformly. The price wedge is calculated using the market price support level and the unadjusted value of production:

$$wedge = \frac{PP}{pw} = \frac{1}{1 - \dfrac{market\,price\ support\ (6)}{Value\ of\ Production\ (3)}}$$

The input subsidy is calculated using the sum of all other payments, and dividing by the adjusted value of production:

$$subsidy = \frac{\sum payments\ (7)-(11)}{Adjusted\,Value\ of\ Production\ (5)}$$

From Table 2.7 we derive the following example numbers:

$$wedge = \frac{1}{1 - \frac{12726}{18321}} = 3.27$$

$$subsidy = \frac{1742}{18577} = 10.35\ \%$$

These wedge and subsidy statistics are used as summary measures of the policy instruments in the modelling simulations. A summary of the statistics used in the base run of the modelling exercises is presented in Table 2.8. In the simulations of policy reforms, these base statistics are adjusted to reflect the change in the wedge or subsidy resulting from the policy reforms. Estimates for the 1985-90 period are entered into the model, providing a basis for the calibration of the model over the historical period.

Manufacturing

The RUNS modelling exercise breaks new ground by including a comprehensive global analysis of non-agricultural distortions. Earlier versions of the RUNS model, in keeping with other general equilibrium exercises, and all the partial equilibrium exercises, relied exclusively on agricultural policy instruments. As a result of not adequately capturing distortions in other sectors, earlier modelling efforts have tended to underplay the economy-wide nature of many reform efforts. The Uruguay Round of the GATT marks a major step forward precisely because it covers interventions across different sectors. Similarly, structural adjustment programmes, adopted by over 60 developing countries and formerly centrally planned economies, aim to address economy-wide distortions. Capturing these distortions is thus a major challenge for general equilibrium modelling.

The relative depth of modelling of agricultural distortions and the apparent weakness in the measurement and modelling of distortions in other sectors is indicative of two interrelated developments. Analytical attention has been concentrated on agriculture because in OECD countries this sector is regarded as the most distorted and because agricultural conflicts have become the focus of heated exchanges which threaten to undermine the GATT. That is why there have been increased efforts to attain consistent data on agricultural distortions.

Manufacturing and other non-agricultural sectors, by contrast, are seen in the OECD countries to be less distorted and for the most part have not been the source of the same degree of conflict as associated with agricultural trade. With a lower priority attached to liberalisation of these sectors, international organisations have not developed a comparative database for non-agricultural distortions. In the absence of a data bank, such as that available on agriculture from the OECD and USDA, modelers have tended to omit analysis of manufacturing distortions or to make *ad hoc* assumptions as to the level and incidence of such distortions. Thus the development for the RUNS project of a consistent and comprehensive database for the measurement of distortions in manufacturing trade is a significant advance.

The RUNS Trade Control Measure (TCM) database is a computerised tabulation of worldwide tariff and non-tariff measures[48]. The primary use of the database is for assigning initial values of non-agricultural distortions in the RUNS base equilibrium. The model specifies tradable price distortions in terms of *ad valorem* equivalent rates, and does not explicitly include other distortions, such as quantitative restrictions and voluntary export restraints. For this reason, the non-manufacturing database provides tariff rates or *ad valorem* equivalent estimates of non-tariff measures, when these are available. In the case of non-tariff measures, the database provides frequency estimates and partial ad valorem computations based on price comparisons. The database is constructed and maintained at the country level and then aggregated into the 22 RUNS regions with an automatic trade-weighted aggregation facility. The TCM information covers four of the five non-agricultural sectors in RUNS. While it has been possible to construct a database for energy, equipment, fertilizers, and other manufacturing, the dearth of information has frustrated attempts to devise a consistent database for trade in services.

Apart from data availability, the most serious constraint to the calibration of RUNS with the TCM is methodological. The model is specified with *ad valorem* price distortions on imports to and exports from every regional sector. Non-tariff measures constitute the vast majority of TCMs around the world. These are rarely specified in *ad valorem* terms. Attempts to translate their observed static effect on prices into percentage terms are fraught with methodological and theoretical difficulties. Most authors agree that it may be possible to estimate static *ad valorem* effects, but in practice these exercises have seldom been undertaken. Given the uncertainty, the widest possible interpretation has been given to the data. The database lists separately average import tariffs, average other import charges, non-tariff frequency on imports, quantitative restrictions frequency on imports, and measures of sectoral price disparity. These can be used separately or together, through the adoption of formulae for weighting the frequencies into tariff equivalents. However, given the considerable degree of uncertainty surrounding the development of the weights, it has been decided in the current version of the model simply to use the average import tariffs. (For example, a low frequency, indicating that non-tariff barriers are applied to a small proportion of imports need not imply a low distortionary effect; to the extent that the barriers are placed on key items they could have a greater distortionary effect on the economy than may be the case in a country with a high frequency.)

The average import values used in the model are presented in Table 2.9. The calculations are 1986 values trade-weighted by origin. For example, the EEC tariffs differentiate between the country of origin; the figure presented for the EEC averages these tariffs on the basis of the value of the trade with the different regions.

The difficulties associated with the measurement of economic distortions are well known. In recent years a number of international organisations, including the OECD, the World Bank and UNCTAD, have addressed the issue with a view to providing transparent and comparable data. Their efforts have been most successful in the area of agriculture, where a comprehensive data set now exists for OECD countries. Simultaneously, a manufacturing trade matrix has been developed which provides the basis for a matrix of manufactured trade. Manufacturing trade control measures, which hitherto have not been consistently collected or modeled, have been included as an integral element in the RUNS project. The construction of a trade in services database and the inclusion of improved indices for non-tariff measures is on the future agenda of the project. For the purposes of this volume, the most transparent and widely recognised of the measures are used. For manufacturing, these are average trade-weighted import tariffs. For agriculture, they are derivatives of the producer and consumer subsidy equivalent measures.

Notes

1. General Equilibrium Model.
2. A full description of the model is provided in Ginsburgh and Waelbroeck (1981).
3. A similar approach had been used independently earlier by Peter Dixon in his Harvard dissertation. See Dixon (1975).
4. Hicks (1976).
5. Simple models of this type had been developed in the academic world and described in journal articles; none had become tools for forecasting and policy analysis.
6. The Minimum Standard Models were soon replaced by Revised Minimum Standard Models (RMSMs, pronounced rimsims); however, those were still crude Harrod-Domar growth models, to which complex descriptions of foreign debt borrowing and repayment schedules were attached.
7. See Cheetham, Gupta and Schwarz (1979).
8. Those were computable general equilibrium models of the type pioneered by Adelman and Robinson (1978) and by Shoven and Whalley (1984); the solution procedure used the very simple Gauss-Seidel algorithm whose the effectiveness had been demonstrated, for example, by Ginsburgh and Waelbroeck (1976, 1979), rather than the fixed-point and other sophisticated (and complicated) algorithms that were all the rage at the time.
9. The basic reference is Gunning *et al.* (1984).
10. See for example Barro and Grossman (1971), (1976).
11. Preobrazhensky (1956).
12. Varuna used an Armington (1969) system for all commodities.
13. Linneman and Keyzer (1979).
14. However, this device is used differently in the two models.
15. The political and legal situation in the former Soviet Union is changing rapidly. The OECD Secretariat recommended (3 June 1992), using the term New Independent States of the ex-Soviet Union (NIS). However, this would exclude the three Baltic Republics which we have not split from the former Soviet Union.
16. The OECD-country aggregate does not include Turkey, which is a Member of the OECD. Turkey is included in the Mediterranean aggregate.
17. The price elasticity of supply is given by:

$$\varepsilon = \beta \frac{PP}{PP - Pc}$$

18. Wheat, rice, coarse grains, sugar, coffee, cocoa, tea, oils, other food, cotton, other non-food.

19. Beef, veal, and sheep meat, other meats, dairy, and wool.

20. Given the assumption of identical input structure for all crops, the average input price in crops is identical. However, the model includes a sector-specific input subsidy which in turn makes the input price sector-specific.

21. The latter are Armington products and therefore subject to substitutability between domestic and imported goods.

22. See Lluch (1973).

23. See Deaton and Muellbauer for a derivation of some of the properties of the ELES consumption system.

24. The value $Yd - \sum pc_j \theta_j$ is sometimes referred to as the supernumerary income.

25. The income and price elasticities are given by:

$$\eta_i = \mu_i \frac{Yd}{pc_i C_i} \qquad \varepsilon_i = \frac{\theta_i(1-\mu_i)}{C_i} - 1$$

where η is the income elasticity and ε is the price elasticity. In the calibration process, these elasticities are exogenous and used to calibrate the other parameters of the ELES.

26. The price of a Toyota is the same for all countries, but if country *i* purchases mainly Yugos, and country *j* mainly Toyotas, the world price of cars of country *i* will be less than the world price of country *j*.

27. There is a tremendous amount of ongoing research on modelling trade. One line of approach is to use different aggregation functions which may have better tracking properties than the ubiquitous CES, for example, the almost ideal demand system (AIDS). See Robinson *et al.* (1992). Another line of approach is to model trade using more refined specifications. This approach relies on the new trade theories and is closely integrated with models of oligopolistic behaviour and increasing returns to scale emanating from the industrial organisation literature. The key theme in this approach is to model product differentiation at the firm level rather than at the country level. See Krugman for some of the theoretical aspects. For empirical applications, see Burniaux and Waelbroeck, Venables and Smith, de Melo and Roland-Holst, and Delorme and van der Mensbrugghe, amongst others.

28. The migration function has its antecedents in an article by Harris and Todaro.

29. A simple example. Assume the initial price is 1, and demand is 10 per cent greater than supply. If δ is equal to 1, the new price will be 10 per cent higher, i.e. 1.1. If δ is 0.1, the new price will be only 1 per cent higher, i.e. 1.01. In either case, the higher price will cause demand to fall and supply to rise, thereby closing the gap.

30. See Armington (1991), Burniaux and van der Mensbrugghe, and King.

31. This assumption is relaxed in a later chapter.

32. All the accumulation and growth equations explicitly take into account the time gap between simulation periods.

33. Given the mathematical nature of this exercise, there are obviously consistency requirements.

34. This section was originally written by Will Martin and a more complete discussion can be found in Martin *et al.*

35. See for example, Willig (1976), McKenzie and Pearce (1976), Chipman and Moore (1980), Vartia (1983), and Shonkwiler (1991).

36. See for example, Dixon *et al.* (1982), and Martin (1990).

37. Fullerton (1991).

38. See Helpman (1978).

39. See for example, Ballard (1990), Fullerton (1991), and Mayshar (1990).

40. The base simulation is the only simulation with endogenous government savings/surplus. In other words, we allow the base simulation to calculate the future level of government savings/deficit through the year 2002. In all subsequent policy simulations, the government balance is assumed to be fixed at the level calculated in the base simulation and the household direct tax rates are the instruments used to achieve the fixed government balance.

41. The values currently used in RUNS are based on estimates from the mid-1980s. The sample size was more restricted than it would be today, both in time and across regions.

42. Formally the world price of energy is given by: $P_{ener} = P^{*}_{ener}$ POECD. If the price of manufacturing exports of OECD countries increases by 10 per cent, the nominal price of energy also increases by 10 per cent. The exogenous real price of energy, P^{*}_{ener}, is determined outside the model.

43. This is to some extent influenced by the concept of the consumer subsidy equivalent (CSE).

44. Since the level of stocks is not accounted for, there is no difference (from a modelling point of view) between change in stocks and downstream loss of production through waste and inefficiency.

45. See Brown and Goldin for a discussion of these trends.

46. These numbers represent net financial flows. In other words, they are the negative of the net trade balance in goods and services.

47. The Council at Ministerial level, May 13, 1987. See OECD, 1990a, page 3.

48. The database and associated methodology was developed by David Roland-Holst, under contract to the World Bank. This section draws on David Roland-Holst, "Estimates of Non-Agricultural Trade Control Measures for Applied General Equilibrium Analysis", mimeo, Mills College, September 1991. The paper provides a full discussion of the methodology and the database.

Table 2.1. **Regional Composition of RUNS**

1. South Asia (LIA)
   Afghanistan, Bangladesh, Bhutan, Burma, Kampuchea, Democratic Republic of Korea, Laos, Maldives, Mongolia, Nepal, Pakistan, Sri Lanka, Viet Nam.
2. China (CHN)
3. India (IND)
4. East Asia and the Pacific (UIA)
   Brunei, Fiji, French Polynesia, Hong Kong, Republic of Korea, Macao, Malaysia, New Caledonia, New Hebrides, Papua New Guinea, Philippines, Singapore, Taiwan, Thailand, Tonga.
5. Indonesia (IDN)
6. Sub-Saharan Africa (AFR)
   Angola, Benin, Botswana, Burkina Faso, Burundi, Cameroon, Cape Verde, Central African Republic, Chad, Comoros, People's Republic of the Congo, Côte d'Ivoire, Equatorial Guinea, Ethiopia, Gabon, The Gambia, Ghana, Guinea, Kenya, Lesotho, Liberia, Madagascar, Malawi, Mali, Mauritania, Mauritius, Mozambique, Namibia, Niger, Reunion, Rwanda, Sao Tome and Principe, Senegal, Seychelles, Sierra Leone, Somalia, Sudan, Swaziland, Tanzania, Togo, Uganda, Zaïre, Zambia, Zimbabwe.
7. Nigeria (NGA)
8. South Africa (ZAF)
9. Maghreb (MAG)
   Algeria, Morocco, Tunisia
10. Mediterranean (MED)
    Cyprus, Arab Republic of Egypt, Israel, Jordan, Lebanon, Libya, Malta, Syrian Arab Republic, Turkey.
11. Gulf Region (OIL)
    Bahrain, Iraq, Islamic Republic of Iran, Kuwait, Oman, Qatar, Saudi Arabia, United Arab Emirates, Yemen Arab Republic, People's Democratic Republic of Yemen.
12. Other Latin America (LAT)
    Anguilla, Antigua and Barbuda, Argentina, The Bahamas, Barbados, Belize, Bermuda, Bolivia, Chile, Columbia, Costa Rica, Cuba, Dominican Republic, Ecuador, El Salvador, French Guiana, Grenada, Guadeloupe, Guatemala, Guyana, Haiti, Honduras, Jamaica, Martinique, Netherlands Antilles, Nicaragua, Panama, Paraguay, Peru, Puerto Rico, Saint Kitts and Nevis, Saint Lucia, Saint Vincent and the Grenadines, Suriname, Trinidad and Tobago, Uruguay, Venezuela, Virgin Islands.
13. Brazil (BRA)
14. Mexico (MEX)
15. United States (USA)
16. Canada (CAN)
17. Australia/New Zealand (ANZ)
18. Japan (JPN)
19. European Community (EEC)
    Belgium, Denmark, France, Federal Republic of Germany (including the former German Democratic Republic), Greece, Ireland, Italy, Luxembourg, Netherlands, Portugal, Spain, United Kingdom.
20. European Free Trade Area (EFT)
    Austria, Finland, Iceland, Norway, Sweden, Switzerland.
21. European Economies in Transition (EET)
    Albania, Bulgaria, Czechoslovakia, Hungary, Poland, Romania, Yugoslavia.
22. Former Soviet Union (FSU)
    Armenia, Azerbaijan, Belarus, Estonia, Georgia, Kazakhstan, Kirgizstan, Latvia, Lithuania, Moldova, Russia, Tajikistan, Turkmenistan, Ukraine, Uzbekistan.

Table 2.2. **Commodity Composition of RUNS**

Agriculture		Non-Agriculture
Food	Non-Food	
Wheat	Wool	Other Manufacturing
Rice (paddy)	Cotton	Energy
Coarse Grains[a]	Other non-food[b]	Services
Sugar (refined)		Equipment Goods
Beef, Veal and Sheep Meat		Fertilizers
Other Meats[c]		
Coffee		
Cocoa		
Tea		
Vegetable Oils[d]		
Dairy and Dairy Products		
Other Food[e]		

a. Maize, rye, barley, oats, sorghum, millet and other grains.
b. Tobacco, sisal, jute, etc.
c. Pork, poultry, eggs, and other meats.
d. Oil seeds, oils, and oil cakes
e. Fruits, vegetables, beverages, etc.

Table 2.3. **Time Coverage of RUNS**

1985	1993
1986	1996
1987	1999
1990	2002

Table 2.4. **Decomposition of Price Wedge Effects**

	Net Importer	Net Exporter
$\frac{pp}{pw} < 1$	Import Subsidies (-)	Export Taxes (+)
$\frac{pp}{pw} > 1$	Import Tariffs (+)	Export Subsidies (-)

Table 2.5. **Average Annual Production, Population, and GDP Trends, 1990-2002**

(Percentage)

	LIA	CHN	IND	UIA	IDN	AFR	NGA	ZAF	MAG	MED	OIL	LAT
Wheat	3.1	4.0	1.8	0.0	-	2.5	2.5	2.5	0.0	1.0	0.0	2.8
Rice	2.9	3.9	2.9	2.9	3.5	2.3	8.6	1.9	2.0	2.0	2.4	4.6
Coarse Grains	2.1	4.0	0.6	4.0	2.9	2.1	0.8	1.4	2.1	2.1	2.6	1.9
Sugar	2.9	7.7	2.6	4.6	3.7	3.4	6.9	2.8	15.1	4.4	5.1	1.7
Beef, Veal, & Sheep Meat	2.7	7.6	2.7	2.7	2.0	1.8	1.8	2.1	2.7	2.1	2.6	1.2
Other Meats	3.5	6.5	5.8	4.7	7.7	2.5	3.3	4.3	5.4	4.9	8.3	3.3
Coffee	2.7	10.2	4.4	7.1	4.6	0.5	1.9	-	-	-	-0.7	2.5
Cocoa	1.8	-	28.3	9.2	10.0	1.6	-2.4	-	-	-	-	1.6
Tea	0.4	7.6	2.7	8.0	2.6	5.8	-	7.4	-	10.9	5.8	2.2
Oils	2.6	5.1	1.5	8.8	6.1	0.8	-1.6	0.4	3.0	3.2	1.0	5.1
Dairy	2.3	4.2	3.5	7.4	7.5	2.6	1.4	-0.2	3.9	1.9	2.2	2.0
Other Food Products	2.5	3.5	2.8	5.0	1.7	2.4	2.6	3.0	0.6	3.1	4.2	2.1
Wool	1.8	3.1	1.0	3.6	-	1.1	-	-1.7	5.3	2.1	-0.2	0.5
Cotton	4.0	4.8	1.1	2.7	6.9	2.4	-4.0	7.1	0.5	1.2	-1.4	0.9
Other Agriculture	0.3	5.9	1.3	1.2	2.4	2.1	-1.9	1.0	2.9	1.8	1.0	1.1
Food Crops	2.8	3.9	2.6	5.1	3.3	2.3	2.6	2.4	2.5	3.0	2.6	2.6
Food Livestock	2.7	6.6	3.6	4.4	5.5	2.1	2.3	2.2	3.8	2.6	4.6	1.9
Population	2.5	1.4	1.8	1.6	1.8	3.2	3.2	2.4	2.6	2.2	3.3	1.8
Total Labour	2.4	2.2	1.6	1.9	1.9	2.6	2.7	1.9	3.3	2.0	3.6	2.0
Total GDP	5.0	6.6	4.6	6.7	5.9	3.8	3.7	2.8	4.5	4.3	2.4	4.3

Table 2.5. (continued)

	BRA	MEX	USA	CAN	ANZ	JPN	EEC	EFT	EET	FSU	GBL
Wheat	2.0	0.0	4.9	2.2	2.7	1.0	2.5	2.1	2.1	1.0	2.4
Rice	9.2	2.4	4.2	-	7.4	0.9	1.1	-	2.5	8.3	3.3
Coarse Grains	3.5	2.2	2.3	3.0	4.1	-6.6	2.5	2.9	2.1	2.4	2.6
Sugar	3.8	2.3	1.0	-1.2	2.7	3.2	2.9	2.3	1.0	0.3	2.8
Beef, Veal, & Sheep Meat	2.1	3.1	1.1	1.3	2.3	5.2	1.9	1.4	2.2	2.7	2.2
Other Meats	4.1	5.6	1.1	2.5	2.4	3.6	2.7	2.1	2.9	2.8	3.5
Coffee	1.8	2.9	-6.9	-	-	-	-	-	-	-	2.3
Cocoa	4.2	2.5	-	-	-	-	-	-	-	-	3.3
Tea	0.9	-	-	-	-	0.8	-1.9	-	-	5.3	4.2
Oils	4.9	-0.2	3.6	7.7	7.1	-1.4	2.8	3.4	3.6	0.7	3.6
Dairy	3.6	4.9	0.5	-0.4	0.1	4.4	1.2	0.2	1.8	1.8	1.4
Other Food Products	3.6	4.2	1.8	2.5	2.8	0.6	1.0	0.0	1.0	1.1	2.1
Wool	0.4	-0.9	-4.3	-3.4	1.6	-	0.4	0.1	1.5	1.1	1.3
Cotton	1.0	-3.5	0.0	-	16.1	-	1.2	-	-3.3	1.9	2.4
Other Agriculture	3.2	-0.3	-1.5	-0.5	-1.0	-1.5	1.9	-1.1	1.5	2.5	2.2
Food Crops	4.9	2.9	2.5	3.6	3.3	0.7	1.8	1.8	1.6	1.2	2.6
Food Livestock	3.2	4.0	0.8	0.5	1.3	4.2	1.7	0.7	2.4	2.3	2.3
Population	1.8	1.8	0.9	0.9	1.3	0.4	0.2	0.3	0.4	0.7	1.6
Total Labour	1.9	2.7	1.5	1.8	1.9	0.4	0.5	1.0	0.3	0.9	1.8
Total GDP	4.2	4.8	2.5	2.6	2.5	3.7	2.8	3.0	3.7	3.7	3.3

1. The regional abbreviations are defined in Table 2.1.
2. For the 15 agricultural commodities, these figures represent the production trends.
3. The final column represents a weighted global average. The respective 1990 values are the applied weights.
4. The Food Crop and Food Livestock rows refer to weighted averages of the respective commodity growth rates. The 1990 production levels are used as weights.
5. Dashes indicate non-applicable values.

Table 2.6. **Projections of Net Foreign Transfers**

($ billions, 1985)

	1985	1986	1987	1990	1993	1996	1999	2002
LIA	10	6	5	2	2	2	2	3
CHN	13	9	0	2	19	50	103	184
IND	5	6	7	5	7	8	10	11
UIA	-17	-26	-33	-5	-12	-26	-43	-71
IDN	-3	1	-1	2	3	3	4	6
AFR	1	5	6	4	3	1	-1	-3
NGA	-6	-1	-3	-2	0	-1	-2	-3
ZAF	2	-6	-6	-3	-2	-1	-1	-1
MAG	1	3	-1	-4	-5	-7	-9	-12
MED	11	12	11	6	2	1	-2	-6
OIL	-3	-12	-12	-46	-33	-36	-40	-46
LAT	0	-2	1	1	0	-8	-20	-41
BRA	-16	-6	-9	7	8	7	7	3
MEX	-9	-6	-10	5	9	11	6	-6
USA	117	145	157	62	93	96	105	146
CAN	2	-8	-8	9	-12	-16	-21	-20
ANZ	-2	-6	-7	6	7	9	12	12
JPN	-52	-93	-79	-87	-74	-82	-101	-124
EEC	-46	-50	-26	8	-12	-4	2	-11
EFT	-3	-2	6	1	-8	-6	-3	-7
EET	-2	-13	-18	21	12	11	14	18
FSU	-5	44	21	8	-7	-12	-21	-32

Note: The number 0 means zero or a quantity less than half the unit shown and not known more precisely.

Table 2.7. **PSE Data for the United States, Dairy Sector, 1985**

(1)	Production ('000 T):	65 200
(2)	Producer Price ($/T):	281
(3)	Value of Production ($M):	18 321
(4)	Direct Payments($M):	256
(5)	Adjusted Value of Production($M):	18 577
(6)	Market Price Support($M):	12 726
(7)	Direct Payments($M):	256
(8)	Reduction of Input Costs($M):	685
(9)	General Services($M):	330
(10)	Sub National($M):	291
(11)	Other($M):	180
(12)	Gross Total PSE($M):	14 468
(13)	Gross Unit PSE($/T):	222
(14)	Gross Percentage PSE(%):	79

Table 2.8. **Base Run Policy Instruments**[a]

	Price Wedge				Input Subsidies			
	Crop	Lvst	Tree	Fibr	Crop	Lvst	Tree	Fibr
LIA	1.13	1.04	0.71	0.92	2.7	2.0	0.0	4.3
CHN	0.65	0.65	1.00	0.96	2.6	0.0	0.0	1.3
IND	0.84	1.00	1.00	0.83	17.4	0.0	0.0	18.0
UIA	2.79	1.57	1.00	1.00	10.6	11.7	0.0	0.0
IDN	1.18	1.00	1.00	1.00	4.0	0.0	0.0	0.0
AFR	1.25	1.00	0.91	0.91	4.3	0.0	1.4	0.0
NGA	1.13	1.00	0.86	1.65	2.7	0.0	0.6	13.3
ZAF	1.35	1.34	1.30	1.30	4.1	0.0	0.0	0.0
MAG	1.24	1.14	1.00	1.00	1.0	0.0	0.0	0.0
MED	1.11	1.00	1.00	0.81	11.9	0.0	0.0	12.1
OIL	3.91	2.41	2.13	0.71	0.0	0.0	0.0	0.0
LAT	1.08	1.00	0.52	1.00	1.9	0.1	5.3	0.0
BRA	1.04	0.84	0.90	0.80	20.8	3.8	0.0	0.0
MEX	1.24	0.97	1.00	1.02	7.1	0.4	0.0	6.7
USA	1.06	1.49	1.00	1.00	19.3	6.9	0.0	0.8
CAN	1.11	1.71	1.00	1.00	15.6	18.9	0.0	0.0
ANZ	1.05	1.15	1.00	1.00	11.5	3.5	0.0	5.3
JPN	3.48	2.36	1.00	1.00	20.4	13.6	0.0	0.0
EEC	1.50	2.19	1.00	1.00	36.5	8.4	0.0	0.0
EFT	3.08	3.30	1.00	1.00	11.7	22.2	0.0	0.0
EET	1.34	1.22	1.00	1.00	3.2	3.4	0.0	0.0
FSU	1.09	0.99	1.00	0.95	4.7	6.1	0.0	12.0

a. See appendix for full tables.

Note: Crop: Wheat, Rice, Coarse Grains, Sugar, Oils
Lvst: Beef, Veal, & Sheep Meat, Others Meats, Dairy
Tree: Coffee, Cocoa, Tea
Fibr: Wool, Cotton.

Table 2.9. **Average Import Tariffs on Urban Goods**

	Manuf.	Energy	Eqpt.	Fert.	Average
LIA	76.0	31.0	46.0	0.0	59.7
CHN	51.0	8.0	29.0	6.0	43.0
IND	106.0	54.0	86.0	51.0	87.2
UIA	6.0	3.0	6.0	5.0	5.3
IDN	27.0	3.0	24.0	0.0	24.6
AFR	22.0	13.0	17.0	6.0	19.3
NGA	29.0	10.0	20.0	5.0	24.7
ZAF	21.1	0.0	8.1	15.0	12.2
MAG	31.0	7.0	14.0	2.0	24.5
MED	17.0	3.0	23.0	2.0	16.7
OIL	8.0	6.0	8.0	0.0	7.8
LAT	29.0	14.0	18.0	7.0	22.5
BRA	68.0	23.0	53.0	10.0	41.5
MEX	18.4	4.1	16.8	0.2	17.0
USA	3.9	0.6	3.1	0.0	3.1
CAN	4.7	3.5	4.1	0.0	4.5
ANZ	12.0	1.0	7.0	0.0	10.2
JPN	1.8	2.6	1.3	0.0	2.3
EEC	4.3	0.4	4.4	1.7	3.4
EFT	1.0	0.0	1.0	0.0	0.8
EET	15.0	5.0	13.0	5.0	12.0
FSU	0.0	0.0	0.0	0.0	0.0

Chapter 3

Analysis of Trade Liberalisation

Introduction

The trade liberalisation debate has a long history. Modern trade theory and empirical work on liberalisation have focused on developing countries, especially on the debate between the import substitution (IS) and the export promotion (EP) models of development. The EP model appears to have gained broad acceptance, both in theory and in practice. In the early 1980s, with the onset of the debt crisis, economists switched their emphasis towards the problems of structural adjustment. Once again, the theory and empirical evidence leaned towards trade reform and opening up of domestic economies (albeit often under the pressure of conditionality programmes). Most empirical studies of trade reform and structural adjustment have relied on single country models and for the most part have assumed an exogenous rest-of-the-world component, with at best, downward sloping export demand curves. While these models have proven to be useful, they are of limited value for trying to analyse the consequences of global trade reform like that envisaged in the Uruguay Round of GATT negotiations.

Global models are fundamental because they pick up the **endogenous** changes in world prices, as well as indicating the global changes in world trade patterns. As noted in Chapter 1, there have been three general equilibrium models of global trade reform: IIASA, RUNS, and WALRAS. All three have emphasized agricultural trade reform. The IIASA model has a sophisticated description of agricultural production and significant resources were expended in developing an appropriate specification and estimation. The non-agricultural sectors were collapsed into one large aggregate, so it is somewhat limited for looking at the larger trade reform issues. WALRAS, while focusing on agricultural trade liberalisation, has limited modelling of agricultural production, modelling only two agricultural sectors. The WALRAS study concentrated on the effects on the non-agricultural sectors of an agricultural trade reform scenario. The WALRAS study also limited the modelling to the OECD regions; the non-OECD countries were aggregated together and not modeled as a fully specified region. Further, the WALRAS model is a comparative static model and does not capture the dynamic effects of trade liberalisation. An important advance of the WALRAS model, was the development and use of detailed agricultural policies. The PSE data, supplied by the OECD Agricultural Directorate, was broken down into six major agricultural price policy instruments, and other non-price instruments were implemented as well including quotas and land set-asides. The RUNS model has some key features from both the IIASA model and the WALRAS model. The RUNS model is global, with 22 regions, dynamic, has strong emphasis on agriculture (with 15 agricultural sectors), incorporates the non-agricultural economy, has a diverse set of policy instruments, and importantly, is based on an up-to-date database.

The following sections analyse the bases of the more important simulations of this volume — global trade reform, both partial and full. The trade reform scenarios have been split into both agricultural and non-agricultural components, as well as liberalising both sectors simultaneously. This enables the decomposition of the different effects. The basic reference simulations assume no labour market imperfections. Economists and economic modelers have struggled with the problem of representing labour market imperfections in models. It is desirable therefore to present the basic results before taking into account the complications induced by unemployment and its implementation. In the latter part of this chapter, the reform simulations are run again, with labour market imperfections. These simulations can thus be compared and analysts and policy makers can choose the results which match their biases. The main reasons for introducing unemployment are the obvious persistence of unemployment in many regions of the world, and the linkage between food prices and real urban incomes. While the modelling of unemployment in RUNS is *ad hoc*, there is an element of user flexibility in the model which allows the analyst to assume different degrees of labour market friction in individual regions.

Two main elements help identify the winners and losers from trade reform. One is the level of the distortions. In agriculture, the largest distortions are in some of the OECD regions, notably the EC, EFTA, and Japan, as well as in some of the high income NIEs. These regions will tend to gain from trade reform because the high agricultural distortions prove to have high economy-wide costs which are not fully reflected in the direct fiscal and consumer budgets. The second element is the relative trade position of each region[1]. Regions which are major food importers are likely to suffer from agricultural trade reform if trade reform leads to higher world food prices. On the other hand, food exporters will gain from higher food prices. In the following sections, we will see how these two elements interact to provide the overall worldwide outlook following trade reform.

In the context of the Uruguay Round of GATT trade reform negotiations, clearly the multi-sectoral trade reform scenarios are the most relevant for providing insight into the likely consequences of a successful conclusion of such negotiations. With this in mind, we have developed an important data set of bilateral trade measures for the non-agricultural sector[2]. First, however, we will analyse the consequences of agricultural trade reform only, and then, separately, the effects of non-agricultural trade reform alone. This will provide insight for the final section, where both sectors are liberalised.

Agricultural Trade Reform

Agricultural trade reform has proven to be one of the most difficult areas of the trade negotiations. In fact, the Uruguay Round is the first time that the GATT multilateral negotiations have included agriculture and, to a large extent, it is agriculture which has proven to be the stumbling block standing in the way of a successful conclusion. The reasons for this difficulty are complex and vary from region to region, from country to country. Amongst the industrialised economies the traditional reasons for protection have been food security, protection of rural incomes, maintenance of the rural economy, and price stabilization. More recently, agricultural trade policies also have been used strategically, particularly by the United States and the EC, each region battling for market share. This has produced high rates of agricultural protection in the industrialised countries, agricultural trade wars, increasing fiscal and consumer costs, and a reduction in world agricultural prices as *ex ante* supply exceeds demand. The reduction of protection of agriculture has also been hindered by domestic forces, such as the considerable influence of farm interests in the United States Congress, especially the Senate. There is little agricultural trade friction amongst the developing countries. However, several large (and small) developing countries have taken an increasingly active role (for example, as participants in the Cairns Group) in the Uruguay Round to defend their interests. In much of the developing world, agriculture tends to be taxed. This has the effect of reducing domestic production and increasing domestic demand, i.e. if anything, it stimulates imports. The main exceptions in the developing world are the large food exporters, particularly in Latin America. These countries compete on the same market as the OECD countries and are penalised by agricultural policies of the OECD countries: they are faced with reduced market shares and low commodity prices. All regions have a stake in agricultural trade reform, though, as indicated by some of the simulations, some regions may lose in the short run from reform.

Partial Agricultural Trade Reform

A successful conclusion of the Uruguay Round will lead to a partial trade reform which will be implemented throughout most of the remainder of the 1990s. In the context of RUNS, partial trade liberalisation has been modeled as follows:

- Agricultural tariff equivalents are reduced by 30 per cent for all agricultural commodities in all regions (including regions which are not currently members of the GATT). If a country protects its agriculture, this implies a 30 per cent reduction in import tariffs or a 30 per cent reduction in export subsidies[3]. If a country is taxing its agriculture, this implies a 30 per cent reduction in its import subsidy or a 30 per cent reduction in its export tax[4]. The latter is unlikely to be a major issue at the GATT because it is trade-creating, rather than a trade impediment. However, further pressure for trade reform comes from other multilateral institutions, which are promoting trade reform for reasons of efficiency, and often make trade reform a condition for obtaining loans for structural adjustment. The reduction in the tariff rate is assumed to occur entirely in the year 1993, and the new rate is held constant for the rest of the simulation period at the lower level.
- All agricultural input subsidies are reduced by 30 per cent.

Land set-aside policies are assumed to remain the same, in both the United States and the EC, though changes in land set-asides could have supply-side implications. No changes are made to the technical progress coefficients[5]. While the actual partial trade reforms are likely to be more complex than the reforms implemented within the context of the RUNS model, the model will capture the major directional changes in both prices and trade volumes.

Under partial **agricultural** trade liberalisation, the world price rises for many of the major commodities: wheat, coarse grains, sugar, meats, vegetable oils, and dairy products. Table 3.1 reproduces the change in world agricultural prices for different reform scenarios. In many regions, particularly the OECD regions, the production of these commodities is significantly protected, and the consumer price is high. A reduction in the rate of protection in these countries leads to a reduction in production and a rise in world prices. This phenomenon is reinforced on the consumption side. A lowering of the domestic price leads to an increase in consumption, and strengthens the rise in the world price. There are also some notable exceptions to these trends: coffee and cocoa, and to a lesser extent, rice. The major producers of coffee, cocoa, and rice tend to tax the production of these commodities. Under partial liberalisation, producers will increase production as the domestic price rises. This leads to a global rise in production and therefore to a reduction in world prices.

The changes in world prices already indicate some of the regions which stand to gain from agricultural trade reform. Exporters of grains, beef, dairy products, and sugar, will benefit from the improvement in the agricultural terms of trade. Importers of these same commodities will face a deterioration in their terms of trade. The importers of food also tend to be major exporters of coffee and cocoa. This further aggravates the deterioration in the terms of trade, leading to even larger losses.

The figures in Table 3.2 reflect some of these notions. It presents the changes in real income, shown as a change in welfare in the year 2002, as a percentage of the base simulation GDP in the year 2002[6]. Almost all regions gain in real income, some quite significantly. The regions which do not fare well include most of sub-Saharan Africa, Indonesia, and the Mediterranean regions. Indonesia, though a grain exporter, is mainly exporting rice whose price declines. Likewise it exports coffee and cocoa, also commodities which decline in price. On the other hand, Indonesia imports wheat, meats, and dairy products which are all increasing in price. These two effects combine to provide a significant decline in Indonesia's terms of trade. Moreover, rural production in Indonesia is protected. This is a consequence of its food self-sufficiency policy. The reduction in the level of protection leads to a contraction in rural income, which is only partially compensated by an increase in urban income since the rural economy still represents a significant share of the overall economy.

In terms of welfare gains, partial agricultural trade liberalisation leads to a per annum global gain of $190 billion (1992 dollars)[7]. Of this amount, $120 billion (1992 dollars) accrues to the OECD countries and $70 billion (1992 dollars) to the developing regions. Amongst the losing regions, total losses are less than $2 billion (1992 dollars). In other words, there is ample scope for compensating the losing regions from the gains of the better off regions, in particular the OECD countries.

Full Agricultural Trade Reform

As a basis for comparison, we have simulated the consequences of full agricultural trade liberalisation. This is similar to the above simulation, except that all domestic prices are set to world agricultural prices, and all input subsidies are set to zero.

The changes in world prices are in general amplified by comparison to the partial reform scenario. Cereal prices which increase by 18 per cent in the partial reform, increase by 30 per cent under complete agricultural reform. Meat and dairy prices increase from 10 per cent to 27 per cent, and the price of sugar increases by as much 60 per cent. The increase in cereal prices may be higher than reflected in some other analyses. Demand in the highly protected OECD countries will increase, particularly in the feed sector. The drop in feed prices will induce a switch to feed. This is particularly true in the other meats sector. A relaxation of the land set-aside programme would also lead to a reduction in the price rise of cereals. The price of coffee and cocoa decrease somewhat more by about 10 per cent. The only shift in sign is the price of rice which declined by 2 per cent in the case of a partial liberalisation, but increases by almost 6 per cent in the case of full liberalisation.

The consequence for income gains also tends to be greater, the gainers gain more, the losers lose more. In the developing regions, the main beneficiaries are regions like China, India, and Low Income Asia which tend to tax agriculture. Given the high percentage of the rural population, these regions gain significantly from lower taxation and higher world prices. Other beneficiaries include the food exporting regions such as Latin America and South Africa. Both of these regions benefit from higher world agricultural prices and greater market shares. The OECD countries do very well. The European regions and Japan gain because of the high distortions which affect directly consumer and government budgets. Moreover, since agricultural protection is implicitly a tax on manufacturing, with its removal resources flow into the urban sector where Europe and Japan have a comparative advantage. The food-exporting OECD countries are aided significantly by agricultural trade liberalisation, although the gains for the United States are small.

In monetary terms, full agricultural liberalisation leads to a per annum global income gain of $430 billion (1992 dollars). Of this, $250 billion (1992 dollars) accrues to the OECD countries, and $180 billion (1992 dollars) to the rest of the world. The losses are also greater, reaching a value of $21 billion (1992 dollars). Once again, however, compensation mechanisms can easily be devised which leave all regions better off.

Non-Agricultural Trade Reform

In this section, we will analyse the consequences of trade reform in the non-agricultural sectors alone[8]. The main element to consider in the reform of the urban sectors is that we are using estimates of import tariffs which indicate that tariffs are relatively high in many developing countries, and very low in the OECD countries. However, our tariff estimates do not embody two phenomena. The estimates ignore the effects of non-tariff barriers (NTBs), which can be significant, particularly in some sectors and within the OECD regions. Therefore our estimates are likely to underestimate the actual trade barriers as well as the potential gains from trade reform. On the other hand, the estimates of import tariffs are based on 1985 data. There is increasing evidence that many countries, particularly developing countries, have already undertaken significant steps towards reducing trade barriers. In this context, we may be overestimating the gains from trade reform, particularly amongst the developing regions.

Partial Non-Agricultural Trade Reform

The first reform scenario consists of a partial trade liberalisation, similar to that of the Uruguay Round negotiations. In the RUNS model, this has been modeled as follows:

> Import tariffs on non-agricultural commodities are all reduced by 30 per cent. Note that the import tariffs in RUNS are sector- and region-specific. For example, India's import tariffs on manufactured goods may differ depending on the region of origin. An initial 100 per cent tariff on goods from the United States will be reduced to 70 per cent, while an initial 20 per cent tariff on goods from Africa will be reduced to 14 per cent.

All agricultural instruments are unchanged from their levels of the base simulation.

The results of manufacturing trade liberalisation are less striking than the results from agricultural trade liberalisation. In most regions, the welfare improvements are small, and the list of losing regions is larger. Most of the Asian regions are better off. The rural regions in the larger countries are much better off as the cost of inputs decreases significantly. The average manufacturing import tariffs vary from 43 per cent to 87 per cent in Asia. Given the high share of the rural sector in these economies, the overall benefit in these regions is positive, even if the urban sector suffers a loss. The losses in the urban sector are somewhat mitigated by lower domestic prices for imports. In many developing regions, the economy suffers an overall loss. The losses incurred in the urban sector are not compensated by the gains in the rural sector. Apart from Brazil, tariff rates to begin with are significantly lower than the tariff rates in Asia. The relative decrease in the cost of inputs is therefore diminished. The share of the rural economy is also not as high as in Asia (except in Africa). Finally, world agricultural prices decrease slightly as demand shifts from food to manufactured goods. The combination of these three items mitigates the gain of the rural economy, enough to make the countries suffer an overall loss from manufacturing trade liberalisation.

While these results may appear to be somewhat worrisome, it is necessary to point out here that a model like RUNS is somewhat limited in several aspects. The closure rule which implements a fixed trade balance forces countries to undertake a real devaluation. As import tariffs are reduced, domestic demand for imports increases putting pressure on the trade balance. This forces countries to undertake a real exchange rate devaluation in order to increase their exports. However, evidence shows that a credible policy of trade reform, like that undertaken in Chile or Mexico, for example, often leads to significant inflows of capital as investment opportunities become more attractive. Moreover, opening up of domestic markets induces producers to innovate, search out niche markets, develop new products, and increase quality in order to meet possibly more stringent world trade standards. Again, this is a factor of trade development which is not captured by RUNS[9]. Also, as mentioned above, we believe we are underestimating the levels of trade barriers in the OECD countries and the reform simulation ignores services, for which neither consistent nor comprehensive data exist (neither for trade volumes nor for trade barriers).

Overall manufacturing trade reform is beneficial for the OECD countries. Since import demand is increasing in the rest of the world, manufacturing exports of OECD countries increase and this provides a boost to the urban economy. The main exceptions are the food-exporting economies of Australia/New Zealand and Canada. World agricultural prices decrease somewhat leading to a negative terms-of-trade shock. Furthermore, they are net importers of manufactured goods which tend to increase in price, further deteriorating the terms of trade. Finally, as their main trading partners are other OECD regions, they do not benefit as much from the increase in imports from non-OECD countries.

The total gains only amount to $29 billion (1992 dollars), or 15 per cent of the gains from partial agricultural liberalisation. Of this, $18 billion (1992 dollars), or about 60 per cent of the gains accrue to the OECD countries. Within the regions of non-OECD countries, the total gains are $23 billion (1992 dollars) and the total losses are $12 billion (1992 dollars).

Full Non-Agricultural Trade Reform

In this section we summarise the results of full manufacturing liberalisation. The results of the previous section tend to be amplified. In particular, food prices which decreased by roughly 2 per cent in the partial reform scenario, now decrease by about 8 per cent. In those regions with very high tariff distortions, the removal of the tariffs, and therefore the reduction in production costs, more than compensates for the reduction in food prices. In the regions where subsistence farming is still prevalent, the removal of import tariffs has little impact on the cost of production. In those regions where the tariffs are low to begin with, the drop in world agricultural prices is enough to drop the profitably of farming, leading to significant losses in the rural sector. The big gainers in the rural sector are China, India, and Brazil.

In most of the non-OECD countries, the urban sector loses out to increased competition and a mandatory reduction in the real exchange rate. The lone exception is Upper Income Asia. All the OECD regions benefit from increasing manufacturing exports except for Australia/New Zealand and Canada.

The global welfare gains sum to $81 billion (1992 dollars), an 180 per cent improvement over the partial welfare gains, but significantly less than the gains from full agricultural trade reform. The gains in the OECD countries sum to $64 billion (1992 dollars). The positive gain in the non-OECD countries amounts to $70 billion (1992 dollars), however the losses add up to $53 billion (1992 dollars).

Multi-Sector Trade Reform

The previous two sections analysed the consequences of trade reform by sector: agriculture and non-agriculture. In this section, we combine the two, and implement trade reform in both sectors. The first simulation looks at the results of partial trade reform, as would be likely to occur at the successful conclusion of the Uruguay Round. As above, we have simply assumed a 30 per cent, across-the-board reduction of all tariffs (and input subsidies), on **all** commodities. The next simulation, indicates the maximum possible gains from complete removal of all distortions in the RUNS model.

Partial Trade Reform

The figures in Tables 3.4 and 3.5 indicate the changes in world prices and in real incomes from the multi-sector partial trade reform. The changes in world prices by and large reflect the changes in world prices observed when reform is limited to the agricultural sector only. In other words, for most agricultural products, there is a rise in the world price, with declines in rice, coffee and cocoa. However, the price rises are dampened and the price decreases are amplified. While the supply-side mechanisms function as before, the liberalisation of the manufacturing sector leads to a shift in consumption away from agricultural commodities to manufacturing commodities, thereby causing a relative decrease in the price of agricultural goods (compared to the trade reform of agriculture alone).

The real income gains tend to be cumulative. Countries which gain under both agricultural and manufacturing trade reform individually, add up their gains when both sectors are reformed simultaneously. In some cases the income changes cancel out, and in a few cases the losses cumulate. The overall income gains reach $213 billion (1992 dollars), only slightly more than the gains from partial agricultural trade reform on its own. The OECD countries reap 64 per cent of the gains, or $135 billion (1992 dollars). Total income improvement in the non-OECD countries is $85 billion (1992 dollars), and the losses sum to $7 billion (1992 dollars).

Tables 3.6 and 3.7 provide an indication of the changes in the structure of trade resulting from partial trade reform. In the base simulation in the year 2002, the total value of agricultural trade is 10 per cent of total world trade. This varies significantly across regions. The regions with the largest share of agricultural exports are China, India, all of Latin America, Australia/New Zealand, and the former centrally planned economies. Countries with significant agricultural import shares are China, India, Africa (except for South Africa), Mexico, the former Soviet Union, and to a lesser extent the Mediterranean and Gulf regions. In terms of food self-sufficiency (as opposed to agricultural self-sufficiency), Africa, and Other Developing are both net food importers, while Low Income Developing imports crops and exports livestock, and the former centrally planned economies export crops and import livestock. The OECD countries are food self-sufficient. In 2002, agricultural exports represent only 6 per cent of total exports, and 3 per cent of total imports.

Under partial trade reform, the global share of agricultural trade falls from 10 per cent to 9 per cent. There are certainly many reasons for this, but one can expect that, in general, food consumption will decrease with a rise in food prices, and in most developing countries there will be a substitution to consumption of manufactured goods and services as import tariffs are reduced. Among the OECD countries, there are no dramatic changes in the agricultural share of exports or imports. Except for Australia/New Zealand, all the OECD regions see a drop in self-sufficiency. The drop is particularly noticeable in livestock where the PSEs tend to be the highest. Amongst the developing countries, the share of agricultural exports as a percentage of total exports increases in China, India, other Latin America, and Brazil. There are relatively small improvements in self-sufficiency ratios in most developing regions.

Full Trade Reform

Full trade reform indicates the most gains which can be achieved by removing all distortions in all sectors (excluding trade in services). What held true in the previous section holds even more in the case of full liberalisation. World prices in general increase, but are dampened by a shift in demand away from food as the domestic price on non-agricultural commodities decreases. Those prices which have a tendency to decline under agricultural trade reform, such as rice, coffee, and cocoa, decline even more.

The total global income gains sum to $450 billion (1992 dollars) per annum. This is not quite a cumulative increase of the two previous sectoral liberalisations which would be $511 billion (1992 dollars). The gains of the OECD countries add up to $290 billion (1992 dollars). The positive gains in the non-OECD countries sum to $201 billion (1992 dollars), while the aggregate losses are $40 billion (1992 dollars).

Table 3.8 provides an indication of the changes in world trade patterns under full liberalisation. Agricultural trade increases from 10 per cent to 11 per cent of total world trade. Among the OECD countries (except for Australia/New Zealand), there are very significant drops in self-sufficiency rates, particularly in livestock. Both the United States and the EC maintain their export status in food crops, but the EC becomes a net importer of livestock (and livestock products). For the OECD as a whole, crop self-sufficiency drops from 1.12 to 1.06, while livestock self-sufficiency drops from a surplus of 1.05, to a deficit of 0.89. This drop has only negligible consequences on the trade balance, with the share of agricultural exports falling from 6 per cent to 5 per cent, while agricultural imports increase from 3 per cent to 7 per cent, as a share of total imports.

For the developing countries, the changes are much greater. Both China and India become much larger exporters of agricultural commodities, and import more non-agricultural commodities (as a share of total imports). This does not make them self-sufficient in food crops (though the self-sufficiency ratios increase). There is a significant increase in livestock exports as they replace OECD production. Latin America also increases substantially its export of livestock, with only minimal changes in food crop self-sufficiency. Sub-Saharan Africa (including Nigeria), also picks up some of the new shares of the livestock market, but sees a decline in food crop self-sufficiency. Other Latin America sees an improvement in food crop exports, and agricultural exports increase from a 20 per cent share of total exports, to a 29 per cent share. Brazil also increases significantly its share of agricultural exports, from 59 per cent to 69 per cent, mainly through an increase in livestock exports, tree crops, and other non-food agricultural commodities.

For different reasons, these simulations indicate the importance of agriculture in the context of the Uruguay Round, although one should keep in mind the low level assumed in non-agricultural tariffs amongst the OECD countries. If we were to incorporate NTMs, the relative significance of the reduction of non-agricultural tariffs on world welfare would increase. Nonetheless, for many developing countries, agriculture remains an important part of the economy, in terms of GDP, employment, trade, income distribution, and share of consumer budget. The evolution of world prices and world trade will have a significant impact on virtually all developing countries. While agriculture is of much less importance in terms of GDP and employment in the OECD countries in general, the high level of protection in many of them and the large budgetary allocations for agricultural policies give an importance to agriculture which is disproportionate to its share of the real economy.

Trade Reform and Unemployment

Subsequent chapters will focus on specific regions and specific topics of analysis. Because of the importance of unemployment in many regions, this section will introduce the results of multi-sectoral reform, both partial and full, incorporating elements of partial real wage rigidity. Within the modelling community, and more generally amongst development economists, modelling of unemployment has stimulated a wide spectrum of views concerning first, the existence and level of unemployment, and secondly, if it exists, the appropriate strategy for modelling labour markets. In light of these controversies and in keeping with the tradition of other general equilibrium modelling exercises, unemployment was not incorporated in the base version of the model, whose results were presented above. While those simulations describe the results of trade reform in the absence of all labour market imperfections, in analysing the perspectives of developing countries, it is necessary to consider the rigidities in the urban labour market and how these rigidities affect the results of trade reform.

The modelling of unemployment in the RUNS model is fairly simple. First, it is assumed that unemployment only exists in the urban sector, i.e. rural labour is always paid its marginal labour product. In the urban sector, unemployment is generated via a semi-rigid real wage mechanism, so that wages are not fully flexible. The model assumes that the real wage is a weighted average of a target real wage and the equilibrium real wage. This is described by the following equation:

$$rw = \omega\, rw^r + (1-\omega) rw^e$$

where rw is the real wage, rw^r is the target real wage, rw^e is the equilibrium real wage[10], and ω is a weight parameter. If ω is equal to 1, then the real wage is **fixed**, because the target real wage is exogenous and reflects the institutional framework in each individual country, such as unions and public sector employees[11]. If ω is equal to 0, then the real wage is the equilibrium real wage. In general, ω is between 0 and 1. Therefore, the equilibrium real wage will have some influence on the level of the actual real wage.

The existence of labour market rigidities will have an effect on the outcome of trade reform. If trade reform leads to lower domestic prices, this relieves pressure on real wage rigidity, leading to a reduction in unemployment and a significant gain in urban and total GDP. If on the other hand, trade reform leads to an augmentation of internal prices, and hence to a rise in the nominal wage, this would lead to a rise in unemployment and a rise in the inefficiency of urban factors. The extent to which the benefits of trade reform are affected by the labour market will depend on several factors, namely: the degree of rigidity of the real wage, the degree to which the changes in world prices are reflected in domestic prices, and the elasticity governing rural-to-urban migration. In this chapter, we continue to assume that the price transmission is perfect, so that all changes in world prices are transmitted 100 per cent to the domestic market. If price transmission is zero, i.e. if a region follows an insulated price policy, then trade reform undertaken by other regions will have little direct effect on unemployment, and the impact of trade reform falls on the government revenue side. Rural-to-urban labour migration will have an impact on the overall level of unemployment. To the extent that trade reform leads to an increase in rural incomes in developing countries, this will lead to a reduction in rural-to-urban migration and therefore a reduction in unemployment.

Partial trade reform entails the same basic elements as above. All trade measures, both agricultural and non-agricultural are reduced by 30 per cent, as are the agricultural input subsidies, and the government deficit is exogenous. As shown in Table 3.9, under the partial trade reform scenario, world agricultural prices will in all cases be higher in 2002 with unemployment than without unemployment (see Table 3.4 for comparison). Prices of commodities which rise under partial trade reform will rise more, and those which decline, decline by less or even rise. The reason for the higher level of world agricultural prices when unemployment is present is the fact that real incomes in each region are significantly greater leading to higher demand.

Table 3.10 presents the changes in real incomes. A comparison of Tables 3.5 and 3.10 reveals that incorporating the unemployment assumption leads to much greater gains from trade reform than assuming labour market-clearing with full employment. The Maghreb and the Mediterranean regions, Brazil, Canada and Mexico continue to lose from global partial trade reform, though the losses in income are much lower. The next several chapters will discuss in more detail some of the regional results.

The full liberalisation scenario not only includes the removal of all trade distortions and input subsidies, but also the removal of labour market distortions, in other words, fully flexible wages. The overall conclusions for the partial trade reform case are similar for the full liberalisation scenario. World agricultural prices tend to be higher in the case of full trade reform with unemployment than in the case of full trade reform without unemployment. The reason for this is the same. Full trade reform with unemployment leads to higher income gains and therefore to higher demand. Table 3.10 indicates the gains in income from full liberalisation. The gains are very large in all regions.

The following chapters will develop in more depth some of the regional results, with emphasis on regional trade reform and other more region-specific simulations. In the regional chapters which follow, all simulations assume the existence of labour market imperfections. In other words, the simulation results should be compared to the results presented in Tables 3.9 and 3.10, and not to the earlier results which assumed perfectly flexible wages. Note that under the partial liberalisation scenario, there is no assumption of reform of the labour market; therefore, the assumption of wage rigidity will play an important role in analysing the consequences of trade reform. Under full liberalisation, it is assumed that labour markets are also liberalised. In other words, the full liberalisation scenario indicates the maximum attainable gains from moving towards an economy without distortions, be they internal or external.

Higher Growth of OECD Countries

In this section, we present the results of higher growth of OECD countries, and its effect on trade and growth in the rest of the world. This is not a trade reform simulation similar to the simulations described above. However, it is of interest because it is often stated that higher growth of OECD countries would serve as a locomotive, pulling the rest of the world to increasing growth. The simulation allows for an increase in the growth rate of the six OECD regions[12]. Table 3.11 presents the changes in overall growth rates for the six OECD regions. Growth rates in the OECD countries improve by between 1.3 per cent and 1.8 per cent.

The global impact of higher growth of OECD countries is favourable, but the greater part of the real income gains accrue to the OECD regions. By 2002, the real income of OECD countries will improve by 18 per cent, while the improvement for the developing regions ranges from negligible to 4.2 per cent. The low-income developing regions would not significantly benefit from this shock. The urban economies of the low-income developing regions suffer from two effects: increasing competition from imports as the price of exports of OECD countries decreases, and an increase in food prices which puts pressure on the urban wage.

World agricultural prices increase because of increasing demand from the OECD countries via an income effect. The increase in world agricultural prices is passed on to farmers, leading to an increase in rural GDP and farm incomes. While all regions are faced with more competition from cheaper imports from OECD countries, in the higher income developing-country regions, this competition is more than offset by increased exports to the OECD countries.

Overall, however, this simulation provides little comfort for those who believe that faster growth in the OECD countries is a panacea for the developing countries' growth problems. Growth in the developing countries is not pulled very strongly by the OECD countries, and one must be concerned by the small or negative effects on the poorest regions. Failure to achieve a more significant pass-through is partially a result of the existing distortions in the world trading system, which impede the developing countries from fully exploiting their comparative advantage.

The low transmission effect, though initially a surprise, is consistent with the model structure and its data. The developing-country regions which do the best, like Far East Asia, have a high degree of openness and a high percentage of their exports going to the OECD countries.

The locomotive effect depends on more than just the trade transmission effect. Foreign direct investment, and other sources of foreign capital are important components of growth in the non-OECD countries. Moreover, while the higher growth of the OECD countries was generated by an exogenous shift in productivity, the underlying causes of the productivity shift, would surely be transmitted to the developing-country regions via technology transfers[13].

Conclusion

Existing trade distortions are costly to the global economy. Agricultural distortions, in particular, undermine the growth potential of virtually all countries, except for those dependent on large food imports and/or exports of tropical tree crops. In all cases of agricultural trade reform, world prices for most food crops will increase as the negative supply response in the heavily protected regions is not met by a large enough positive supply response from those regions where agriculture is not protected. The main exceptions are rice and the tropical tree crops whose main producers tend to be taxed. Manufacturing liberalisation tends to lower relative food prices as consumption shifts from food to the cheaper manufactured goods.

The gains from agricultural trade liberalisation would be significant. A partial reform would lead to a gain of $190 billion (1992 dollars), while a full reform could lead to global gains of at least $450 billion (1992 dollars). While not negligible, the gains from manufacturing trade liberalisation are not as significant. However, the results from the RUNS simulation probably suggest a lower bound since the model does not incorporate trade barriers in services or the increasing importance of non-tariff barriers, particularly by the OECD countries. The modelling of trade in RUNS is limited by its use of the Armington assumption and the closure rule. In an annex to this chapter, several sensitivity simulations were performed varying the trade elasticities from their base values. The sensitivity analysis suggests that the conclusions for the partial trade reform scenario are not sensitive to changes in the trade elasticities.

The benefits of trade reform are distributed unevenly, across regions and within regions, creating a potential for international and domestic conflicts. However, the overall gains from trade are great enough so that it would be possible to institute measures which would enable all countries and both the urban and rural sectors to benefit from higher world growth.

Incorporating labour market distortions does not modify the basic results, but instead magnifies them. Higher world food prices are beneficial to the large rural sector of many developing countries, while lower domestic food prices in the developed countries and higher income developing countries leads to a reduction in unemployment in the urban sector.

An increase in growth of the OECD countries, which is generated by an exogenous shift in the urban production possibility frontier only provides marginal benefits to the rest of the world, except for those regions which have high trade penetration with the economies of OECD countries. This simulation does not take into account other transmission mechanisms, such as foreign resource transfers and technology flows. However, it does show that the trade transmission mechanism is limited in scope.

In the following chapters we will focus on the three Latin American regions, Africa, China, India, and the former Soviet Union, providing only a cursory look at the remaining regions. The term **Other Latin America** will be used to designate the large other Latin American aggregate region (in the tables it will have the regional abbreviation LAT). Brazil and Mexico will be designated by the abbreviations BRA and MEX, respectively. Africa will designate four of the RUNS regions, incorporating Sub-Saharan Africa (AFR), Nigeria (NGA), South Africa (ZAF), and the Maghreb (MAG). In many of the following tables, the world is subdivided into six regions:

Africa	Sub-Saharan Africa, Nigeria, South Africa, the Maghreb
Low Income	Low Income Asia, China, India
Latin America	Other Latin America, Brazil, Mexico
Other Developing	Upper Income Asia, Indonesia, Mediterranean, Gulf Region
OECD	USA, Canada, Australia and New Zealand, Japan, EC, EFTA
Other	Eastern and Central Europe, Former Soviet Union.

Notes

1. The trade position of a region is not always easy to categorise since there are 15 agricultural commodities. A region may be a net food exporter in value terms, but may be importing some key agricultural commodities. The RUNS model is also a dynamic model, and therefore the relative trade position of a region may shift over time as either its supply increases faster than its demand, or the converse.
2. See Roland-Holst.
3. Note that agricultural commodities are assumed to be perfect substitutes across the world, that is, Europe's wheat is the same as wheat from Canada. A region is therefore either an importer or an exporter. Agricultural border policies are measured as a price wedge between the domestic price and the world price. The interpretation of a country's trade policy instrument will depend on the country's net trade position.
4. In terms of the model, we have the following equation (assuming perfect tariffication):

   $pp = pw\,(1 + \tau)$

   where *pp* is the domestic price, *pw* the world price, and τ is the tariff/tax. A reduction of 30 per cent involves reducing τ by 30 per cent. This will have non-linear effects on the price wedge. For example, if the original tariff is 100 per cent (and all prices are set to 1), the original price wedge *(pp/pw)* is 2.0, and the 30 per cent reduction leads to a tariff of 70 per cent, or a price wedge of 1.7. The price wedge decreases by 15 per cent. If the original tariff is 50 per cent, the new tariff is 35 per cent and the price wedge decreases by 10 per cent (from 1.5 to 1.35).
5. This assumption is relaxed in a later chapter.
6. Chapter 2 describes the measure of welfare in more detail.
7. The welfare figures in this chapter will be inflated to 1992 US dollars from their 1985 values given by the model. We used the World Bank's MUV inflation rate as the multiplicative factor.
8. We will use the terms non-agriculture and urban interchangeably.
9. See Krugman etc. for a discussion of the new trade theories.
10. While *rwe* is designated as the equilibrium real wage, it is not the true equilibrium real wage. It is the real wage which equilibrates the urban labour market *ceteris paribus*, i.e. given unemployment exists. The true equilibrium real wage is the real wage which equilibrates the labour market without unemployment.
11. The reference real wage is determined by the model in the dynamic calibration phase. An unemployment scenario is predetermined for all regions and time periods which includes the weight parameters. The reference real wage is calculated to be consistent with the

exogenous scenario. After the dynamic calibration phase, unemployment is endogenous and the reference real wage is exogenous. See Burniaux and van der Mensbrugghe for a more complete description.

12. This was accomplished by adding 1 per cent to the urban technological growth factor. See Burniaux and van der Mensbrugghe, Annex 6.

13. See OECD (1991a), for example.

Table 3.1. **World Agricultural Prices: Agricultural Reform Only**
(Per cent change in 2002 from base simulation)

	PLIBA	FLIBA
Wheat	5.9	30.2
Rice	-1.9	5.6
Coarse Grains	3.6	19.0
Sugar	10.2	59.3
Beef, Veal and Sheep	4.7	27.0
Other Meats	1.0	9.9
Coffee	-6.1	-11.4
Cocoa	-4.0	-9.7
Tea	3.0	17.5
Vegetable Oils	4.1	17.7
Dairy Products	7.2	52.6
Other Food	-1.7	-2.2
Wool	2.0	9.8
Cotton	3.7	15.6
Other Agriculture	5.9	27.1

Note: Column titles refer to the different simulations. PLIBA represents partial agricultural trade reform. FLIBA represents total agricultural trade reform (although no changes in FSU consumer subsidies).

Table 3.2. **Per Cent Changes in Real Income: Agricultural Reform Only**

	PLIBA	FLIBA
Low Income Asia	0.4	1.5
China	1.8	4.3
India	0.3	2.0
Upper Income Asia	1.9	5.2
Indonesia	-0.2	-0.5
Other Africa	0.0	-0.3
Nigeria	-0.1	-0.2
South Africa	1.1	1.8
Maghreb	0.0	0.1
Mediterranean	-0.2	-1.4
Gulf Region	0.6	-1.7
Other Latin America	1.2	4.2
Brazil	0.1	0.6
Mexico	0.2	0.5
United States	0.2	0.3
Canada	0.4	0.9
Australia/New Zealand	0.5	2.5
Japan	0.7	1.7
European Community	1.3	2.4
European Free Trade Area	1.4	3.1
European Economies in Transition	0.4	1.0
Former Soviet Union	0.1	0.9

Note: The figures represent per cent changes in real income. This is measured as the change in welfare in the year 2002 divided by the value of GDP in the year 2002 in the base simulation.

Table 3.3. **Per Cent Changes in Real Income: Manufacturing Reform Only**

	PLIBM	FLIBM
Low Income Asia	0.2	-0.1
China	0.8	2.4
India	0.3	0.2
Upper Income Asia	0.7	2.8
Indonesia	-0.6	-2.3
Other Africa	-0.1	-0.6
Nigeria	-0.3	-1.5
South Africa	-0.4	-1.5
Maghreb	-0.5	-2.4
Mediterranean	-0.2	-1.0
Gulf Region	-0.1	-0.2
Other Latin America	-0.5	-2.2
Brazil	0.1	-0.1
Mexico	-0.2	-0.7
United States	0.0	0.1
Canada	-0.2	-0.8
Australia/New Zealand	-0.2	-1.1
Japan	0.3	1.1
European Community	0.2	0.6
European Free Trade Area	0.0	0.1
European Economies in Transition	-0.3	-1.1
Former Soviet Union	0.0	0.2

Note: The figures represent per cent changes in real income. This is measured as the change in welfare in the year 2002 divided by the value of GDP in the year 2002 in the base simulation.

Table 3.4. **World Agricultural Prices: Multisectoral Reform**
(Per cent change in 2002 from base simulation)

	PLIB	FLIB
Wheat	3.5	16.9
Rice	-5.0	-8.7
Coarse Grains	1.5	8.7
Sugar	8.0	46.6
Beef, Veal & Sheep	2.8	17.8
Other Meats	-1.2	-0.5
Coffee	-8.2	-19.8
Cocoa	-5.7	-16.6
Tea	0.1	2.1
Vegetable Oils	1.7	6.1
Dairy Products	5.1	40.9
Other Food	-3.8	-11.6
Wool	-0.1	-0.3
Cotton	0.9	1.6
Other Agriculture	2.9	11.4

Note: Column titles refer to the different simulations. PLIB represents partial multisector multilateral trade reform. FLIB represents total multisector multilateral trade reform (although no changes in FSU consumer subsidies).

Table 3.5. **Per Cent Changes in Real Income: Multisectoral Reform**

	PLIB	FLIB
Low Income Asia	0.6	1.3
China	2.5	4.5
India	0.5	1.8
Upper Income Asia	2.6	8.2
Indonesia	-0.7	-2.6
Other Africa	-0.2	-0.9
Nigeria	-0.4	-1.8
South Africa	0.6	0.1
Maghreb	-0.5	-2.3
Mediterranean	-0.4	-2.4
Gulf Region	0.5	-1.0
Other Latin America	0.6	1.3
Brazil	0.3	0.4
Mexico	0.0	-0.4
United States	0.2	0.3
Canada	0.2	0.0
Australia/New Zealand	0.1	1.0
Japan	0.9	2.7
European Community	1.4	2.8
European Free Trade Area	1.4	3.0
European Economies in Transition	0.1	-0.1
Former Soviet Union	0.1	0.9

Note: The figures represent per cent changes in real income. This is measured as the change in welfare in the year 2002 divided by the value of GDP in the year 2002 in the base simulation.

Table 3.6. **Self-Sufficiency Ratios in Base Simulation (2002)**

Export/Import Ratios in Base Simulation (% in 2002)

	Self-sufficiency Ratios				Export-Import Ratios	
	Crops	Livestock	Tree Crops	Other Agric.	Non-Ag. Export	Non-Ag. Imports
Low Income Asia	0.95	1.07	1.19	0.95	88	81
China	0.80	1.23	1.46	1.12	48	48
India	0.97	1.17	1.13	0.85	45	56
Upper Income Asia	1.10	0.83	2.06	0.41	97	97
Indonesia	1.00	1.14	4.86	0.69	80	88
Sub-Saharan Africa	0.94	0.88	3.57	2.30	80	78
Nigeria	0.94	0.70	6.69	0.81	98	77
South Africa	1.24	0.98	0.32	1.25	82	95
Maghreb	0.91	0.83	0.00	0.60	94	73
Mediterranean	0.99	0.77	0.87	1.08	90	83
Gulf Region	0.65	0.72	0.27	0.32	99	82
Other Latin America	1.21	1.00	2.45	1.51	80	98
Brazil	1.19	1.05	2.68	0.96	41	93
Mexico	0.93	1.12	2.44	0.65	77	74
United States	1.37	0.90	0.00	1.21	87	96
Canada	1.51	0.99	0.00	0.99	93	98
Australia, New Zealand	1.59	1.81	0.00	7.58	60	99
Japan	0.71	1.11	0.15	0.17	99	92
European Community	1.15	1.12	0.00	0.49	95	99
European Free Trade Area	0.74	0.97	0.00	0.05	100	97
European Economies in Transition	1.28	0.97	0.00	0.74	74	92
Former Soviet Union	1.13	0.78	0.41	0.95	82	60
Africa	0.95	0.88	3.16	1.65	87	80
Low Income	0.89	1.15	1.34	1.04	58	53
Latin America	1.15	1.03	2.70	1.19	72	90
Other Developing	0.96	0.80	1.60	0.68	96	91
OECD	1.12	1.05	0.01	0.96	94	97
Other	1.10	0.87	0.20	0.88	78	76
Total	1.00	1.00	1.00	1.00	90	90

1. The self-sufficiency ratios represent the ratio of domestic production to domestic demand. A rate of over 1 indicates an exporting country.
2. The numbers in the fifth column represent the percentage of non-agricultural exports (in value), to the total value of exports. The sixth column represents the percentage of non-agricultural imports to the total value of imports.

Table 3.7. **Self-Sufficiency Ratios in PLIB (2002)**
Export/Import Ratios in PLIB (% in 2002)

	Self-sufficiency Ratios				Export/Import Ratios	
	Crops	Livestock	Tree Crops	Other Agric.	Non-Ag. Exports	Non-Ag. Products
Low Income Asia	0.94	1.09	1.34	0.99	90	84
China	0.83	1.29	1.30	1.06	46	58
India	0.97	1.22	1.11	0.88	43	60
Upper Income Asia	1.06	0.80	1.99	0.39	98	97
Indonesia	0.98	1.20	4.87	0.72	81	87
Sub-Saharan Africa	0.93	0.92	3.48	2.38	82	80
Nigeria	0.93	0.74	6.70	0.81	99	78
South Africa	1.23	0.96	0.34	1.28	83	95
Maghreb	0.92	0.84	0.00	0.61	93	73
Mediterranean	0.98	0.80	0.90	1.13	91	84
Gulf Region	0.62	0.67	0.26	0.32	100	81
Other Latin America	1.23	1.02	2.77	1.56	78	99
Brazil	1.18	1.16	2.65	1.04	39	94
Mexico	0.92	1.17	2.33	0.70	77	75
United States	1.34	0.86	0.00	1.22	88	96
Canada	1.51	0.93	0.00	1.02	94	97
Australia, New Zealand	1.60	1.82	0.00	7.60	60	99
Japan	0.67	1.03	0.15	0.18	100	91
European Community	1.13	1.06	0.00	0.53	97	99
European Free Trade Area	0.72	0.87	0.00	0.05	100	96
European Economies in Transition	1.28	0.95	0.00	0.78	74	90
Former Soviet Union	1.11	0.79	0.41	0.96	84	62
Africa	0.95	0.90	3.13	1.69	88	81
Low Income	0.91	1.19	1.31	1.02	56	62
Latin America	1.16	1.07	2.80	1.24	70	91
Other Developing	0.94	0.79	1.56	0.68	96	91
OECD	1.10	1.01	0.01	0.98	95	97
Other	1.09	0.87	0.21	0.89	80	76
Total	1.00	1.00	1.00	1.00	91	91

1. The self-sufficiency ratios represent the ratio of domestic production to domestic demand. A rate of over 1 indicates an exporting country.
2. The numbers in the fifth column represent the percentage of non-agricultural exports (in value), to the total value of exports. The sixth column represents the percentage of non-agricultural imports to the total value of imports.

Table 3.8. **Self-Sufficiency Ratios in FLIB (2002)**
Export/Import Ratios in FLIB (% in 2002)

	Self-sufficiency Ratios				Export/Import Ratios	
	Crops	Livestock	Tree Crops	Other Agric.	Non-Ag. Exports	Non-Ag. Imports
Low Income Asia	0.94	1.21	1.66	1.04	83	86
China	0.93	1.53	1.07	0.99	32	80
India	0.98	1.44	1.08	0.95	27	67
Upper Income Asia	0.90	0.76	2.08	0.25	97	91
Indonesia	0.95	1.35	4.85	0.80	83	87
Sub-Saharan Africa	0.89	1.07	3.27	2.52	80	79
Nigeria	0.92	0.88	6.76	0.76	98	80
South Africa	1.19	0.95	0.36	1.34	84	93
Maghreb	0.97	0.90	0.00	0.64	87	71
Mediterranean	0.93	0.96	0.97	1.24	92	86
Gulf Region	0.50	0.41	0.21	0.34	100	68
Other Latin America	1.28	1.14	3.16	1.67	71	97
Brazil	1.19	1.52	2.75	1.23	31	92
Mexico	0.88	1.35	2.14	0.80	73	75
United States	1.30	0.76	0.00	1.25	90	92
Canada	1.52	0.75	0.00	1.09	94	95
Australia, New Zealand	1.69	1.92	0.00	7.47	57	99
Japan	0.51	0.78	0.16	0.19	100	86
European Community	1.07	0.86	0.00	0.61	98	95
European Free Trade Area	0.57	0.55	0.00	0.06	100	91
European Economies in Transition	1.26	0.93	0.00	0.88	70	82
Former Soviet Union	1.06	0.86	0.42	0.94	85	65
Africa	0.93	0.98	3.06	1.75	86	80
Low Income	0.96	1.35	1.26	1.00	42	79
Latin America	1.17	1.22	2.92	1.36	62	90
Other Developing	0.87	0.76	1.51	0.62	96	86
OECD countries	1.06	0.89	0.01	1.01	95	93
Other	1.06	0.91	0.22	0.90	78	75
Total	1.00	1.00	1.00	1.00	89	89

1. The self-sufficiency ratios represent the ratio of domestic production to domestic demand. A rate of over 1 indicates an exporting country.
2. The numbers in the fifth column represent the percentage of non-agricultural exports (in value), to the total value of exports. The sixth column represents the percentage of non-agricultural imports to the total value of imports.

Table 3.9. **World Agricultural Prices: Multisectoral Reform with Unemployment**
(Per cent change in 2002 from base simulation)

	PLIBU	FLIBU
Wheat	4.0	19.0
Rice	-4.3	-6.7
Coarse Grains	2.2	10.7
Sugar	8.7	50.1
Beef, Veal and Sheep	3.7	22.5
Other Meats	-0.7	2.0
Coffee	-7.2	-17.6
Cocoa	-4.8	-13.7
Tea	1.1	5.7
Vegetable Oils	2.6	9.3
Dairy Products	5.9	45.5
Other Food	-3.2	-9.6
Wool	0.4	1.6
Cotton	1.5	3.9
Other Agriculture	3.8	14.5

Note: Column titles refer to the different simulations. PLIBU represents partial multilateral trade reform incorporating unemployment. FLIBU represents total multilateral trade reform (although no changes in FSU consumer subsidies). In FLIBU, labour market reform is also included.

Table 3.10. **Per Cent Changes in Real Income: Multisectoral Reform with Unemployment**

	PLIBU	FLIBU
Low Income Asia	3.5	5.1
China	4.3	6.5
India	0.2	6.4
Upper Income Asia	7.2	13.4
Indonesia	2.3	4.5
Other Africa	0.7	5.0
Nigeria	1.1	6.1
South Africa	0.8	8.6
Maghreb	-0.7	9.0
Mediterranean	-0.4	6.4
Gulf Region	2.4	1.2
Other Latin America	1.4	9.6
Brazil	-0.1	3.7
Mexico	-0.9	1.8
United States	0.7	4.3
Canada	-0.3	3.2
Australia/New Zealand	1.2	7.3
Japan	2.3	4.4
European Community	3.6	9.0
European Free Trade Area	3.0	5.1
European Economies in Transition	0.9	5.4
Former Soviet Union	0.0	6.6

Note: The figures represent per cent changes in real income. This is measured as the change in welfare in the year 2002 divided by the value of GDP in the year 2002 in the base simulation. For example, in the partial trade reform simulation, the change in welfare in Mexico is estimated to be $4 billion in the year 2002, which is roughly 0.9 per cent of Mexico's baseline GDP in 2002.

Table 3.11. **Comparison of OECD Growth Rates (%)**
Average 1990-2002 Annual Growth Rates

	Base	Higher Growth
USA	2.5	3.9
Canada	2.6	4.0
Australia/New Zealand	2.5	4.0
Japan	3.7	5.0
EC	2.8	4.5
EFTA	3.0	4.3

Table 3.12. **Impact of Higher OECD Growth on Key Variables**
(% change in the Year 2002 from the base simulation)

	Real Income	Rural Value Added	Urban Value Added	Rural/ Urban Income	Food Prices	Terms of Trade
Africa	1.6	0.0	-0.7	-1.4	-0.3	1.4
Low Income Regions	0.3	0.5	0.0	1.7	1.4	2.4
Latin America	1.7	0.2	0.2	-2.1	-0.2	2.6
Other Latin America	3.5	0.2	1.5	-3.6	-0.5	3.2
Brazil	0.9	0.4	0.1	0.2	0.5	5.0
Mexico	1.0	-0.4	-2.0	-2.5	-1.4	-0.2
Other Developing Regions	3.1	0.7	0.5	-1.3	0.6	1.5
OECD Regions	18.5	2.6	19.7	-4.8	6.8	-1.8
Other	0.8	0.8	-0.4	1.4	1.6	2.4
Total	12.3	1.1	13.4	-1.4	2.9	n.a.

Annex

Sensitivity Analysis of the Trade Elasticities

In the RUNS model, and virtually all other applied general equilibrium models, the import demand and export supply elasticities are key parameters. As noted in Chapter 2, import demand in RUNS is modeled using the Armington assumption, with product differentiation according to region of origin. The implementation of the Armington assumption is a two-tiered CES. Demand for an import aggregate is determined at the top level as an imperfect substitute for home goods. At the second tier, the aggregate import demand is allocated across the different regions of the model, again using a CES aggregation function. For each region, there are two elasticity of substitution parameters per sector, or a total of 10 elasticities[1].

The export supply specification is symmetric. Domestic suppliers maximise revenues of selling goods locally or abroad based on the relative price on the two markets and subject to a transformation frontier. Similar to import demand, a constant elasticity of transformation function is used, implying there are 5 elasticities per region. (We do not assume that foreign markets are differentiated by region. The exporter perceives the rest of the world as a homogenous market.) The total number of trade elasticities per region is 15, and the total for the RUNS model is 330.

All modelers are faced with the problem of assigning values to these parameters. While literature searches and own estimations provide some indication of the parameter values, they both present problems. Literature searches do not provide complete or consistent estimates. Among other problems, regional and sectoral aggregations differ. Econometric estimates have in general been quite poor. Data is inconsistent, time series are short, it is difficult to separate volume and price data from value data, and it is difficult to control for macroeconomic and microeconomic phenomena such as exchange rate disequilibria and non-tariff barriers. Faced with these problems, like as most modelers, we have made informed guesses about the value of the trade elasticities.

In order to gauge the importance of the base elasticities, we undertook a (limited) series of sensitivity simulations, perturbing the trade elasticities from their base values. There is an increasing literature on sensitivity analysis in the context of CGE modelling[2]. CGE modelers have shied away from systematic sensitivity analysis. The models are often large and require significant resources and time to solve. Computers and algorithms have improved over time, but systematic sensitivity analysis, of the type done in Monte Carlo simulations is still not practicable for most models. If we were to assume that the trade elasticities each had a known distribution function, we could design an experiment by generating random values according to the distribution function and resolving the model for each random experiment. A simple experiment would be to assign a high and a low value to each parameter estimate and to run a simulation with each possible combination. In RUNS, this would imply 2 330 simulations, an impossibly high number. Harrison and Vinod suggest taking a random sample of all the possible combinations (with replacement). This reduces significantly the number of simulations. While the example in their paper was enlightening, the model tested had only 52 variables, which they solved 15 000 times. The full version of RUNS has 77 000 variables, and takes about 10 minutes to solve. We therefore chose a very reduced sample size of 7 simulations (including the base shock).

Three sets of experiments were designed. All experiments involved the same policy shock, partial multilateral and multisectoral trade reform, which was described earlier in this chapter. In the first set, the Armington CES import demand elasticities were reduced by 50 per cent, and increased by 50 per cent (both the first and second level simultaneously). Table A3.1 provides only a summary of the results. It shows that the RUNS model, if summarised by the gain in real income, is very insensitive to the Armington elasticities alone. World income does not change, and there are some minor variations in some of the regions. It appears that the regions which do worse with higher elasticities are the big agricultural exporters, notably other Latin America and Australia/New Zealand. With higher Armington elasticities, consumers will shift more easily into manufacturing imports which induces a crowding out of food purchases.

The second experiment involved perturbing the export supply elasticities, again, they were both decreased and then increased by 50 per cent compared to their base values. Table A3.2 presents the results from this experiment. The real income gains are virtually unchanged from the base shocked simulation in both sensitivity simulations. In the final experiment, both the Armington and the CET elasticities were perturbed simultaneously, first divided by two, and then increased by 50 per cent. The resulting income gains were slightly more sensitive in this case, with the change in global real income ranging from 0.6 per cent with lower elasticities, to 0.8 per cent with higher trade elasticities.

Due to the limited nature of these experiments, these simulations do not provide conclusive evidence of the robustness of the RUNS results with respect to the trade elasticities. However, we feel confident that the base values of the trade elasticities are not the critical elements of the RUNS model. Further diagnostic testing of the RUNS model would be useful to determine the robustness of RUNS to other critical elements, such as the rural and urban production elasticities, and also the model's robustness to alternative specifications[3].

Notes and References

1. Agricultural commodities are assumed to be homogeneous. Implicitly this means that the elasticity of substitution is infinite.
2. For example, see van der Mensbrugghe *et al.*, and Harrison and Vinod.
3. Some of these issues will be covered in van der Mensbrugghe and Burniaux.

Table A3.1. **Impact of Partial Multilateral Liberalisation on Real Income Sensitivity with Respect to the Armington Elasticities**

(% change in the Year 2002 from the base simulation)

Armington Elasticities	-50%	BASE	+50%
Low Income Asia	0.4	0.6	0.8
China	2.3	2.6	2.8
India	0.6	0.6	0.5
Upper Income Asia	1.7	1.8	1.9
Indonesia	-0.6	-0.6	-0.5
Other Africa	-0.2	-0.2	-0.1
Nigeria	-0.3	-0.4	-0.4
South Africa	-0.3	-0.3	-0.3
Maghreb	-0.4	-0.4	-0.4
Mediterranean	-0.5	-0.4	-0.3
Gulf Region	0.0	0.5	0.6
Other Latin America	1.1	0.6	0.5
Brazil	0.2	0.3	0.3
Mexico	0.1	0.0	-0.1
United States	0.2	0.2	0.2
Canada	0.4	0.4	0.4
Australia, New Zealand	0.3	0.3	0.2
Japan	1.0	0.9	0.8
European Community	1.3	1.4	1.5
European Free Trade Area	1.4	1.6	1.6
European Economies in Transition	0.1	0.2	0.3
Former Soviet Union	0.1	0.0	0.0
Africa	-0.3	-0.3	-0.3
Low Income	1.6	1.7	1.8
Latin America	0.4	0.3	0.3
Other Developing	0.5	0.8	0.9
OECD	0.7	0.8	0.7
Other	0.1	0.1	0.1
Total	0.7	0.7	0.7

Notes: This table shows the percentage change in real income from partial multilateral and multisectoral trade reform. The middle column refers to the results of the policy shock using the base elasticities. The first column shows the results from the policy shock when the Armington elasticities are 50 per cent of the base values. The third column refers to the results of the policy shock when the Armington elasticities are increased by 50 per cent.

Table A3.2. **Impact of Partial Multilateral Liberalisation on Real Income Sensitivity with Respect to the CET Elasticities**
(% change in the Year 2002 from the base simulation)

CET Elasticities	-50%	BASE	+50%
Low Income Asia	0.5	0.6	0.6
China	2.6	2.6	2.6
India	0.5	0.6	0.6
Upper Income Asia	1.8	1.8	1.9
Indonesia	-0.6	-0.6	-0.6
Other Africa	-0.2	-0.2	-0.2
Nigeria	-0.4	-0.4	-0.4
South Africa	-0.3	-0.3	-0.3
Maghreb	-0.5	-0.4	-0.4
Mediterranean	-0.4	-0.4	-0.4
Gulf Region	0.4	0.5	0.5
Other Latin America	0.6	0.6	0.7
Brazil	0.3	0.3	0.3
Mexico	0.0	0.0	0.0
United States	0.2	0.2	0.2
Canada	0.4	0.4	0.4
Australia, New Zealand	0.2	0.3	0.2
Japan	0.8	0.9	0.9
European Community	1.4	1.4	1.4
European Free Trade Area	1.5	1.6	1.6
European Economies in Transition	0.2	0.2	0.2
Former Soviet Union	0.0	0.0	0.0
Africa	-0.3	-0.3	-0.3
Low Income	1.7	1.7	1.7
Latin America	0.3	0.3	0.3
Other Developing	0.8	0.8	0.8
OECD	0.7	0.8	0.8
Other	0.1	0.1	0.1
Total	0.7	0.7	0.7

Notes: This table shows the percentage change in real income from partial multilateral and multisectoral trade reform. The middle column refers to the results of the policy shock using the base elasticities. The first column shows the results from the policy shock when the CET elasticities are 50 per cent of the base values. The third column refers to the results of the policy shock when the CET elasticities are increased by 50 per cent from the base values.

Table A3.3. **Impact of Partial Multilateral Liberalisation on Real Income Sensitivity with Respect to BOTH Trade Elasticities**

(% change in the Year 2002 from the base simulation)

BOTH Trade Elasticities	-50%	BASE	+50%
Low Income Asia	0.3	0.6	0.9
China	2.3	2.6	2.8
India	0.6	0.6	0.5
Upper Income Asia	1.7	1.8	1.9
Indonesia	-0.6	-0.6	-0.5
Other Africa	-0.2	-0.2	-0.1
Nigeria	-0.3	-0.4	-0.4
South Africa	-0.4	-0.3	-0.3
Maghreb	-0.4	-0.4	-0.3
Mediterranean	-0.5	-0.4	-0.3
Gulf Region	0.0	0.5	0.6
Other Latin America	1.1	0.6	0.5
Brazil	0.2	0.3	0.3
Mexico	0.0	0.0	0.0
United States	0.1	0.2	0.2
Canada	0.4	0.4	0.4
Australia, New Zealand	0.3	0.3	0.2
Japan	1.0	0.9	0.8
European Community	1.3	1.4	1.5
European Free Trade Area	1.4	1.6	1.6
European Economies in Transition	0.1	0.2	0.3
Former Soviet Union	0.1	0.0	0.0
Africa	-0.3	-0.3	-0.3
Low Income	1.5	1.7	1.8
Latin America	0.4	0.3	0.3
Other Developing	0.5	0.8	0.9
OECD	0.7	0.8	0.8
Other	0.1	0.1	0.1
Total	0.6	0.7	0.8

Notes: This table shows the percentage change in real income from partial multilateral and multisectoral trade reform. The middle column refers to the results of the policy shock using the base elasticities. The first column shows the results from the policy shock when both trade elasticities are reduced 50 per cent from the base values. The third column refers to the results of the policy shock when both trade elasticities are increased by 50 per cent from the base values.

Chapter 4

Latin America

Introduction

Latin American specialists need no reminder of the historical significance of agriculture in the region. Until the Second World War, agriculture dominated economic and political life in most Latin American countries. The desire to escape dependence on primary commodity exports gave rise to a growing bias in favour of manufacturing, beginning in the 1940s. The continuing diversification away from primary commodity exports in recent years is strikingly illustrated by the share of the major primary commodity exports in total exports. This ratio fell from 50 per cent in 1972-76 to barely 18 per cent in 1983-87[1].

However, this impressive change created its own problems. In the post-World War II period import-substitution industrialisation policies severely penalised agriculture. The policy of subsidising industry at the expense of agriculture contributed to the debt crisis and mounting structural imbalances in Latin American economies. Not surprisingly, the stabilization and adjustment assistance in the 1980s has been associated with the rediscovery that agriculture plays an important role.

Agriculture in Latin America is now penalised much less than in the 1970s. This change and other factors outlined below enabled agriculture to perform well in the 1980s despite sharply declining terms of trade. In the 1990s, agriculture is expected to strengthen its position further, providing a solid base for economic growth and alleviating poverty.

Although now on a more equal footing with industry in terms of taxation, agriculture remains neglected in public expenditures. The restoration of public expenditures on public goods — notably agricultural research — is vital if Latin America is to enjoy continued agricultural growth.

Agriculture Growth Profile

In the past 40 years there have been some remarkable changes in the agricultural sector in Latin America. Annual agricultural growth averaged 3 per cent and production per agricultural worker grew by 2.4 per cent per year. This primarily reflected increasing capitalisation rather than, as is commonly assumed, an expansion of the land frontier; fertilizer and tractor use rose by over 5 per cent per year, while land use grew by 1 per cent a year, well below the expansion of output.

Other sectors grew even more rapidly than agriculture, so that sector's share of GDP was cut by half and its share of total regional exports declined from two-thirds to one-third. Imports of agricultural goods (mainly wheat and rice) have continued to hover above 10 per cent of total imports, so the region remains a major net agricultural exporter. The regional picture of course conceals, so to speak, considerable differences among countries. In Brazil, Mexico and elsewhere, part of the population consumes imported food.

There has been a significant diversification of both agricultural production and trade. The share of traditionally exported products — cotton, coffee, cocoa and sugar — has fallen to under half of total production and trade, giving way to new products which initially were oriented to the domestic markets, such as meat, poultry, and soybeans. After outpacing domestic demand, production has been oriented towards exports. At the same time, more favourable domestic incentive structures have encouraged non-traditional exports, like fruit and flowers, even though the OECD countries have maintained barriers to these imports.

Rural employment and income structures have also undergone fundamental change. Over one-third of the regional population has moved from rural to urban areas in the post-World War II period. Simultaneously, rural labour increasingly has entered the wage market and land tenure has adjusted to reflect property rights.

Agriculture and Debt

Although there is a general familiarity with the main characteristics of the Latin American debt crisis, agriculture's role in it nevertheless remains neglected. Industrial import-substitution policies were associated with direct and indirect subsidies for industry by penalising agriculture. The redirection of the region's resources to urban industrialisation lowered the cost of urban real wages and increased the value of industrial output relative to food and agricultural products. As a result, there was slower rural growth and of agricultural exports. The industrial import-substitution policies, which entailed agriculture's neglect, accounted in no small part for the growing structural imbalances and associated dependence on foreign capital which gave way to the debt crisis.

The strength of agricultural performance in the crisis years of the 1980s has served as a stabilizing influence on economic activity and incomes and provided a solid base for the repayment of debt. Despite declining domestic and international prices, agricultural production and exports have reached record levels.

Economic Crisis and Agriculture

Import substitution and the associated penalisation of agriculture are at the heart of the structural imbalances which in the 1980s were reflected in the explosion of debt and macroeconomic instability. External factors — notably successive oil price shocks, sharp increases in global interest rates, slowing of demand in the OECD countries and falling commodity prices of course cannot be dismissed. However, these external difficulties were compounded by domestic policy errors, especially concerning the inter-sectoral balance and support for agriculture.

In part, the relative neglect of agriculture results from a perception of its remarkable robustness. Penalisation of agriculture apparently has not been associated with a slackening of its growth. In the 1950-80 period, agricultural growth lagged behind GDP growth, but nevertheless recorded a 3 per cent per year improvement. In the 1980-90 period, agriculture became the leading sector, insulating incomes, and the economy as a whole, from an even more dramatic slump in activity. Table 4.1 provides a summary of the principal indicators.

The crisis of the 1980s brought to an end a remarkable three decades of sustained economic expansion which in the 1970s was reflected by an annual GDP growth of 5.2 per cent. The driving force was industry, while agriculture, squeezed by import-substitution policies, lagged behind at a less thAn 3 per cent growth rate. The crisis of the 1980s reversed this picture. While GDP growth fell to under 1 per cent, agriculture became the leading sector, recording an average annual growth of approximately 2 per cent.

In part, the relative strength of agriculture in the 1980s reflects the positive impact of reductions in taxation of the sector. In particular, reductions in indirect taxes associated with exchange rate overvaluation and industrial subsidies were important. However, the strength of agriculture and the Latin American experience reflect of a more generalised phenomenon. An analysis of agriculture's performance in the course of the economic cycle in other developing countries and in OECD countries reveals the relative stability of agriculture: it grows less rapidly in times of rapid growth and suffers a more modest decline in times of downturn.

Among the main factors explaining the relative performance of agriculture and industry is the fact that the price-elasticity of agriculture is close to zero in the short run, and that this leads, in a recession, to a fall in the relative prices of agricultural goods, even though the fall in demand for industrial goods is greater. Galbraith and Black (1938), Schultz (1945) and others have suggested that the medium-term price-elasticity of agricultural supply is also very low. This is due to the prices of primary factors of production (land and labour) and the maximising behaviour at the farm level which, in the context of the relatively competitive structure of agriculture, leads to a fuller utilisation of capital stock than in industry. Factor price flexibility was shown in the 1980s, when wages and rents declined faster in the agricultural sector than in the industrial sector. To the extent that agricultural land has no alternative use, its price elasticity of supply is zero, implying that as long as the rent to land is positive, all available land will be utilised. Similarly, previously accumulated capital assets (buildings, tractors, forests, etc.) will be utilised as long as the additional income obtained from their utilisation covers at least part of the fixed cost, thereby minimising losses. In industry, by contrast, oligopolistic pricing strategies tend to be premised on the recovery of full costs, and in the case of reduced demand are associated with lower capacity utilisation. This is evident with industrial inputs into the agricultural sector (fertilizers, tractors, etc.). With output prices falling more rapidly than input prices, farmers reduce their purchases of current inputs, substituting primary factors with more flexible prices — land and labour — for new capital goods. As a result of this substitution, lower levels of farm savings and income tend not to be associated with a corresponding fall in output. Indeed the evidence of the 1980s suggests that in Latin America producer prices fell sharply and that rural-urban terms of trade deteriorated, but that agricultural output fell much less than industrial output. Agriculture thus provided a cushion for the fall in GDP. It also has provided a foundation for strengthening export performance and maintaining rural and urban incomes by increased output in face of falling prices.

Indirect Taxation

In recent years, there has been growing awareness of the significance of the indirect distortions affecting inter-sectoral relations. Schiff and Valdés found that during the 1960-85 period agriculture suffered from a net drain of resources in all 15 middle- and low-income countries they studied; indirect taxation averaged 22 per cent of the agricultural output and direct taxes 8 per cent[2]. The five Latin American countries sampled broadly mirrored the pattern in other regions, with indirect taxes accounting for 21 per cent and direct taxes 6 per cent.

These findings are striking because they highlight the extent to which indirect, economy-wide policies influence agricultural incentives. The evidence, despite its considerable shortcomings, points to the indirect effects dominating the direct effects and the two together draining almost one-third of agricultural GDP.

The question of who benefits is of course important, industry and the urban sector in general benefit directly from rural taxation and subsidies for the industrial sector and urban infrastructure and services (average industrial protection over the corresponding period was estimated at around 20 per cent).

The extent to which urban consumers and, through the real wage effect, employers, benefit from lower food prices varies considerably from country to country. In general, food- exporting countries tend to set domestic prices below world prices and, by imposing producer price ceilings and export taxes, induce their farmers to sell output at below world market prices. In Latin America, these taxes averaged 13 per cent of the value of the output of exportables. For importables, the situation is rather different. Producers of these products in Latin America tend on average to enjoy a level of protection of around 14 per cent.

In general, exchange rate overvaluation, which benefits non-tradables relative to tradables, penalises agriculture. For agricultural exports the argument is well known, but the case against overvaluation is much broader; food crop producers also tend to be penalised by competition with products imported, at prices below those that would prevail at an equilibrium exchange rate.

Domestic policy distortions in Latin America thus have severely constrained the profitability of agriculture. In the 1980s there was a diminution of these distortions. Not surprisingly, this process was accompanied by a succession of record harvests in agriculture, and, in the context of economic crisis, agriculture has become a leading sector in the regional economy. Nevertheless, agricultural growth remains severely constrained by external developments, notably the failure of the OECD countries to respond to the liberalisation challenge. The interaction of domestic reforms and external developments is examined in the next section, using the results from RUNS.

The 1985 Base Data Set

Table 4.2 presents some of the key statistics for the three Latin American regions. Two caveats should be kept in mind when looking at these tables. The base data are derived from national income and product accounts, national input/output tables, and FAO data. All data in national currencies are converted to 1985 dollars. The dollar to national currency exchange rate in 1985 is probably not an accurate reflection of the true underlying relative values. The second caveat concerns the agricultural data. All FAO data are evaluated first at **world** prices and then converted to national prices using estimated price wedges. Again, neither the 1985 level of world prices, nor the price wedge may accurately reflect the true **equilibrium** values.

Rural GDP as a share of total GDP varies from 10 per cent in Mexico to 16 per cent in Brazil. In all three regions, agriculture employs between 28 and 33 per cent of the labour force. The regional differences show up in per capita incomes. In Brazil, the ratio of rural and urban incomes is about 52 per cent. In Mexico, however, rural income per capita is roughly one-fifth of urban income. For the rest of Latin America, the rural/urban income ratio is 40 per cent.

There is a wide regional difference in export income as well. Agricultural exports represent a significant 43 per cent of total export income in Brazil. In Mexico, it is only 9 per cent, while it is 23 per cent for the rest of Latin America. All regions' agricultural imports are relatively low, with Mexico's share reaching 10 per cent of total imports.

In 1985 Brazil's total trade surplus was over $16 billion, with a net agricultural trade surplus of $12 billion. Mexico also had a surplus of roughly $9 billion. However, Mexico was a net food importer. The rest of Latin America was relatively close to trade balance equilibrium, but it was a large net exporter of agricultural products with a surplus of $14 billion.

Tables 4.3a-c, present an overview of the structure of agricultural production, exports, and imports for all three regions/countries. For Other Latin America, production is characterised by sugar, meat, and other food, and to a lesser extent coffee, oils and dairy products. Sugar, however, dominates export revenues, followed by coffee and other food. The main imports are dairy products and other meats.

Production in Brazil is more diversified than in Other Latin America. Coffee, oils and other food each represent over 20 per cent of export revenues, with sugar, meat, cocoa, and oils earning most of the rest. The largest import is wheat, accounting for 64 per cent of the total agricultural import bill.

In Mexico, meat and other food production account for 57 per cent of the value of production, followed by coarse grains, oils, and dairy products. Other food accounts for 59 per cent of export revenues, with coffee adding an additional 30 per cent. The largest import item is oils, followed by coarse grains and dairy products.

While rural GDP is a relatively small share of total GDP, the importance of agriculture, as noted above, for Latin America cannot be overemphasized. Agriculture is a major export earner is for both Brazil and Other Latin America. In Mexico, agriculture is not a large export earner, however, the relatively large rural population and its low income makes income distribution a critical issue.

The External Environment

The base simulation of RUNS incorporates a series of judgements of the basic growth rates in the economy: total GDP, agricultural production, and population. Table 4.4 presents the overall growth rates for the base simulation. As readily seen, the 1985-90 period saw weak overall economic growth. During this period, only Brazil had a small increase in per capita GDP, with Other Latin America losing roughly 0.4 per cent. In both Brazil and Mexico, the rural economy outpaced the urban economy, reflecting the trends observed above. The projections for the rest of the century are more optimistic, with per capita incomes increasing by between 2.5 per cent and 3 per cent annually.

The fastest growing parts of the agricultural sector in Other Latin America are projected to be rice, other meats, and oils. In Brazil the fastest growth sectors will be in wheat, coarse grains, sugar, other meats, cocoa, oils, dairy products, and other foods. Coffee production is expected to decrease somewhat. The fastest growing subsectors in Mexico will be wheat, meats, dairy products, and other foods.

The second main external element driving the model is the path of external (exogenous) net foreign savings. Table 4.5 presents the path for the three Latin American regions and the United States. These projections derive from the World Bank's GEM model. In as much as they are projections, the levels for the latter years should probably be viewed as somewhat speculative[3]. According to these projections, Brazil and Mexico will benefit from positive inflows throughout the 1990s, while the rest of Latin America will be subject to increasing outflows as debt is repaid.

Table 4.6 presents some of the key agricultural price wedges (i.e. the ratio of the domestic price to the world price), agricultural input subsidies, and the non-agricultural tariffs in each of the three Latin American regions. A wedge below 1 is essentially a tax on agriculture, a wedge greater than 1 is equivalent to a subsidy.

Combining Tables 4.3 and 4.6, we can deduce the following for the three Latin American regions:

- Other Latin America taxes exports of wheat, coffee and oils. It subsidises exports of sugar and rice.
- Brazil taxes exports of beef, coffee, oils, and cotton. It taxes imports of wheat, rice, and coarse grains.
- Mexico taxes imports of wheat, and coarse grains. It subsidises exports of other food and cotton.

While some agricultural sectors tend to benefit from a degree of protection, it is clear from the non-agricultural tariffs presented in Table 4.6 that manufacturing is the overall beneficiary of a high rate of protection, particularly in Brazil, with more moderate tariffs in other Latin America, and even lower tariffs in Mexico. The negative effects of these high rates of manufacturing protection are well known, and as we have seen in

Chapter 3, Latin America suffers from non-agricultural trade liberalisation as reduction or elimination of import tariffs requires a real devaluation in the urban sector in order for these countries to achieve their trade balance constraint.

The Key Results of the Base Simulation

The base simulation reflects the assumptions concerning the key trends of the economy. It also assumes that policies remain unchanged. The agricultural supply trends, the total GDP trends, and the population trends were presented and discussed above. Tables 4.7a-c present some of the key variables for each region for two simulation periods, 1985 and 2002.

Other Latin America's rural GDP share increases over time while the rural population share decreases. The combination of these two effects leads to a closing of the income gap between the rural and urban populations. The relative weight of agricultural exports falls from 19.2 per cent in the base year to 18.9 per cent in 2002, while the import share increases from 1.2 per cent to 1.4 per cent. Nonetheless, agricultural trade remains in surplus.

The structure of agricultural production does not change drastically. The shares of sugar and meats decline somewhat, while there is an increase in dairy products and other food (note that these shares represent value shares, therefore they reflect changes in both volumes and relative prices). The structure of exports does not change remarkably either. Oils and other foods increase their share of export earnings, with a fall in sugar, coffee and beef. The import structure changes dramatically. Note however, that both exports and imports are net values (i.e. the difference between domestic supply and domestic demand). A number calculated by subtraction is extremely volatile. Also note that total imports of agricultural products is low to begin with, less than $1 billion, increasing to $4.4 billion. The main import shifts from dairy products to tea, coarse grains, and beef[4].

Brazil's profile differs from Other Latin America over time. Initially the rural share of total GDP increases somewhat, but it drops to 13 per cent by the year 2002. The rural labour share decreases fairly constantly, which leads to an increase in the rural/urban income parity. However, the rural/urban income parity index peaks early, with a declining index from 1993 onwards. On the trade side, agricultural exports account for an increasing share of export revenues, achieving a 61 per cent share in 2002. Agricultural imports increase from a minor 5 per cent share to a 7 per cent share of total imports.

The production structure shifts slightly, with small decreases in production share in many sectors, and the largest share increase in the other foods and rice sectors. The import structure changes completely. However, overall agricultural imports remain negligible as Brazil is nearly self-sufficient in all agricultural commodities in the base period and becomes a net exporter of all commodities except for cotton and wool. Cotton imports make up the bulk of agricultural imports in the year 2002.

The rural share of GDP in Mexico increases from 10 per cent to 10.6 per cent, while the rural share of the labour force decreases from 33 per cent to 23 per cent. The latter is influenced by rural-to-urban migration which is a function of relative incomes. The rural/urban income parity starts at a very low level of 22 per cent, but rises to 39 per cent by 2002. The relative increase in rural incomes is related to the relative weight of agricultural exports. Initially, Mexican exports are weighted heavily towards manufacturing exports (a 93 per cent share). In order to remain competitive internationally, Mexico's factor prices in the urban sector must be compressed, particularly due to the compression of world energy prices. Rural factor prices, on the other hand, partly benefit from a reduction in input costs, notably feed costs in the livestock sector, while at the same time do not face the same competitive pressures as the urban factors. As a result, the share of agricultural exports increases from 7 per cent to 23 per cent. At the same time, the share of agricultural imports in the total import bill increases to 26 per cent from 10 per cent. By 2002, however, Mexico becomes a net aggregate agricultural exporter.

The structure of production shifts perceptibly more than in the two other Latin American regions. Sectors with declining shares include wheat, coarse grains, sugar, and oils. The shares of livestock production along with other food increase quite substantially. There is an even more radical shift in the export structure, with a large decrease in the share of coffee revenues. The largest export earner becomes the beef sector with a 47 per cent share in 2002. The change in the agricultural import structure is less significant, with only one sector becoming important, other meats with a 20 per cent share.

The Simulations

Multilateral Multi-sector Partial Trade Reform

The overall conclusion of the partial trade reform scenario, including both agricultural and non-agricultural reform, was presented earlier in Chapter 3. This and subsequent sections will focus more specifically on the three Latin American regions.

There are several mechanisms which help to explain the winners and losers from trade reform. The first mechanism is the terms of trade. Many developing regions are net agricultural exporters. An increase in the world price of agricultural products will improve their terms of trade, leading to a positive income effect which may offset entirely, or in part, the negative consequences due to the increase in food prices.

The second mechanism involves the rise in farm incomes. It has been argued by Adelman, amongst others, that the rise in farm incomes leads to an increase in the demand for manufactured products in a way which is conducive to accelerated industrialisation[5]. Indeed if one analyses the current situation in the former Soviet Union, it appears that farmers are holding back production due to the lack of supply of consumer goods for which they could use their income.

The third mechanism involves the intricate interplay between the rural and urban economies. An increase in food prices will affect the urban economy via the wage mechanism. To the extent that real wages are semi-rigid, the increase in food prices will lead to a rise in wages relative to the price of urban output, a decrease in the demand for labour, a decrease in urban output and an increase in unemployment.

Table 4.8 presents some of the key macroeconomic indicators in various regions. Other Latin America benefits from a small gain in its terms-of-trade. It exports many agricultural commodities which increase in price, except for coffee. The higher producer prices lead to higher rural output and higher rural incomes. While the higher food prices could have a depressing effect on the urban economy, and lead to a reduction in manufacturing protection, the urban economy improves because of lower unemployment and the links between the rural and urban economies.

Brazil fares much more poorly. It suffers a terms-of-trade loss of 2.1 per cent. Brazil relies more on coffee and cocoa exports for its agricultural export revenues, and the prices of these commodities fall, as does the price of other foods, such as orange juice. While the price of these commodities is falling, producer prices in grains are also falling due to a reduction in protection. Together, these elements produce a decline in farm incomes in Brazil. The urban sector also suffers a net loss. Manufacturing protection rates are very high, an average of 41 per cent, compared to 22 per cent for Other Latin America, and 17 per cent for Mexico. The reduction in protection puts a strain on urban competitiveness which is only partially offset by lower domestic prices. Brazil also relies heavily on agricultural exports, and thus with a loss of competitiveness in agriculture, Brazil undergoes a real devaluation in order to meet its balance-of-payments constraint.

Mexico has increases in both rural and urban GDP which mask a loss of real income (i.e. welfare as opposed to GDP) in the urban sector, which is greater than the gain in the rural sector. Mexico suffers from a terms-of-trade loss which lowers national income. The rural sector benefits from higher producer prices for dairy products and livestock, while lower prices for grains also benefit the livestock sector. The high non-agricultural tariffs were also a tax on agriculture, and a reduction in these tariffs boosts agricultural exports from Mexico.

These results do not compare favourably with the no unemployment scenario, except for Other Latin America. Other Latin America sees a significant improvement in its terms of trade, which provides a counterweight to the negative effects of higher food prices and their impact on urban unemployment. For Brazil and Mexico, the higher food prices and the obligatory higher competitiveness of the urban sector lead to significant real devaluations, which reverse the gains from trade reform under the no unemployment alternative. In both countries, the rural sector is effectively taxed by urban protection, and while the rural sector does better in Mexico than in Brazil, in part, this can be attributed to Brazil's large exports of coffee and cocoa.

Full Multilateral Liberalisation

Table 4.9 presents the key results for the full liberalisation scenario. Global real income increases by over 6 per cent as compared with the base case simulation in the year 2002. All regions witness an improvement in real income. Most regions also have a gain in both the rural and urban economies, the main exceptions being Brazil, high-income developing countries and the OECD countries.

Brazil turns out to be a special case, and shows how the aggregate statistics can sometimes be misleading. While real rural value added in Brazil goes down, this is exclusively due to substitution towards rural factors and away from rural surplus.[6] All rural factors increase: labour, land, and equipment, in both volumes and values. Rural incomes increase significantly, as shown by the rural/urban income parity index which increases by 16 per cent. In fact, despite the high level of protection of certain agricultural crops, other agricultural sectors are taxed and, except for the tree crops, these sectors benefit from the rise in both the world price and a decline in the level of taxation. Net agricultural trade in Brazil goes up significantly. The high protection of domestic manufacturing, which is an indirect taxation of Brazilian agricultural exports, is removed with the elimination of import tariffs. The exportable surplus also increases dramatically as domestic consumers shift consumption from agricultural goods to manufactured goods which become significantly cheaper in relative terms.

Similar changes also occur in the two other Latin America regions but in differing degrees. Other Latin America has different protection rates than Brazil so one expects to see less price variation. However, Other Latin America has a higher level of base unemployment, and the removal of unemployment leads to a significant increase in urban GDP. Mexico, relying heavily on petroleum, sees a smaller gain in welfare due to a negative terms-of-trade shock. Nonetheless, Mexico gains overall. The elimination of unemployment leads to an increase in urban value added, while the rural sector benefits from higher world prices and a reduction in the implicit taxation induced by the non-agricultural tariffs.

Unilateral Liberalisation in Latin America

In recent years, a number of Latin American countries have significantly reoriented their trade policies while simultaneously undertaking domestic structural adjustments: notably Chile, Mexico and Argentina. Their adjustments have, by and large, been undertaken unilaterally, with few parallel concessions from key trading partners. To assess the impact for Latin America as a whole, we have simulated full unilateral trade liberalisation, both agricultural and non-agricultural, by the three Latin American regions, accompanied by the removal of domestic distortions in the labour market.

As Table 4.10 shows, the results of full unilateral liberalisation in the three Latin American regions are very positive, with highly positive gains in both the rural and urban economies (except for the rural economy in Brazil). The impact on the rest of the world is also primarily positive. The elimination of import tariffs leads to a significant increase in volume of trade. The increase in imports will obviously have a negative impact on the competitiveness of domestic goods. On the other hand, the reduction of import tariffs will significantly decrease the cost of intermediate consumption, in both the rural and urban sectors, leading to a positive supply shock. Moreover, since this is accompanied by the removal of labour market distortions, the domestic economies are able to utilise fully their resources.

Comparing these results with the full multilateral global liberalisation at the world level, the main difference is the reduction of world prices under partial liberalisation. This is beneficial in general for many countries in the aggregate as it reduces agricultural import bills, and relieves pressure on the urban labour markets. However, the terms-of-trade shock is negative for Other Latin America and Brazil, largely due to the reduction of world agricultural prices. Mexico, on the contrary, is a net food importer, so it benefits from a lower food import bill and, unlike in global full liberalisation, the price of energy will not change significantly because there will be only slight changes in the price of manufacturing exports of the OECD countries. From a comparison of the two full liberalisation scenarios we can conclude that Latin America can reap most of the gains from reform on a unilateral basis, as the experience of Chile and Mexico illustrates.

Increase in Net Foreign Transfers

While Latin America has slowly been emerging from the debt crisis, most Latin American countries are still not benefiting from the flow of funds witnessed in earlier periods.

The role of foreign transfers has been widely discussed and thus it was considered useful to determine the impact of changes in foreign transfers as compared to changes in trade policies. To assess the impact of an increase in foreign transfers we have simulated an increase in net transfers of $3 billion to each of the three regions/countries, starting in 1993, and through the remaining periods. The residual capital flow is financed by the six OECD regions and Upper Income Asia in proportion to the absolute value of their net transfers. The overall impact for the world economy is neutral, as shown in Table 4.11. However, all regions lose slightly except for the three Latin American regions. The regions with the largest losses are the OECD regions and Upper Income Asia due to a reduction in their overall investment levels. The other regions decline to a lesser extent as a reaction to slower growth in the OECD countries.

The increase in the net transfer scenario is particularly beneficial to the three Latin American regions, because this inflow stimulates investment directly due to model closure. Brazil's gains accrue almost immediately, whereas in the rest of Latin America the benefits are more gradual, gains in Mexico really only appearing in the year 2002. It is the urban sector which grows the most, particularly in Other Latin America. While the investment is divided between the rural and urban sectors, it is the urban sector which tends to benefit the most, particularly from a demand effect. Rural investment leads to an increase in demand for urban goods, or in other words, the increase in rural investment leaks to the urban sector.

Increase in Rural Investment

Over the years there has been a debate on the role of agriculture in development and the role of rural investment as an engine of economic growth. In order to assess the implications of increased rural investment we undertake a simulation in which rural investment is increased by $3 billion in each region in each period, from 1993 forwards. Rather than extract this additional investment from the urban sector, these funds are directly financed from external sources. The foreign aid is financed by the six OECD-country regions and Upper Income Asia in proportion to the absolute value of their net transfers.

From Table 4.12, it can be seen that the overall response in Latin America is positive, with an aggregate increase in real income of 1.4 per cent in the year 2002 as compared with the base simulation. In all three regions, both rural and urban value added increase significantly. The increase in rural investment increases the capacity of rural production. It also has several feedbacks in the urban sector. First, there is an increased demand for urban goods, particularly equipment (e.g. tractors). Second, there is a small decrease in the price of food which relieves the pressure on wages in the urban sector. Third, the external financing eases the balance-of-payments constraint, which permits financing of more imports.

While growth is not as important in this scenario as in the previous scenario, in part, this can be attributed to the fact that the economies are in a second-best situation, with continuing distortions in the agricultural and non-agricultural product markets, as well as in the urban labour market.

Higher Growth in OECD Countries

As initially presented in Chapter 3, the global impact of higher growth in OECD countries would be favourable, but the bulk of the real income gains accrue to the OECD countries. By 2002, the real income of the regions of OECD countries will improve by 18 per cent, while the aggregate improvement for Latin America is only 2 per cent. The low-income developing regions would actually not significantly benefit from this shock. The urban economies of the low-income developing regions suffer from two effects: increasing competition from imports as the price of OECD countries' exports decreases, and an increase in food prices which puts pressure on the urban wage.

World agricultural prices increase because of increasing demand from the OECD countries through an income effect. The increase in world agricultural prices is passed on to farmers and this leads to an increase in rural GDP and farm incomes. While all regions are faced with more competition from cheaper imports from OECD countries, in the higher income developing regions this competition is more than offset by increased exports to the OECD countries.

Of the developing countries, Other Latin America tends to do particularly well, in large part due to a significant improvement in its terms of trade. This allows Other Latin America to sell less agricultural commodities abroad, but at a higher price, leading to an increase in domestic supply. The higher domestic supplies reduce (in relative terms) the price of food, leading to a relaxation of the real wage constraint and an increase in urban productivity.

Overall, however, this simulation provides little comfort for those who believe that faster growth in the OECD countries is the panacea for the developing countries' growth woes. Growth in the developing countries is not pulled very strongly by the OECD countries, and one must be concerned by the small effects on the poorest regions. Failure to achieve a more significant pass-through is partially a result of the distortions in the world trading system which impede the developing countries from fully exploiting their comparative advantage.

Conclusion

In the introduction to this chapter on Latin America, we sketched the traditional importance of agriculture in the development and growth of Latin America. We have recalled the sustaining role of agriculture as an anchor for the economy during tumultuous economic periods, as demonstrated during the 1980s, and as a leading export earner for the economies of Latin America.

Six simulations were undertaken: a partial multilateral trade reform, a full multilateral trade reform, a full unilateral trade reform, an improvement in foreign net transfers towards Latin America, an increase in rural investment, and higher growth in

OECD countries. The simulations indicate that complete liberalisation, either unilateral or multilateral, coupled with eliminating domestic distortions, leads to the largest increase in growth in the three Latin American regions. Irrespective of the final outcome of the Uruguay Round, these simulations indicate that the Latin American countries would benefit significantly from a unilateral removal of trade barriers. Note that neither liberalisation scenario implies a change in net transfers of resources from the benchmark levels. Increasing net transfers to Latin America is also very positive for Latin America, though in this simulation the benefits accrue more to the urban economy than to the rural economy. The model does not explain how to achieve this increase in transfers, whether by foreign aid, negotiated debt reductions, capital repatriation, increasing foreign direct investment, or a combination of all four. Clearly some of the solutions to the net transfer problem rely on providing a domestic environment conducive to voluntary investment and repatriation, while others rely on the willingness of the creditor countries to relax repayment requirements. An increase in rural investment is beneficial to the economies of Latin America and would only impose a small burden on the rest of the world.

Higher growth rates in the OECD countries also lead to an improvement in real incomes in Latin America, with a fairly balanced growth both in the rural and urban economies. In this simulation, however, it is striking that real incomes that are 18 per cent higher in the OECD countries in 2002 only lead to a 2 per cent increase in Latin America. Moreover, this simulation does not improve real incomes in the poorer developing regions. Furthermore, this simulation assumes no change in trade distortions which prevent developing countries from fully realising their comparative advantage. In addition, this growth was engendered exogenously. The potential for higher growth in the OECD countries will depend on a number of factors: the consolidation of the EC's internal market and the expansion of the EC to include EFTA and possibly some of the eastern European economies; the ability of the eastern European and Soviet economies to overcome the difficulties in the transformation to market economies; the ability of the US to overcome the crisis in the financial sector and reduce the large public deficit; sustaining research and development expenditures; and the ability of Japan and the industrialised economies of Asia to continue expanding at the same pace as in the 1980s.

The partial liberalisation scenario provides significant improvement for the rural economies in the developing regions, though it may have negative impact in the urban economies for those regions where an increase in food prices leads to a deterioration in capacity utilisation. For Latin America the overall impact is neutral.

These six simulations using the RUNS model focused on Latin America clearly illustrate the interactions between the rural and urban economies; the interactions between trade, macroeconomic policies and agricultural policies; and the interactions between the regions of the world. The simulations show the negative impact of agricultural and industrial trade distortions, which prevent Latin America from fully exploiting its comparative advantage in agricultural production.

Notes and References

1. All agricultural production data comes from FAO data tapes, trade data from the United Nations ComTrade database, and GDP data from the World Bank Tables.
2. The estimates of direct and indirect protection rates are cited in Schiff and Valdés.
3. Our own preliminary results using an alternative closure with endogenous foreign savings has the Latin American aggregate becoming a net importer of capital, but both Brazil and Mexico would be significant exporters of capital.
4. Beef supply is projected to increase by 1.2 per cent per annum, while demand is increasing by 2.7 per cent.
5. Adelman (1984) has called this agricultural demand-led industrialisation. See also Berthélemy and Morrisson (1989).
6. Rural value added is split into two components. The first component includes payments to physical factors: land, labour, farm equipment, and draught cattle. The second component is a residual component which is the difference between farm revenues and all other input costs. This component is called rural surplus in the model. While it is straightforward to calculate real rural GDP using the first component, real rural surplus is more difficult to interpret.

Table 4.1. **Proportions and Growth Rates: Latin America**

	Ya/Y (%) (a)	Yi/Y (%) (b)	Annual Growth Rates (%) GDP (c)	Agriculture (d)	Industry (e)	Comparative Weight & Growth: (a)*(d)=(f)	(b)*(e)=(g)
1965	13.57	35.16					
1966	12.72	35.46	4.26	-2.26	5.17	0.12	0.37
1967	12.60	35.05	5.43	4.43	4.21	0.13	0.37
1968	12.20	36.29	5.58	2.20	9.30	0.12	0.40
1969	11.78	36.28	6.87	3.15	6.85	0.12	0.39
1970	11.15	36.12	6.98	1.33	6.50	0.11	0.38
1971	11.05	36.01	5.69	4.72	5.38	0.12	0.38
1972	10.62	36.19	6.11	1.95	6.64	0.11	0.39
1973	10.20	36.65	7.76	3.47	9.11	0.11	0.40
1974	9.93	36.24	6.12	3.33	4.95	0.10	0.38
1975	9.97	35.34	2.86	3.28	0.31	0.10	0.35
1976	9.69	35.66	5.16	2.27	6.09	0.10	0.38
1977	9.87	35.40	4.93	6.89	4.19	0.11	0.37
1978	9.69	35.32	3.69	1.71	3.43	0.10	0.37
1979	9.31	35.46	6.83	2.64	7.26	0.10	0.38
1980	9.19	35.31	5.52	4.17	5.08	0.10	0.37
1981	9.65	34.13	0.38	5.44	-2.98	0.10	0.33
1982	9.88	33.67	-1.71	0.62	-3.02	0.10	0.33
1983	10.11	32.99	-2.21	0.03	-4.20	0.10	0.32
1984	10.09	33.01	3.61	3.45	3.67	0.10	0.34
1985	10.26	33.07	2.90	4.67	3.09	0.11	0.34
1986	9.65	33.68	3.90	-2.33	5.82	0.09	0.36
1987	10.01	33.46	2.83	6.68	2.15	0.11	0.34
1988	9.88	31.57	5.71	4.37	-0.25	0.10	0.31
1989	9.76	31.18	0.78	-0.44	-0.48	0.10	0.31

Notes: (a) and (b) are respective agricultural share and industrial share of GDP.
The calculation of (f) and (g) are based on the index numbers of the preceding columns.

Source: World Bank Tables.

Table 4.2. **Key Statistics for 1985**

	LAT	BRA	MEX
Rural GDP Share (%)	13.9	16.5	10.0
Rural Labour Share (%)	28.2	27.6	33.2
Rural Income Per Capita ($, 1985)	804	1 019	706
Urban Income Per Capita ($, 1985)	1 974	1 966	3 179
Total Income Per Capita ($, 1985)	1 643	1 705	2 358
Share of Agriculture in Exports	22.5%	42.9%	9.3%
Share of Agriculture in Imports	1.2%	4.4%	9.9%
Agricultural Exports ($ million, 1985)	14 877	12 948	2 596
Agricultural Imports ($ million, 1985)	820	1 400	2 845
Industrial Exports ($ million, 1985)	53 509	19 036	26 165
Industrial Imports ($ million, 1985)	67 443	14 529	17 040
Trade Balance ($ million, 1985)	124	16 055	8 876

Table 4.3a. **Agricultural Structure in Other Latin America (percentages)**

Output		Exports		Imports	
Sugar	11.6	Sugar	36.2	Other Meats	18.1
Total Meat	22.8	Beef	6.3	Dairy Products	81.9
Coffee	3.6	Coffee	15.4		
Oils	6.5	Oils	9.0		
Dairy Products	6.4	Other Food	15.5		
Other Food	36.1				
Total	86.0	Total	83.4	Total	100.0

Table 4.3b. **Agricultural Structure in Brazil (percentages)**

Output		Exports		Imports	
Rice	10.5	Sugar	8.9	Wheat	63.9
Coarse Grains	7.2	Total Meat	9.7	Rice	22.2
Sugar	5.8	Coffee	25.7	Coarse Grains	7.5
Total Meats	14.5	Cocoa	6.3	Dairy Products	6.4
Coffee	8.3	Oils	21.2		
Dairy Products	5.8	Other Food	20.1		
Oils	12.7	Other Non-Food	5.6		
Other Food	26.7				
Total	91.5	Total	98.5	Total	100.0

Table 4.3c. **Agricultural Structure in Mexico (percentages)**

Output		Exports		Imports	
Wheat	3.6	Coffee	29.9	Coarse Grains	25.2
Coarse Grains	12.1	Other Food	59.3	Oils	41.5
Sugar	5.2			Dairy Products	20.9
Total Meats	21.7				
Oils	8.3				
Dairy Products	7.1				
Other Food	35.8				
Total	93.8	Total	89.2	Total	87.6

Table 4.4. **Projected Growth Rates (percentages)**

	1985-1990 Average			1990-2002 Average		
	LAT	BRA	MEX	LAT	BRA	MEX
Rural GDP	-0.2	3.3	1.7	2.4	4.0	3.8
Total GDP	1.4	2.0	1.4	4.3	4.2	4.8
Population	1.8	1.8	1.8	1.8	1.8	1.8

Table 4.5. **Net Foreign Savings ($ billions)**

	LAT	BRA	MEX	US
1990	0.0	6.7	4.6	62.5
1993	0.1	7.4	9.1	92.6
1996	-7.8	7.4	11.0	95.6
1999	-20.3	7.0	6.4	105.1
2002	-40.6	3.1	-6.2	145.9

Table 4.6. **1990 Price Wedges (Index), Input Subsidies (percentages), and Tariffs (percentages)**

	LAT		BRA		MEX	
	Wedge	Subsidy	Wedge	Subsidy	Wedge	Subsidy
Wheat	0.95	1.5	1.55	19.9	1.71	13.1
Rice	2.57	4.7	1.39	31.3	1.00	0.0
Coarse Grains	1.03	4.7	1.16	21.9	1.76	6.4
Sugar	1.30	1.5	1.00	0.0	1.00	0.0
Beef, Veal & Sheep	1.00	0.0	0.78	6.6	0.90	0.5
Coffee	0.45	5.1	0.90	0.0	1.00	0.0
Oils	0.71	0.3	0.86	23.0	0.91	15.6
Other Food	1.00	6.8	1.00	0.0	1.28	5.3
Cotton	1.00	0.0	0.79	0.0	1.02	7.1
Other Manufacturing	29.0	-	68.0	-	18.4	-
Energy	14.0	-	23.0	-	4.1	-
Equipment	18.0	-	53.0	-	16.8	-
Fertilizers	7.0	-	10.0	-	0.2	-

Table 4.7a. **Selected Base Results for Other Latin America (percentages)**

	1985	2002
Rural GDP Share	13.9	20.9
Rural Labour Share	28.2	22.7
Rural/Urban Income Parity	40.7	90.5
Rural Share of Exports	19.2	18.9
Rural Share of Imports	1.2	1.4
Agricultural Production Structure		
Sugar	11.7	8.7
Total Meat	22.8	20.0
Coffee	3.5	2.3
Oils	6.5	6.6
Dairy Products	6.4	9.0
Other Food	36.1	42.2
% of Total Agricultural Production	87.0	88.8
Agricultural Export Structure		
Sugar	37.2	28.1
Beef	6.3	0.0
Coffee	15.4	10.7
Oils	9.0	17.3
Other Foods	15.5	27.5
% of Total Agricultural Exports	83.4	83.6
Agricultural Import Structure		
Other Meats	18.1	0.0
Dairy Products	81.9	0.0
% of Total Agricultural Imports	100.0	0.0

Table 4.7b. **Selected Base Results for Brazil (percentages)**

	1985	2002
Rural GDP Share	16.5	12.8
Rural Labour Share	27.6	16.1
Rural/Urban Income Parity	51.8	76.6
Rural Share of Exports	37.0	60.7
Rural Share of Imports	4.4	7.3
Agricultural Production Structure		
Rice	10.5	15.8
Coarse Grains	7.2	4.0
Sugar	5.8	4.8
Total Meats	14.5	14.0
Coffee	8.3	4.3
Oils	12.7	11.5
Dairy Products	5.8	8.4
Other Food	26.7	30.4
% of Total Agricultural Production	91.5	93.3
Agricultural Export Structure		
Sugar	8.9	1.5
Total Meat	9.7	3.4
Coffee	25.7	15.7
Cocoa	6.3	2.0
Oils	21.2	17.3
Other Food	20.1	11.4
Other Non-Food	5.6	7.2
% of Total Agricultural Exports	98.5	58.7
Agricultural Import Structure		
Wheat	64.2	50.5
Rice	21.8	0.0
Coarse Grains	7.5	0.0
Dairy Products	6.5	0.0
% of Total Agricultural Imports	100.0	50.5

Table 4.7c. **Selected Base Results for Mexico (percentages)**

	1985	2002
Rural GDP Share	10.0	10.6
Rural Labour Share	33.2	23.2
Rural/Urban Income Parity	22.2	39.2
Rural Share of Exports	6.7	22.6
Rural Share of Imports	9.9	25.9
Agricultural Production Structure		
Wheat	3.6	2.1
Coarse Grains	12.1	4.9
Sugar	5.2	4.7
Total Meats	21.7	25.3
Oils	8.3	1.9
Dairy Products	7.1	8.7
Other Food	35.8	48.5
% of Total Agricultural Production	93.8	96.0
Agricultural Export Structure		
Coffee	29.9	6.8
Other Food	59.3	46.2
% of Total Agricultural Exports	89.2	53.0
Agricultural Import Structure		
Coarse Grains	25.2	20.6
Oils	41.5	30.9
Dairy Products	20.9	11.7
% of Total Agricultural Imports	87.6	63.2

Table 4.8. **Impact of Partial Multilateral Trade Reform on Key Variables**
(per cent change in the Year 2002 from the base simulation)

	Real Income	Rural Value Added	Urban Value Added	Rural/ Urban Income	Food Prices	Terms of Trade
Africa	0.6	-0.4	0.1	-1.0	-0.4	-0.2
Low Income Regions	2.9	0.7	0.3	4.6	7.7	8.6
Latin America	0.1	-0.5	0.8	2.6	3.2	-0.9
Other Latin America	1.4	1.3	1.2	2.4	2.4	0.4
Brazil	-0.1	-2.5	-0.5	1.2	2.7	-2.1
Mexico	-0.9	0.9	1.4	8.0	5.0	-2.8
Other Developing Regions	4.0	-6.0	3.4	-13.9	-6.3	0.9
OECD Regions	1.9	-7.7	1.9	-10.2	-7.2	-1.3
Other	0.3	-1.5	0.4	-1.3	-0.4	-2.3
Total	1.9	-3.1	1.7	-3.7	0.2	n.a

Table 4.9. **Impact of Full Multilateral Liberalisation on Key Variables**
(per cent change in the Year 2002 from the base simulation)

	Real Income	Rural Value Added	Urban Value Added	Rural/ Urban Income	Food Prices	Terms of Trade
Africa	6.6	0.8	10.5	0.2	4.9	-4.1
Low Income Regions	6.3	3.7	-0.9	25.3	26.5	15.0
Latin America	5.0	0.0	5.9	13.1	11.5	1.2
Other Latin America	9.6	4.5	9.7	9.9	8.7	1.8
Brazil	3.7	-4.9	1.7	15.9	15.8	1.6
Mexico	1.8	2.9	4.4	20.4	8.3	-3.4
Other Developing Regions	7.9	-24.0	8.3	-27.8	-22.5	-1.9
OECD Regions	5.8	-22.1	5.8	-30.1	-23.7	-4.1
Other	6.2	-3.8	6.8	-0.5	3.6	-2.8
Total	6.1	-9.0	5.8	-6.3	1.4	n.a.

Table 4.10. **Impact of Liberalisation in Latin America on Key Variables**
(per cent change in the Year 2002 from the base simulation)

	Real Income	Rural Value Added	Urban Value Added	Rural/ Urban Income	Food Prices	Terms of Trade
Africa	0.4	-0.4	0.7	-1.8	-0.6	-0.5
Low Income Regions	0.1	-0.1	0.0	0.0	0.0	-0.1
Latin America	4.1	-1.8	6.4	8.1	9.2	-3.0
Other Latin America	7.2	1.3	10.1	4.7	6.8	-5.2
Brazil	2.9	-5.0	2.5	13.6	17.1	-3.7
Mexico	2.5	-0.2	4.7	7.1	0.3	0.1
Other Developing Regions	0.6	-0.8	0.6	-1.7	-0.5	0.2
OECD Regions	0.7	-0.8	0.6	-2.0	-1.7	0.2
Other	0.8	-0.5	1.1	-1.3	-0.8	-0.3
Total	0.9	-0.6	1.0	-0.7	0.1	n.a.

Table 4.11. **Impact of Increase in Net Transfers on Key Variables**
(per cent change in the Year 2002 from the base simulation)

	Real Income	Rural Value Added	Urban Value Added	Rural/ Urban Income	Food Prices	Terms of Trade
Africa	-0.1	0.0	-0.1	0.2	0.0	0.0
Low Income Regions	0.0	0.0	0.0	0.1	0.0	0.1
Latin America	1.9	-0.1	2.2	-2.0	-0.4	-0.2
Other Latin America	2.0	0.1	2.4	-1.9	0.2	-0.2
Brazil	1.6	-0.2	1.7	-1.8	-0.6	0.0
Mexico	2.3	-0.4	2.2	-3.5	-1.2	-0.1
Other Developing Regions	-0.2	0.1	-0.3	0.4	0.1	0.0
OECD Regions	-0.2	0.1	-0.2	0.3	0.2	0.0
Other	-0.1	0.1	-0.1	0.1	0.1	0.0
Total	0.0	0.0	-0.1	0.1	0.0	n.a.

Table 4.12. **Impact of Increase in Rural Investment on Key Variables**
(per cent change in the Year 2002 from the base simulation)

	Real Income	Rural Value Added	Urban Value Added	Rural/ Urban Income	Food Prices	Terms of Trade
Africa	0.0	0.0	0.0	-0.1	-0.1	0.0
Low Income Regions	0.0	0.0	0.0	-0.1	-0.1	0.0
Latin America	1.4	0.4	1.1	-2.4	-1.7	0.3
Other Latin America	1.6	0.8	1.2	-2.1	-1.2	0.4
Brazil	1.3	0.2	1.4	-2.5	-1.6	0.1
Mexico	1.4	0.0	0.7	-3.7	-2.5	0.2
Other Developing Regions	-0.2	0.0	-0.2	0.0	-0.1	0.0
OECD Regions	-0.2	0.0	-0.2	0.1	0.0	0.0
Other	0.0	0.0	0.0	0.0	0.0	0.0
Total	0.0	0.0	0.1	0.1	-0.2	n.a.

Table 4.13. **Impact of Higher OECD Growth on Key Variables**
(per cent change in the Year 2002 from the base simulation)

	Real Income	Rural Value Added	Urban Value Added	Rural/ Urban Income	Food Prices	Terms of Trade
Africa	1.6	0.0	-0.7	-1.4	-0.3	1.4
Low Income Regions	0.3	0.5	0.0	1.7	1.4	2.4
Latin America	1.7	0.2	0.2	-2.1	-0.2	2.6
Other Latin America	3.5	0.2	1.5	-3.6	-0.5	3.2
Brazil	0.9	0.4	0.1	0.2	0.5	5.0
Mexico	1.0	-0.4	-2.0	-2.5	-1.4	-0.2
Other Developing Regions	3.1	0.7	0.5	-1.3	0.6	1.5
OECD Regions	18.5	2.6	19.7	-4.8	6.8	-1.8
Other	0.8	0.8	-0.4	1.4	1.6	2.4
Total	12.3	1.1	13.4	-1.4	2.9	n.a.

Chapter 5

Africa

Introduction

This chapter assesses the future trends of African economies, both in terms of domestic changes and in the context of projected trends in the world economy. It also analyses the main policy variables which could enhance the prospects for rapid, sustainable and equitable growth in Africa.

The Issues

Africa is a continent beset by crises. Until recently, the prevailing view was that the situation, if anything, would get worse. The Economic Commission for Africa observed in 1983 that "the picture that emerges from the analysis of the perspective of the Africa region by the year 2008, under the historical trend scenario, is almost a nightmare... Poverty would reach unimaginable dimensions"[1]. In 1990, former World Bank president Robert McNamara, reflecting on earlier projections, noted that the situation would be even worse than imagined and "that there is little reason to believe that the current development programs will reverse the adverse trends"[2].

In the first three decades following the Second World War, economic growth in Africa on average just managed to exceed the pace of population growth, but in the 1980s per capita GDP declined by about 20 per cent to around $280. Africa's population, estimated at around 600 million, is growing at over 3 per cent per year, so that in order to maintain per capita incomes its economy needs to grow more rapidly than any other continent. The extent to which this may be possible is critically dependent on the performance of primary commodity exports and particularly of agriculture.

The importance of agriculture and rural development cannot be underestimated in Africa. Agriculture accounted for roughly 34 per cent of GDP and over 65 per cent of exports in 1988[3]. Equally importantly, it employs fully 72 per cent of the total labour force. Rural incomes are largely dependent on agriculture, while urban living standards are linked to food availability and prices. In Africa, to a greater extent than in the other continents, economic growth and human development is inextricably bound up with agriculture.

Agriculture remains the foundation of Africa's economic development, and its weakness underlies the poor overall performance. Over the last 20 years the growth in agricultural production trailed behind population growth by almost a percentage point per year. The result was increasing dependence on food imports and declining exports; food imports increased by an average of 5 per cent per annum (and food aid by 6 per cent), and agricultural exports declined at an average rate of 3 per cent per year. This was associated with a loss of up to 50 per cent of Africa's market shares. Despite this declining share, dependence on exports has grown. Agriculture provides more than 75 per cent of the export revenue for 14 sub-Saharan nations and six countries rely on agriculture for over 90 per cent of their export earnings[4].

The success of a number of African countries in overcoming agricultural stagnation and the slightly improved overall performance in recent years provides some room for optimism. Nevertheless, a 1990 United Nations Report, after reviewing this evidence, concludes that "the prospective situation is appalling", with a shortfall of around 50 million tons of cereals projected for the year 2000[5]. Thus the outlook is for a further deterioration of the current catastrophic situation in which over 140 million Africans, or one in four of the continent's inhabitants, are undernourished[6].

The explanation for Africa's economic, and perforce agricultural, stagnation is to be found in a combination of internal and external factors. Of the external factors, attention has focused on the terms of trade. After suffering a gradual secular decline in the entire post-World War II period, the downturn accelerated in the 1980s, so that by the end of the decade the prices for Africa's main export commodities were as much as 40 per cent below their 1980 level[7]. The weakness of commodity prices reflects a combination of factors, all of which have particularly disadvantaged Africa. These include the slowing of world economic growth and the rise in interest rates in OECD countries, and a dramatic increase in the burden of debt, which now exceeds African GDP and is equivalent to 400 per cent of export earnings.

The links between the debt crisis and the fall in the terms of trade have been explored elsewhere[8]. Perhaps the most important link is through the implementation of structural adjustment programmes in African and other developing countries, which aimed to increase (commodity) exports, and facilitated exports of greater quantities at any given world price by devaluation and associated changes in the tradable and non-tradable balances, together with reductions in export taxes and other trade interventions.

As a result of domestic reforms in African countries, farmers have not always received lower prices despite the decline in world prices; the net protection coefficient for the principal exports in 30 African countries fluctuated markedly in the 1980s but around a rising trend, as reductions in taxation (notably through overvaluation and trade taxes) served to offset market declines[9]. Simultaneously, however, it served to increase input prices and squeeze public expenditure, threatening to undermine the effect of the macroeconomic and trade reforms on agricultural technology. In the late 1980s and early 1990s, economic reforms had advanced to the extent that sub-Saharan Africa switched from being a net taxer to almost a net protector of agriculture.

The failure of the African agricultural sector to record higher productivity growth is perhaps the most disturbing of all the trends to emerge from a reading of the African statistics. Given the exhaustion of the land frontier and the high population growth rates, it is perhaps not surprising that the productivity of land and labour has fallen to low levels in Africa. More surprising, however, is the evidence that capital intensity has declined. This is most dramatically reflected in input use and particularly in the application of fertilizers. From a small base, the annual growth rate of fertilizer consumption fell from 11 per cent in the 1960s to 4 per cent in the 1980s, so that Africa's use of fertilizer has fallen from 4 to 2 per cent of global consumption[10].

Economic reforms are widely recognised as an indispensable element in the revitalisation of Africa. A widespread perception of the inadequacy of the public sector has led to an increased emphasis on deregulation and privatisation. To the extent that this has led to an improvement in the productive environment, it has already been reflected in enhanced performance. However, the limitations of the market have quickly been reached, so that policy makers are forced to choose between the inadequacy of the state and the failure of the market to perform a number of key functions. In particular, the ability of agriculture to provide the foundation for enhanced growth has been undermined by the erosion of public sector investment and extension services which ensure that appropriate technologies reach farmers and that their crops reach market.

Within Africa, macroeconomic and trade policy interventions which effect the pivotal rural-urban balance are the key to future growth. However, these interventions are linked in turn to external developments, including the development of world prices and markets and the availability of external sources of capital. Accordingly, it is evident that Africa's economic crisis requires an analysis which is both economy-wide and international in its coverage.

In the following sections we will focus on the four African regions, providing only a cursory look at the remaining regions. We will designate the other African aggregate by the term sub-Saharan Africa. The four African regions will be denoted by the following abbreviations: AFR — sub-Saharan Africa, NGA — Nigeria, ZAF — South Africa, and MAG — the Maghreb.

The Trends

A key statistic for describing the reality in Africa is the rate of self-sufficiency[11]. Table 5.1 presents the self-sufficiency rates for the base year. While overall, sub-Saharan Africa has a self-sufficiency ratio of 1.1, this is almost entirely due to non-food crops: coffee, cocoa, tea, cotton and other non-food crops. Sugar is the only **food** crop in which sub-Saharan Africa is self-sufficient. Both Nigeria and South Africa have relatively low self-sufficiency ratios in a number of key commodities. For Nigeria these include wheat, rice, coarse grains, sugar and dairy products. For South Africa, rice and oils. The Maghreb region has a very low overall self-sufficiency ratio and an aggregate domestic agricultural demand 30 per cent higher than production. Amongst the commodities with a low self-sufficiency ratios are wheat, rice, coarse grains, sugar, meats, oils, and dairy products. Only in the other food category does the Maghreb have a significant exportable surplus.

Tables 5.2a-d, present an overview of the structure of agricultural production, exports, and imports for all four regions. Agricultural output in sub-Saharan Africa is dominated by the other food category (essentially fruits, vegetables, beans, and other food crops), whose share in the value of output is almost 50 per cent. The rest of the output is largely divided into sugar, beef, coffee, and oils. The main exports are coffee and cocoa, which have a combined 69 per cent share of export revenues, with the rest being earned by sugar, tea, cotton and other non-food. The main imports are grains and dairy products.

Output in Nigeria is even more specialised, with the other food category providing 80 per cent of domestic agricultural output. The only export crop is cocoa. The main imports are grains, sugar and dairy products.

South Africa exhibits a greater heterogeneity in output, with livestock representing over 30 per cent of total agricultural output, other food with a 39 per cent share, and significant shares for coarse grains and sugar. Exports are concentrated in sugar, other food, and wool. Imports include rice, oils, coffee and cotton.

The Maghreb also has a fairly diversified agricultural production structure. Other food accounts for 46 per cent, with grains and livestock accounting for the rest. The only export is the other food category. Imports include grains, sugar, coffee, and dairy products.

Table 5.3 presents the import and export structure for each region in the non-agricultural sectors. A striking fact revealed by the trade structure is the almost complete lack of intra-African trade. One easily sees that Africa's main trading partners are OECD countries (note that these figures exclude agricultural trade in which the ties between Africa and the OECD countries is probably even closer).

As mentioned in Chapter 2, the base simulation of RUNS incorporates a series of judgements on the basic growth rates in the economy: total GDP, agricultural production and population. Table 5.4 presents the overall growth rates for the base simulation. The growth rates over the 1985-90 period were abysmal, especially in per capita terms. Rural GDP managed to outpace population growth to some extent in South Africa and the Maghreb. For the 1990-2002 period, GDP per capita is assumed to grow slightly. However, it is only again in South Africa and the Maghreb that rural GDP will grow significantly faster than population.

In sub-Saharan Africa, the fastest growing agricultural sectors are projected to be sugar and tea, with output in all other commodities projected to grow less than the population. The two main cash crops, coffee and cocoa, are projected to grow at 0.3 per cent and 1.6 per cent, respectively, per annum. In Nigeria, output of rice, sugar and other meats is expected to grow at a higher rate than population, albeit with significant drops in the output of cocoa, oils, and cotton. South Africa will experience significant growth in wheat, sugar, other meats, tea, other food, and cotton. Finally, in the Maghreb, the leading agricultural sectors will be sugar, beef and other meats, oils, dairy products, and wool.

The second key exogenous element driving the model is the path of external (exogenous) net foreign savings. Table 5.5 presents the path for the four African regions and the United States. Sub-Saharan Africa is projected to have decreasing net transfers for the rest of the decade, while both Nigeria and South Africa will experience a continuous outflow, although remaining close to zero. Net transfers for the Maghreb will also be decreasing.

Data on agricultural policies in Africa are still somewhat sketchy and subject to revision. The overall picture is that agricultural production have been taxed, particularly compared to urban production. While direct taxation may be low, the effects of overvalued exchange rates has had significant indirect effects on farmers. Rural production has also been hurt by public investment policies which have tended to favour urban infrastructure over rural infrastructure. However, agricultural policies are not uniform across countries or across sectors.

Non-agricultural trade tariffs are low compared to the rates of other developing countries. The average tariff rate in sub-Saharan Africa is 19 per cent, in Nigeria, 25 per cent, in South Africa 12 per cent, and in the Maghreb, 25 per cent. These rates may not necessarily reflect the true distortions between world prices and domestic prices due to macroeconomic variables, particularly the exchange rate.

The Key Results of the Base Simulation

The base simulation reflects the assumptions concerning the main trends of the economy. It also assumes, that policies remain unchanged. The trends for agricultural supply, total GDP and the population were presented and discussed above.

In aggregate, rural GDP stays more or less constant, as a share of total GDP. In every region, there is a continuous flow of population from the rural sector to the urban sector, in large part due to the large income differentials. Migration tends to raise the level of per capita incomes, and rural GDP stays roughly constant. The value of agricultural exports increases slightly, whereas imports increase more substantially as food production lags behind population increases. The evolution of trade can be deduced from the self-sufficiency statistics provided in Table 5.6.

For sub-Saharan Africa, the aggregate self-sufficiency ratio decreases from 1.1 to 0.9, that is, it changes from being a net agricultural exporter to a net importer. In most agricultural sectors, particularly food, the self-sufficiency ratios decrease significantly. For example, the level of self-sufficiency drops by 40 per cent in the meat sectors. In Nigeria, the aggregate self-sufficiency ratio decreases by 10 per cent. While import dependency decreases for wheat and rice (in fact, Nigeria starts exporting rice), for most other food items, the self-sufficiency ratio decreases as in sub-Saharan Africa, and there are large increases in meat imports. South Africa, on the other hand, moves from aggregate self-sufficiency to a regime of exportable surplus. It exports wheat and coarse grains, other meats, while other food exports increase. In the Maghreb, the aggregate self-sufficiency ratio improves slightly, from 0.7 to 0.8. However, the sectoral detail is not homogeneous. The Maghreb increases its import dependency in wheat, coarse grains, and meats. It turns into an exporter of rice, sugar, and wool.

Overall, in terms of agriculture, the picture is not particularly optimistic for the African continent, particularly with respect to some of the key food sectors: grains and meats. In the next few sections, we will analyse alternative scenarios which will modify the projected base line tendencies.

The Simulations

Partial Multilateral Trade Reform

The partial trade reform scenario, assuming unemployment, provides a more positive picture as a whole for the African continent. While international food prices increase, within the region there is a decrease, because Africa tends to protect many agricultural commodities. The reduction in internal food prices relieves pressure on the real wage and leads to an expansion of the urban economy. Pressure on the real wage declines further since the reduction in manufacturing import tariffs tends to reduce the consumer price index.

Rural incomes decrease overall. This is due to several factors. The level of protection is reduced, input subsidies are reduced, and export prices of key commodities — coffee and cocoa — go down. Therefore, despite the increase in the world price of key agricultural commodities, the farmers in Africa do not fare well from partial trade reform. Urban incomes tend to increase, in part, from a reduction in unemployment and, in some regions, due to an increase in the terms of trade. While international food prices increase, international manufacturing prices tend to decrease, and the share of manufactured imports is high in Africa. Nigeria is a special case. One would expect Nigeria to suffer a terms-of-trade loss since the price of energy is linked to the price of the OECD countries' manufactured exports. However, the share of manufactured imports of Nigeria is about 80 per cent in the year 2002, in the base simulation. A large share of its imports emanates from non-OECD countries. To the extent that its trading partners have lower export prices than the OECD countries, Nigeria would tend to gain. If energy is excluded from the terms-of-trade calculation, Nigeria would experience a 4 per cent gain in its terms of trade. Nigeria is also a significant exporter of services (and to a lesser extent fertilizers), which are not included in the numeraire price; i.e. energy prices can increase with respect to the price of services and fertilizers. Over 20 per cent of Nigeria's imports are services and fertilizers.

South African farmers lose significantly as agricultural protection is reduced. The urban economy gains from a 10 per cent decline in unemployment and cheaper manufactured imports. The Maghreb is one of those anomalous regions where both rural and urban GDP increase (in real terms), but total real income decreases.[12] Rural farmers do better in the Maghreb. The protection and subsidy rates tend to be lower than in the rest of Africa, so the drop in protection is more than compensated by the higher world prices. Unlike the rest of Africa, they are not major producers of coffee and cocoa. While food prices increase somewhat in the urban sector, the aggregate consumer price index decreases from a decline in import prices. However, the increase in food prices and the negative terms of trade lead to a decline in urban real income, which is not compensated by the rise in rural real incomes.

Full Multilateral Liberalisation

In this simulation, we compare the results of the previous **partial liberalisation** simulation, with the results of a complete **multilateral** liberalisation of all markets, both agricultural and non-agricultural. We also remove all domestic distortions. Table 5.8

presents the main results for the full liberalisation scenario. Global real income increases by 6.1 per cent as compared with the base case simulation in the year 2002. All regions experience an improvement in real income, with the large gains appearing in South Africa and the Maghreb, and solid gains in sub-Saharan Africa.

For three of the four African regions the rural sector improves under full multilateral liberalisation. Despite the protection rates in certain sectors and the drop in the world price of some commodities, the gains are solid. South Africa is the only region with a rural loss, which can be attributed to the high agricultural protection rates. The urban gains are very impressive, largely due to the removal of labour market imperfections which increases urban productivity. The gains in the urban sector more than offset the negative terms-of-trade shock from higher world food prices. When compared to the simulations with no unemployment, we see that the incorporation of unemployment significantly modifies the interpretation of full liberalisation if it includes domestic structural adjustment as well.

Full Unilateral Liberalisation in Africa

In the last few years, several African countries have significantly reoriented their trade policies while simultaneously undertaking domestic structural adjustments. These adjustments have by and large been undertaken unilaterally, with few or no concessions from key trading partners. To assess the impact for Africa as a whole, we have simulated full unilateral trade liberalisation, both agricultural and non-agricultural, by the four African regions, accompanied by the removal of domestic distortions in the labour market. Chapter 2 presented the level of non-agricultural tariff rates in Africa. These tariffs are high relative to tariffs of OECD countries, but lower than in many other developing regions.

As Table 5.9 shows, the results of full unilateral liberalisation in the four African regions are very positive, with highly positive gains in both the rural and urban economies (except for the rural economy in South Africa). The impact on the rest of the world is also by and large positive, although small. The elimination of import tariffs leads to a significant increase in trade volume. The increase in imports will obviously have a negative impact on the competitiveness of domestic goods. On the other hand, the reduction in the import tariffs will significantly decrease the cost of intermediate consumption, both in the rural and urban sectors, leading to a positive supply shock. Moreover, since this is accompanied by the removal of labour market distortions, the domestic economies are able to utilise fully their resources.

This simulation compares favourably with the previous full multilateral liberalisation. Africa can reap much of the gain from liberalisation by implementing it unilaterally. In the rural sector, farmers are better off in sub-Saharan Africa and Nigeria under unilateral liberalisation than under multilateral liberalisation. Tree crop prices do not fall as much under unilateral liberalisation, which benefits these two regions. However, farmers in South Africa and, even more, those in the Maghreb, do better under multilateral liberalisation because of the much larger increase in world prices of agricultural commodities which helps to overcome negative effects of the elimination of protection. The gains in the urban economy are similar in both cases. However, urban incomes are slightly improved from the smaller change in food prices and a relative improvement in the terms of trade.

Higher Growth of OECD Countries

Table 5.10 presents the main results for the African regions of an increase in growth in OECD countries. The global impact is favourable, but the bulk of the real income gains accrue to the OECD countries. By 2002, the OECD countries' real income will improve by 18 per cent while, in the aggregate, Africa would see a real income gain of less than 2 per cent. The urban economies of the low-income developing regions suffer from two effects: increasing competition from imports as the price of OECD countries' exports decreases, and an increase in food prices which puts pressure on the urban wage. These latter two effects are compounded by a restraining effect on world energy prices. As the OECD countries experience a real devaluation, this leads to a relative price drop for energy. Since sub-Saharan Africa, Nigeria, and the Maghreb export energy, they suffer from a deterioration in the terms of trade, although in the case of sub-Saharan Africa, this is mitigated by other changes.

World agricultural prices increase because of increasing demand from the OECD countries by an income effect. The increase in world agricultural prices is passed on to farmers and this leads to an increase in rural GDP and farm incomes. While all regions are faced with more competition from cheaper imports from OECD countries, in the higher income developing regions, this competition is more than offset by increased exports to the OECD countries.

Increase in Net Foreign Transfers

In this simulation we undertake an increase in net transfers to each one of the four African regions. Starting in 1993, and through the remaining periods, we assume that net transfers are increased by $3 billion in each region. The residual transfers are assumed to be funded by the six OECD-country and Upper Income Asia in proportion to the absolute value of their initial net transfers.

The overall impact for the world economy is neutral (see Table 5.11). However, all regions lose slightly except for the four Africa regions. The regions with the largest loss are the OECD-country regions and Upper Income Asia due to a reduction in their overall investment levels. The other regions decline to a lesser extent as a reaction to a decline in growth in the OECD countries.

This scenario is particularly beneficial to the four African regions. The gains to the four regions are not uniform, in part, due to the fact that each region is benefiting from the same absolute level of new transfers, while their GDP levels are quite different. The largest gains accrue to South Africa and Nigeria. All four regions have large increases in the urban capital stock and a decrease in unemployment. The impact on the rural sector is small.

Increase in Rural Investment

In this section we transfer the new net transfers directly to rural investment. (In the previous simulation, the new transfers were allocated to the rural and urban sectors in proportion to GDP shares.) Rural investment is increased by $3 billion in each region and in each period from 1993 forwards. The new transfers are again drawn from the OECD countries and Upper Income Asia.

From Table 5.12, it can be seen that the overall response in Africa is positive, with an aggregate increase in real income of 4 per cent in the year 2002 as compared with the base simulation, but less than the 7.4 per cent gain of the previous simulation. In all four regions, both rural and urban value added increases, but the gains are higher in the urban sector. The increase in rural investment increases the rural production capacity. It also has several important feedbacks in the urban sector. First, there is an increased demand for urban goods, particularly investment goods (e.g. tractors), as well as increased intermediate demand (e.g. fuel). Second, there is a small decrease in the price of food which relieves the pressure on wages in the urban sector. Third, since the financing is external, the balance-of-payments constraint is relaxed, permitting easier financing of imports.

Conclusions

Six simulations were undertaken: a partial and full multilateral trade liberalisation; a full unilateral liberalisation, both rural and urban, by the African regions; higher growth in the OECD countries; an increase in net foreign transfers towards Africa; and an increase in rural investment. In all simulations, the overall impact on Africa is positive, though in varying degrees. The partial trade reform scenario has the smallest impact, with a gain in real income of less than 1 per cent, and the Maghreb even loses. The impacts of partial trade reform on income distribution are disturbing. Farmers, in the aggregate tend to lose, in large part due to the heavy reliance on exports of tree crops, and also because of lower protection in some of the other commodities.

Full global trade reform provides a much more significant boost for the African economy, although, the impacts on income distribution are still negative. While in the aggregate farmers are better off, the urban economy improves much more significantly as capacity utilisation in the urban sector improves dramatically. By and large, Africa could reap the gains from full liberalisation by undertaking reforms unilaterally. The urban sector would experience the same gains. The rural sector would improve, but not as much since world prices would not be significantly affected.

Higher growth in the OECD countries provides only a relatively small boost to the African economy, with the higher gains accruing to those countries with the highest level of penetration in the economies of the OECD countries. The impact on urban economies is somewhat negative as the higher world food prices increase pressures on the real wage, which leads to higher unemployment. Segments of the rural sector benefit from higher world agricultural prices.

Increasing the net foreign resources in Africa proves to be very beneficial. An increase in net transfers of $12 billion per year provides a 7.4 per cent boost in real income by the year 2002. Most of the gains accrue to the urban sector. Investment in the rural sector in large part leaks to the urban economy as rural investment is transformed into demand for manufactured and equipment goods. At the same time, increasing mechanisation leads to a reduction in the demand for rural labour and therefore to a reduction in rural wages and an increase in migration to the cities.

Africa is the world's poorest region and its growth prospects through the year 2002 will likely lead to an increase in the income gap between Africa and all other regions of the world. Africa's reliance on primary commodity exports — tree crops, petroleum and minerals — makes it particularly vulnerable to a long-term relative decline in the price of these commodities, as well as to cyclical variations in price. Not all of Africa's problems can be laid on the doorstep of a harsh world environment. Poor policies, both microeconomic and macroeconomic, have been responsible for part of the poor performance of the African economy. A combination of trade reform, both multilateral and/or unilateral, and higher transfers would provide better prospects for the continent. However, most of the scenarios indicate that the gap between rural and urban incomes will increase. Given the endemic poverty of the rural sector, it will be necessary to initiate policies which benefit farmers in order to reduce the income gap.

A reduction in rural taxation, both direct and indirect, would be a step in the right direction.

Notes and Refrences

1. ECA, 1983.
2. McNamara, p. 2.
3. Not including petroleum exports, which although concentrated in nine countries, account for over 60 per cent of Africa's total export earnings. Including oil, commodities account for almost 99 per cent of Africa's exports and approximately 90 per cent of non-oil exports.
4. Akiyama and Larson, p. 6.
5. United Nations, 1990, p. 19.
6. *Ibid.*, p. 19 and Goldin and Brown, 1991, p. 64.
7. United Nations, p. 16. (including petroleum).
8. For example, see Evans, Goldin and van der Mensbrugghe.
9. World Bank and UNDP, pp. 22-23.
10. Delgado and Tshibaka, p. 7. See also Fontaine.
11. The self-sufficiency rate is the ratio of domestic output to total domestic absorption (the sum of household demand, intermediate demand and change in stocks). A ratio greater than 1, indicates a positive net trade position. The use of the self-sufficiency statistic does not imply a value judgement. It is used in this particular context because the net trade position is a significant factor in calculating the impact of trade reform.
12. Real GDP (rural or urban) is measured using standard statistics. Real income is the welfare measure described in Chapter 2, i.e. the economy trade expenditure function. It is a more accurate welfare measure.

Table 5.1. **Self-Sufficiency Ratios (1985)**[a]

	AFR	NGA	ZAF	MAG
Wheat	0.3	0.0	1.0	0.4
Rice	0.6	0.7	0.0	0.2
Coarse Grains	0.9	0.9	1.0	0.8
Sugar	1.3	0.3	1.7	0.1
Beef, Veal & Sheep	1.0	1.0	1.0	0.8
Other Meats	0.9	1.0	1.0	0.9
Coffee	5.0	0.7	0.0	0.0
Cocoa	10.0	-10.0[b]	0.0	0.0
Tea	2.5	0.0	0.4	0.0
Oils	1.0	0.9	0.8	0.6
Dairy Products	0.8	0.5	1.0	0.5
Other Food	1.0	1.0	1.1	1.1
Wool	1.0	n.a.	2.5	0.8
Cotton	2.5	0.4	0.6	0.2
Other Non-Food	2.0	0.8	0.9	0.3
Total	1.1	1.0	1.0	0.7

a. The rate of self-sufficiency is the ratio of total domestic output to total domestic absorption.

b. A negative self-sufficiency ratio simply means that the domestic demand is smaller than the stock reduction.

Source: FAO Supply Utilization Accounts and own calculations.

Table 5.2a. **Agricultural Structure in Sub-Saharan Africa (percentages)**

Output		Exports		Imports	
Sugar	5	Sugar	10	Wheat	21
Beef	12	Coffee	44	Rice	38
Coffee	7	Cocoa	25	Coarse Grains	5
Oils	6	Tea	5	Dairy Products	25
Other Food	47	Cotton	11		
		Other Non-Food	5		
Total	77	Total	99	Total	89

Table 5.2b. **Agricultural Structure in Nigeria (percentages)**

Output		Exports		Imports	
Beef	5	Cocoa	100	Wheat	25
Other Food	80			Rice	22
				Coarse Grains	5
				Sugar	19
				Oils	7
				Dairy Products	12
Total	85	Total	100	Total	90

Table 5.2c. **Agricultural Structure in South Africa (percentages)**

Output		Exports		Imports	
Coarse Grains	12	Sugar	51	Rice	28
Sugar	9	Other Food	35	Coarse Grains	5
Beef	16	Wool	12	Coffee	12
Other Meats	7			Tea	8
Dairy Products	6			Oils	30
Other Food	39			Cotton	9
Total	89	Total	98	Total	92

Table 5.2d. **Agricultural Structure in Maghreb (percentages)**

Output		Exports		Imports	
Wheat	7	Other Food	100	Wheat	19
Coarse Grains	8			Coarse Grains	6
Sugar	6			Sugar	25
Beef	10			Coffee	7
Other Meats	5			Oils	12
Oils	9			Dairy Products	18
Dairy Products	7				
Other Food	46				
Total	98	Total	100	Total	87

Table 5.3. **Export/Import Structure (percentages)**

Africa

	Export Structure		Import Structure	
	Manufacturing	Energy	Manufacturing	Energy
Africa	6	16	3	55
Nigeria	20	0	0	0
South Africa	4	0	0	0
Maghreb	0	0	0	4
OECD	51	62	77	25
ROW	19	22	19	16

Nigeria

	Export Structure		Import Structure	
	Manufacturing	Energy	Manufacturing	Energy
Africa	3	0	45	6
Nigeria	1	0	0	0
South Africa	0	0	0	0
Maghreb	0	0	0	0
OECD	74	37	29	81
ROW	23	63	26	13

South Africa

	Export Structure		Import Structure	
	Manufacturing	Energy	Manufacturing	Energy
Africa	1	0	5	0
Nigeria	0	0	0	0
South Africa	0	0	0	0
Maghreb	0	0	0	0
OECD	90	100	88	65
ROW	9	0	7	35

Maghreb

	Export Structure		Import Structure	
	Manufacturing	Energy	Manufacturing	Energy
Africa	1	1	0	3
Nigeria	0	0	0	0
South Africa	0	0	0	0
Maghreb	0	0	0	0
OECD	60	74	46	69
ROW	39	25	54	27

a. OECD includes all 6 OECD regions. ROW, rest of the world, includes all regions not part of Africa, and not part of the OECD.

b. Manufacturing is an aggregate of three sectors: equipment, fertilizers, and other manufacturing.

Source: Trade shares are based on CEPII data (see CEPII 1988) and own calculations.

Table 5.4. **Projected Growth Rates (percentages)**

	AFR	NGA	ZAF	MAG	AFR	NGA	ZAF	MAG
Rural GDP	2.4	-0.8	4.3	3.4	3.4	3.4	3.3	5.2
Total GDP	2.6	3.0	0.4	-0.6	3.4	3.8	3.3	4.2
Population	3.2	3.2	2.4	2.6	3.2	3.2	2.4	2.6

Table 5.5. **Net Foreign Savings ($ billion)**

	AFR	NGA	ZAF	MAG	USA
1990	4.1	-1.9	-2.7	-3.5	62.5
1993	2.8	-0.2	-1.6	-5.2	92.6
1996	0.7	-0.9	-1.4	-7.0	95.6
1999	-1.2	-2.0	-1.3	-9.4	105.1
2002	-2.9	-2.7	-1.1	-11.4	145.9

Table 5.6. **Final Year Self-Sufficiency Ratios (2002)**

	AFR	NGA	ZAF	MAG
Wheat	0.3	0.2	1.1	0.3
Rice	0.6	1.1	0.0	1.7
Coarse Grains	0.7	0.5	1.3	0.5
Sugar	1.1	0.1	1.4	1.3
Beef, Veal, & Sheep	0.7	0.7	0.9	0.7
Other Meats	0.7	0.6	1.1	0.9
Coffee	3.3	1.0	n.a.	n.a.
Cocoa	5.0	10.0	n.a.	n.a.
Tea	3.3	n.a.	0.8	n.a.
Oils	0.6	0.3	0.6	0.7
Dairy Products	0.8	0.4	0.8	0.5
Other Food	0.9	1.0	1.3	0.8
Wool	0.8	n.a.	1.4	1.1
Cotton	3.3	0.8	1.4	0.1
Other Non-Food	1.4	0.5	0.8	0.3
Total	0.9	0.9	1.1	0.8

Table 5.7. **Impact of Partial Multilateral Liberalisation on Key Variables**
(per cent change in the year 2002 from the base simulation)

	Real Income	Rural Value Added	Urban Value Added	Rural/ Urban Income	Food Prices	Terms of Trade
Africa	0.6	-0.4	0.1	-1.0	-0.4	-0.2
Sub-Saharan Africa	0.7	-0.2	1.0	-0.6	0.7	0.5
Nigeria	1.1	-0.7	-1.6	-7.2	-3.8	1.9
South Africa	0.8	-2.3	1.5	-3.6	-1.2	-1.7
Maghreb	-0.7	1.1	0.2	3.9	1.2	-2.2
Low Income Regions	2.9	0.7	0.3	4.6	7.7	8.6
Latin America	0.1	-0.5	0.8	2.6	3.2	-0.9
Other Developing Regions	4.0	-6.0	3.4	-13.9	-6.3	0.9
OECD Regions	1.9	-7.7	1.9	-10.2	-7.2	-1.3
Other	0.3	-1.5	0.4	-1.3	-0.4	-2.3
Total	1.9	-3.1	1.7	-3.7	0.2	n.a.

Table 5.8. **Impact of Full Multilateral Liberalisation on Key Variables**
(per cent change in the year 2002 from the base simulation)

	Real Income	Rural Value Added	Urban Value Added	Rural/ Urban Income	Food Prices	Terms of Trade
Africa	6.6	0.8	10.5	0.2	4.9	-4.1
Sub-Saharan Africa	5.0	0.7	9.3	0.9	5.2	-2.1
Nigeria	6.1	2.0	7.9	-5.5	2.1	-1.4
South Africa	8.6	-6.4	13.5	-9.4	2.7	-8.5
Maghreb	9.0	7.4	13.5	13.6	9.4	-6.8
Low Income Regions	6.3	3.7	-0.9	25.3	26.5	15.0
Latin America	5.0	0.0	5.9	13.1	11.5	1.2
Other Developing Regions	7.9	-24.0	8.3	-27.8	-22.5	-1.9
OECD Regions	5.8	-22.1	5.8	-30.1	-23.7	-4.1
Other	6.2	-3.8	6.8	-0.5	3.6	-2.8
Total	6.1	-9.0	5.8	-6.3	1.4	n.a.

Table 5.9. **Impact of Full Unilateral Liberalisation in Africa on Key Variables**
(per cent change in the year 2002 from the base simulation)

	Real Income	Rural Value Added	Urban Value Added	Rural/ Urban Income	Food Prices	Terms of Trade
Africa	6.1	0.2	11.6	-0.2	5.4	-3.6
Sub-Saharan Africa	4.7	1.1	9.8	2.1	4.8	-3.6
Nigeria	5.2	4.5	9.7	11.6	11.0	-0.2
South Africa	9.1	-10.8	13.7	-10.9	-2.2	-7.3
Maghreb	8.3	0.3	15.0	-1.9	3.2	-3.4
Low Income Regions	0.0	0.1	0.0	0.0	0.0	0.0
Latin America	0.0	0.1	0.0	0.0	0.1	0.2
Other Developing Regions	0.0	0.1	0.0	0.1	0.2	0.1
OECD Regions	0.0	0.1	0.0	0.1	0.1	0.1
Other	0.0	0.0	0.0	0.0	0.1	0.0
Total	0.2	0.1	0.3	0.0	0.4	n.a.

Table 5.10. **Impact of Higher OECD Growth on Key Variables**
(per cent change in the year 2002 from the base simulation)

	Real Income	Rural Value Added	Urban Value Added	Rural/ Urban Income	Food Prices	Terms of Trade
Africa	1.6	0.0	-0.7	-1.4	-0.3	1.4
Sub-Saharan Africa	1.7	0.4	0.5	-0.6	0.7	2.3
Nigeria	-0.2	-1.6	-4.4	-4.6	-3.0	-0.6
South Africa	2.6	0.5	1.5	-0.8	1.3	3.2
Maghreb	3.8	-0.1	0.7	-4.5	-1.6	-0.3
Low Income Regions	0.3	0.5	0.0	1.7	1.4	2.4
Latin America	1.7	0.2	0.2	-2.1	-0.2	2.6
Other Developing Regions	3.1	0.7	0.5	-1.3	0.6	1.5
OECD Regions	18.5	2.6	19.7	-4.8	6.8	-1.8
Other	0.8	0.8	-0.4	1.4	1.6	2.4
Total	12.3	1.1	13.4	-1.4	2.9	n.a.

Table 5.11. **Impact of an Increase in Net Transfers on Key Variables**
(per cent change in the year 2002 from the base simulation)

	Real Income	Rural Value Added	Urban Value Added	Rural/ Urban Income	Food Prices	Terms of Trade
Africa	7.4	0.4	9.4	-6.1	1.0	-1.2
Sub-Saharan Africa	3.9	0.5	6.3	-3.9	1.3	-1.2
Nigeria	8.8	0.9	11.0	-5.9	1.9	-2.1
South Africa	11.3	0.0	13.4	-11.1	0.2	-1.8
Maghreb	9.2	-0.3	9.4	-9.6	-0.9	-0.3
Low Income Regions	0.0	0.0	0.0	0.1	0.1	0.1
Latin America	0.0	0.0	0.0	0.2	0.1	0.1
Other Developing Regions	-0.3	0.0	-0.4	0.5	0.2	0.1
OECD Regions	-0.2	0.1	-0.3	0.4	0.3	0.0
Other	-0.1	0.1	-0.1	0.2	0.1	0.1
Total	0.0	0.1	0.0	0.0	0.2	n.a.

Table 5.12. **Impact of Increase in Rural Investment on Key Variables**
(per cent change in the year 2002 from the base simulation)

	Real Income	Rural Value Added	Urban Value Added	Rural/ Urban Income	Food Prices	Terms of Trade
Africa	4.0	0.7	3.4	-5.4	-2.1	0.6
Sub-Saharan Africa	2.6	0.7	3.2	-3.8	-0.3	0.0
Nigeria	3.3	-0.8	1.4	-9.8	-5.1	0.5
South Africa	6.4	1.5	6.6	-8.9	-2.9	0.8
Maghreb	6.1	2.6	3.9	-7.2	-4.3	1.3
Low Income Regions	0.0	0.0	0.0	0.0	0.0	0.0
Latin America	0.0	0.0	0.0	0.0	0.0	0.0
Other Developing Regions	-0.3	0.0	-0.3	0.2	0.0	0.0
OECD Regions	-0.2	0.0	-0.2	0.1	0.0	0.0
Other	0.0	0.0	0.0	0.0	0.0	0.0
Total	0.0	0.1	-0.1	-0.2	-0.1	n.a.

Chapter 6

Tropical Product Exporters

Introduction: A Fallacy of Composition in Policy Advice?

This chapter is concerned with the consequences of policy-conditional adjustment assistance being applied simultaneously in several developing countries[1]. Is there a contradiction between individual actions and group outcomes, often referred to in policy discussions as the fallacy of composition? How important is it likely to be empirically? If it is empirically relevant, how can adjustment policies be best adapted to take into account weaknesses in the small-country assumption?

Many developing countries have not embraced trade liberalisation willingly. The burden of debt has nevertheless constrained their choice and — with the drying up of commercial bank lending — increased their reliance on multilateral and bilateral agencies whose lending increasingly has been associated with a reform conditionality. However, the extent of outside pressure should not be exaggerated. Moreover, developing countries are learning some lessons from their development policies which have not worked and, together with the eastern European countries, are now more receptive to the benefits of freer trade. Nevertheless, strong reservations remain. This section focuses on a key concern for the tropical product exporters: the small-country assumption and the possibility of a fallacy of composition in policy advice[2].

Different branches of economics have long been concerned with phenomena where the elasticity of demand for one seller is greater than for the market as a whole. Furthermore, in development economics, a long-running debate has centred on the extent to which reforms undertaken by one country may be rendered ineffective if similar reforms are undertaken by other countries[3]. While much of the recent debate has focused on manufacturing exports from developing countries, analysis of the "small-country assumption" suggests that adverse terms-of-trade consequences of export expansion may be an awkward but appropriate concern for developing countries heavily dependent on primary commodity exports. Our interest is in the possible consequences for developing countries of a removal of the small-country assumption from the formulation of structural adjustment and trade reform[4].

If successful, trade policy reform with structural adjustment may lead to increased traditional and non-traditional exports, as well as more efficient import substitution. However, in the case of traditional primary exports, there is some evidence that the policies may induce comparative static welfare loss because of the fallacy of composition. For example, Karunasekara (1984), identified eight primary commodities for which this is possible — coffee, cocoa, tea, bananas, bauxite, copper, tin and tropical timber. Similarly, Koester *et al.* (1990) found that African cocoa and coffee exporters will not gain by expanding production of those crops, while Panagariya and Schiff (1990b) explored the implications of the argument in the context of strategic behaviour.

The evidence suggests that the countries which would suffer the strongest terms-of-trade effects from developing country trade reform are precisely those poor, typically sub-Saharan, countries which have the weakest trade performance[5]. Trade reforms by these countries, to the extent that they mirror those of their principal competitors, may not improve their position. Thus, on redistributive grounds, there may be a case for allowing some of the costs of trade policy reform to fall on better-off countries.

Despite the mass of empirical work on the relationship between trade policy and economic performance, the evidence regarding the effects of policy reform is inconclusive[6]. In part, this reflects the difficulties of comparative historical analysis, both because it is difficult to measure trade policy variables and their independent influence on growth, and because the full consequences of recent reforms have yet to be seen. The RUNS model provides an opportunity to explore the consequences of policy choices beyond the range of historical experience.

Conceptual Background

Adverse terms-of-trade movements usually decrease welfare in a static context. It is often implied in the Prebisch-Singer tradition that this static result carries over to economic growth. However, with factor input growth, adverse terms-of-trade movements can be associated with output growth, which can either improve or decrease welfare. In any case, a single country can only do something about its "terms-of-trade problem" when it has independent market power, that is, when the small-country assumption does not hold and it has an imperfectly elastic demand curve for one or more export products.

The analysis of welfare- and revenue-maximising export taxes in the literature, when a single country faces a less than perfectly elastic demand curve for its exports, has usually been carried out in the context of a two-country general equilibrium [Johnson (1950-51), Tower (1977)]. In policy terms, however, although export taxes have been recognised as one of the very few cases where optimal intervention requires a trade tax, optimal export taxes have not been recommended in practice for two reasons. First, because of the free-rider problem which occurs when two or more countries face a less than perfectly elastic demand schedule for a homogeneous product (so that other producers would benefit when taxes were raised). Second, because in the context of a cosmopolitan rule-based international trading system, there is no place for the long-run legitimisation of the collective monopoly power of one country or group of countries, even if the free-rider problems associated with co-operative solutions could be overcome.

The cosmopolitan view was easier to defend in the context of rapidly growing world trade. However, when a group of countries with market power and export taxes on their chief export crops are also some of the poorest in the world, for example, cocoa producers, the cosmopolitan view may be challenged from a poverty perspective[7]. In the context of slower growth of world output and trade, the status of policy recommendations on trade policy reform in structural adjustment programmes requires further analysis[8]. Should the costs of trade policy reform which increase global welfare be borne by the countries in question? Can the Bretton Woods institutions overcome the free-rider problems involved in taking into account the combined monopoly power of such poor producing countries when formulating policy-conditional structural adjustment assistance? Could this be done without undermining a rule-based world trading system?

In their recent analysis of the sequencing of trade policy liberalisation, Papageorgiou *et al.* (1991, Vol. 7) make an argument for the use of selective incentives where trade liberalisation has employment implications, to allow a longer period for adjustment in larger and labour-intensive industries. We suggest that the argument should be extended to include the selective retention of some level of export taxes when the chief exporting countries individually face a substantially less than perfectly elastic demand curve for exports, when collective action in reducing existing levels of export taxes could have significant welfare costs and when the countries concerned are poor. The argument is particularly pertinent when the policy conditionality driving the export tax reform is imposed by the Bretton Woods institutions whose job is to assist in the financing of both stabilization and structural adjustment. If it is in the long-run interests of a cosmopolitan rule-based world trading system to remove export taxes, even when welfare-reducing for the poorer countries concerned, there appears to be an argument for a slower rate of reduction of export taxes and other trade policy instruments while other policies are being reformed. There may also be a case for additional adjustment assistance to offset the costs of early trade policy reforms, or for export tax reduction to be carried out only in the context of renewed growth in the world economy and multilateral trade policy reform. Usually, negotiating "chips" in multilateral trade negotiations are tariff reductions, which are widely believed by trade economists to be welfare-enhancing even if carried out unilaterally. When multilateral trade policy reform is clearly welfare-reducing for some of the poorer countries involved, surely there is a case for some compensatory transfers, financing or access to markets. For the tree crops, the removal of tariff escalation facing processed exports would be an obvious compensatory trade policy reform.

The extension of the earlier literature on optimum export taxes to strategic behaviour has only just begun [see Panagariya and Schiff (1990a, b) and their contribution to this volume]. This new literature uses a partial equilibrium framework because a general equilibrium approach is said to be analytically intractable, especially if growth is also considered. However, a first exploration of the general equilibrium issues in an empirical context is carried out here using RUNS, focusing mainly on coffee and cocoa.

In its present formulation, the RUNS model has an endogenously specified behavioural mechanism governing agricultural export taxes in which the target variables are farm gate prices in each country or region; there is no behavioural mechanism to incorporate strategic behaviour. What is done in the preliminary results reported is to explore the model's implications for growth and the terms of trade for two types of overall structural adjustment shocks: changes in the degree of wage flexibility, to simulate a drop in the real wage and a lowering of the urban-rural real wage differential; and changes in trade policies for a subgroup of developing countries which include the main producers of tropical beverages or tree crops.

These countries first have the shock of an across-the-board change in the export taxes on their tree crops, with and without wage policy changes. Then there is a policy shock in which only one of the regions pursues policy changes. To understand the model's results, the next two subsections review the optimal tax arguments in the context of co-operative and strategic behaviour, paying particular attention to the relationship between actual export tax revenues and the optimal welfare and revenue taxes.

Optimum Export Taxes and Actual Behaviour

Panagariya and Schiff (1990a, b) examine the problem of optimum and revenue-maximising export taxes in the context of a three-country partial equilibrium model with myopic, Nash and co-operative behavioural assumptions. The competitive outcome always leads to a higher level of output than either of the co-operative taxing outcomes, and the co-operative revenue-maximising tax is always higher than the profit-maximising tax[9]. The welfare outcomes of the Nash revenue- and Nash profit-maximising solutions cannot be uniquely ranked. For higher elasticities of supply, the Nash revenue-maximising tax has the higher welfare, but for lower elasticities of supply, the Nash profit-maximising solution has the higher welfare outcome.

If one of the countries has a real exchange rate depreciation, this is equivalent to a downward shift in the country's, and the world's, supply curve. The optimum taxes will increase, as will the Nash profit and Nash revenue taxes, but the rankings of the optimum co-operative profit- and revenue-maximising taxes will not change[10].

Similarly, on account of the Lerner symmetry condition, the introduction of tariff or other forms of protection for import-competing production will lead to an appreciation of the real exchange rate, an upward shift in the export supply curve and a lowering of the optimal export taxes. In a general equilibrium context, exploitation of a country's monopoly power in trade can be achieved either through export taxes, import protection, or some combination of both.

Exploration of the implications of strategic behaviour by export-taxing governments in the countries producing tropical beverages is very much in its infancy. It is too early to tell how closely the pattern of actual export taxes matches that predicted by the Panagariya and Schiff multicommodity model of strategic behaviour of the governments of cocoa-producing countries. For the present purposes, it is sufficient to draw on their work, developed in a partial equilibrium context, to understand the implications of exogenously imposed patterns of export tax changes on applied general equilibrium growth models such as RUNS. These implications can now be analysed.

When a group of countries has monopoly power in their export market, lowering their export taxes below the co-operative optimal levels can lower export tax revenue. The lower export taxes will be associated with higher domestic prices and higher levels of output of the exported product, lower profits and, when domestic consumption of the exported product is small, lower levels of welfare. Furthermore, the lower profits in export production may lead to a lower level of investment and lower growth. Moreover, if the loss of export tax revenue lowers total savings (public and private) because of redistributive and budgetary effects, there can be additional adverse consequences for growth.

When a single country, or one group of countries, alone lowers its export tax, the optimal tax structure will be lowered for the remaining countries. In the absence of retaliation, lower export taxes in the single country or subgroup of countries may, or may not, be revenue- or profit-enhancing. The outcome will depend on the relationship between existing tax structures and the optimal tax for the subgroup of countries acting alone, given the tax levels of the remaining countries. The effects on growth will follow from the revenue and profit effects discussed above.

The removal of other distortions such as tariff protection or exchange rate overvaluation, leading to an exchange rate depreciation, will tend to increase the optimal export tax. In themselves, the removal of other distortions may enhance or reduce revenue and welfare, depending on whether the changes move the economy closer to or away from the optimal export taxes. The growth effects following the removal of other distortions will depend critically on the effects of the changes on gross savings, as noted above. However, the removal of export taxes will be welfare-enhancing for the world economy as a whole.

These results are used in interpreting the initial set of policy shocks reported for the RUNS model in the next section.

The Empirical Estimates

The tree crop supply and demand elasticities used in the RUNS model are discussed and compared with those used in other studies in the Appendix to this chapter. As a first attempt to use the RUNS model to explore structural adjustment issues, a base-run scenario was developed consistent with current World Bank projections for macro growth and foreign capital flows, and with wage inflexibility which roughly reproduces the base levels of unemployment. Two types of shocks were then considered. The first was designed to simulate the effects of changing the degree of wage flexibility on the real exchange rate and growth, and the second to simulate the effects of changes in the price-wedges affecting tree crop exports for different combinations of the major tree crop exporters.

Within the RUNS model, as already indicated, there is no explicit exchange rate variable or monetary instrument. This means that it is not possible to model the effects of a deviation of the real exchange rate from its equilibrium value as frequently occurs when there is macroeconomic disequilibrium. However, the RUNS model can capture the effects of varying degrees of wage rigidity on the equilibrium real exchange rate and on growth. In the Armington world of universal but imperfect tradability in non-agricultural commodities, there is no real exchange rate, as conventionally defined, that is, the ratio of the price of non-tradables to tradables.

However, it is possible to define an Armington-world counterpart to the conventional definition by measuring the relationship between domestic prices and the prices of imports[11]. To model the shock of a change in export taxes levied by tropical beverages producers (tree crops in RUNS terminology), the 1993 price wedges for these commodities were cut by 25 per cent from the 1990 level with full pass-through of world price changes starting in 1993. This is done in varying combinations with the other policy shocks. Finally, in order to explore the consequences of a single country (or group of countries) cutting export taxes, the final policy shock lowers all African tree crop export taxes by 25 per cent after 1993.

The characteristics of the base run and the five different policy shocks considered are as follows:

Base Run: Underlying World Bank projections of growth and capital flows to 2002; labour market rigidities roughly reproduce base-year rates of unemployment; constant export taxes from 1993.

Shock I: Base run plus more flexible urban employment in Africa, Latin America, Mediterranean and Low Income Other Asia from 1993.

Shock II: Base run plus 25 per cent cut in tree crop export taxes in Africa, Latin America, Mediterranean and Low Income Other Asia from 1993.

Shock III: I and II combined.

Shock IV: Sensitivity test with both base run comparator and policy shock II calculated with cocoa and coffee supply elasticities doubled.

The essential characteristics of the base run and the policy shock simulations are set out in Table 6.1. The main results for the present set of policy shock simulations for the major producers of coffee and cocoa crops are set out as a percentage change in the 2002 level for each of the variables considered. The reported results include GDP growth rates, trade volume, rural and urban incomes and factor prices, country or regional terms of trade, world prices of tree crops, real exchange rates, tree crop net trade, and tree crop tax income. The changes of latter results are reported in billions of 1985 dollars.

Overall world GDP growth to 2002 is 3.2 per cent per annum and world trade growth is 3.5 per cent in the base run. The effects of the policy shocks considered are presented as deviations from the base run for each of the policy simulations.

The results of the first policy experiment are shown under I. The pattern of the marked increase in GDP and trade volumes from the elimination of labour market distortions in this policy simulation reflect the higher initial levels of measured unemployment in Africa and the rest of Latin America. For Africa, Low Income Asia and the rest of Latin America, where the growth stimulus is greatest, there are relatively large adjustments in the overall terms of trade and the real exchange rate accompanying increased labour market flexibility. Whilst the accuracy of the base projections of unemployment and the feasibility of eliminating labour market distortions must be heavily qualified, it is interesting to note from simulation I that effects on tree crops of sharply increased growth in the countries experiencing the shock is relatively small. There are many other possibilities for adjustment to the higher growth outside of the tropical beverages. In the absence of a policy shock, which increases the world demand for tropical beverages, the export tax and terms-of-trade effects of increased growth in the main supplying countries for coffee and cocoa are minor.

It would be interesting to know the extent to which the effects of the policy shock can be attributed to static efficiency gains and to longer-run growth. In the present formulation of the RUNS model it is not possible to make an accurate separation of these effects since investment is endogenously determined and will exert some influence on current levels of output. However, some indication of the comparative static effects is given by comparing the orders of magnitude of the effects in 1993, the first year of their policy shocks, and in 2002, the final year considered. Thus, in the case of policy shock I, about 75 per cent of the relative GDP effect occurs in Africa in the initial year, and in the remaining countries 40 per cent to 50 per cent of the relative GDP effect occurs in the initial year.

Policy shock II was designed to throw light on the revenue and welfare implications of cutting tree crop export taxes in a context of longer-run growth. The 25 per cent cut in the 1993 price wedge for tree crops was not applied to India and China, as the analysis focuses on the major producers of coffee and cocoa. In the case of the latter crops, there is a significant decline in world prices, tax revenues for the major producing countries and in GDP for Africa. The decline in tree crop export tax revenue per annum for the countries shown in Table 6.1 is $800 million (1985 prices) by the year 2002, compared with the base run.

If the GDP effects for the rest of Latin America and Africa were traced back to the major producing countries within these regions, the percentage fall in GDP would be very much higher. In absolute terms the changes in GDP are large. For Africa, Brazil and the rest of Latin America, the aggregate decline is $8.3 billion.

There are obviously many ways in which countries could offset the negative effects of an across-the-board cut in export taxes. One of these is considered in policy shock III, which combines shock I, the removal of labour market imperfections, with the cut in export taxes considered in shock II. In so far as I is possible and realistic, the results for shock III show that the negative effects of the export tax cut can be offset by faster growth arising from policy changes in the countries concerned. Other alternatives, such as an increase in transfers from developed countries during some transition period, trade policy reform in the developed countries affecting the processing of tree crops, or faster developed country growth, have yet to be explored.

A final set of calculations was made. It may be legitimately argued that the econometric estimates of the supply elasticities used and reported in the Appendix are too low. It should be recalled that, in the context of an applied general equilibrium growth model, the relevant elasticities are the short-run estimates; the model itself, through investment, allows for a long-run supply response. As a sensitivity check, the supply elasticities for coffee and cocoa were doubled in size and shock II was rerun with the larger elasticities and an appropriately adjusted base simulation, reported as shock IV in the last column of Table 6.1. In effect, the size of the short-run elasticities used in shock IV are similar to the econometrically estimated long-run supply elasticities which can be found in the literature.

Conclusions: Developing Countries' Concerns

The international dimensions of adjustment are not fully understood and models such as RUNS have a special role to play in capturing the interaction of different national policies. The policy simulations using the RUNS model obtained so far suggest that the order of magnitude of the annual tax revenue and GDP loss arising from a 25 per cent across-the-board cut of tree crop export taxes is very substantial for the crops considered; the immediate GDP losses for this policy change alone amount to over 5 per cent of total ODA to developing countries. These results need further refinement and extension, but the overall orders of magnitude are unlikely to change.

The results suggest that in contrast with present practice, co-ordinated policy-conditional assistance needs to take into account explicitly the removal of the small-country assumption. The fallacy-of-composition issue is a valid concern for policy makers in tree-crop-exporting developing countries. Stabilization could be provided through continued use of trade policy instruments, such as export taxes, and this could enhance the possibility of success of other adjustment measures. For these countries, there may well be a case for special treatment, allowing for a slower rate of reform of selective trade interventions during a transition period. Alternatively, the tree crop producers might request compensation for reforms which are in the general interest, either in the form of additional ODA or, trade policy reform in developed countries with respect to downstream processing of tree crop products. The essential is ensuring that the legitimate concerns of developing countries are met without eroding the wider commitment to freer trade, including reductions in the OECD countries' protectionism. Reducing this protectionism will facilitate the diversification of developing country exports, improve their terms of trade, and offset the threat of a fallacy of composition in the policy advice of OECD countries to developing countries.

Appendix A

The Elasticities Used for Tree Crops

In so far as the empirical results from the RUNS model have a bearing on the policy consequences of the fallacy of composition as it affects the tropical beverages, it is important that the supply and demand elasticities used for tree crops in RUNS are roughly in conformity with the range of estimates obtained econometrically from other studies, and are in line with the values used in other tree-crop modelling exercises. Table 6A.1 summarises the RUNS elasticities and those used in some other studies.

Not all of the elasticities shown in Table 6A.1 are comparable; for example, the price elasticities from the Panagariya and Schiff (1990a, b) study on cocoa are country-based, whereas the RUNS values are for total world exports. However, the country-level price elasticities implied by the export shares in RUNS for cocoa are somewhat higher than the values used by Panagariya and Schiff (1990a, b). On the other hand, the RUNS price elasticities of demand are somewhat lower than assumed by Mabbs-Zeno and Krissoff (1990) for cocoa and tea. Overall, the price elasticities of demand used in RUNS are close to the range of estimates found in the Karunasekera survey. On the supply elasticities, the RUNS values are near the low end of the range found by Karunasekera (1984), which is to be expected since the relevant econometrically estimated supply elasticities used in RUNS are short-run; the long-run supply elasticities being implicit in the model's solutions. The use of lower-bound estimates of supply elasticities in RUNS can also be justified in the light of recent discussions of the role of non-price factors affecting export supply [see Lipton (1987)][12]. Given that the supply and demand elasticities for tree crops used in the RUNS model are roughly in the range used in other studies, the main role of RUNS is to provide a systematic background of general equilibrium effects associated with the policy shocks examined.

Notes and References

1. This chapter draws extensively on David Evans, Ian Goldin and Dominique van der Mensbrugghe, "Trade Reform and the Small Country Assumption" in Goldin and Winters, (eds.), *Open Economies: Structural Adjustment and Agriculture*, Cambridge University Press, Cambridge, 1992.
2. Often the substance of economic analysis is about differences between individual and collective outcomes. The phrase "fallacy of composition" is used in policy discussions to refer to the failure of policy analysis to identify situations in which individual and collective interests diverge.
3. Milestones in the debate include: Prebisch (1950) and Singer (1950) whose export pessimism was challenged by Krueger (1961), Balassa (1971) and Bhagwati (1978a, b). Lewis (1980) countered the optimistic challenge in the light of the apparent slowing of growth in OECD countries, arguing that it would be better for developing countries to promote South-South trade, while Cline (1982) showed that without greater access to markets of developed countries, developing countries could not hope to emulate the dynamic Asian economies. Riedel (1984, 1988) and Balassa (1987) countered that there was no correlation between developing country exports and rates of growth of OECD countries, and that with effective price and exchange rate policies, international demand no longer represents a significant constraint on developing country export growth, but this view has recently been challenged by Faini *et al.* (1990b).
4. World Bank and IMF adjustment programmes generally make small-country assumptions. See, for example, in Michaely (1986), Krueger (1978), Goldstein (1986), Thomas and Nash (1990) and World Bank (1988, 1989, 1990). Note that the small-country assumption is an extreme case of the elasticity proposition by which the elasticity of demand for one seller is much greater than the market as a whole.
5. See Koester, I., H. Schafer and A. Valdés (1990); and UNCTAD (1989).
6. See Evans (1991).
7. For documentation of the collapse of tropical product commodity prices in the 1980s, see UNCTAD (1989, Annex Table 4).
8. For example, see Bateman *et al.* (1990), which recommends the removal of cocoa export taxes in Ghana.
9. Note that in the absence of domestic consumption of the exportable, the profit-maximising tax is also welfare-maximising.
10. For some types of non-linear demand curves, it is possible for the optimal taxes to decrease. However, the result in the text will hold the linear and for the constant own price elasticities implied by the ELES used in the RUNS model.

11. For a discussion of indexes relating to the real exchange rate calculated on the export and the import side, see Devarajan *et al.* (1991). In the RUNS model, there is a perfect elasticity of transformation between production for domestic and export markets so that tax-inclusive domestic and export prices are the same and only the import-side real exchange rate index is relevant.

12. Our supply elasticities are derived by the International Trade Division of the World Bank.

Table 6.1. **Main Results for Countries Subject to Policy Shocks**

	% p.a. Base	% change in level 2002 I	II	III	IV
GDP (deflated by consumption price index)					
Africa	3.10	6.20	-2.08	6.16	-1.14
Low Income Asia	3.81	4.06	0.38	4.03	1.91
Brazil	4.06	2.57	-0.10	2.50	-0.35
Latin America	2.93	8.17	0.25	8.20	-0.36
OECD	2.67	-0.04	-0.02	-0.03	-0.35
World	3.21	0.96	-0.02	0.96	-0.31
Trade Volume (imports + exports)					
Africa	3.07	5.62	-0.51	4.86	-0.22
Low Income Asia	4.21	4.72	0.25	4.70	2.16
Brazil	3.35	1.36	-0.07	1.33	-0.32
Latin America	2.72	5.54	0.32	5.72	-0.16
OECD	2.93	0.24	-0.02	0.26	-0.48
World	3.53	0.98	0.00	0.99	-0.58
Rural-Urban Parity					
Africa		-2.11	-0.11	-2.25	-0.20
Low Income Asia		-1.44	-0.54	-1.46	-1.01
Brazil		0.15	0.11	0.26	0.22
Latin America		-1.67	0.62	-0.98	1.16
Terms of Trade (excluding oil)					
Africa		-3.41	0.54	-3.74	-0.41
Low Income Asia		-2.49	-0.07	-2.51	-1.94
Brazil		-0.08	-0.44	-0.52	-0.40
Latin America		-2.48	-0.29	-2.63	0.09
World Prices					
Coffee		0.28	-4.73	-4.47	-4.10
Cocoa		0.02	-2.89	-2.87	-3.62
Real Exchange Rates (ratio domestic prices of importables to prices of imports)					
Africa		-5.23	1.26	-4.32	-0.10
Low Income Asia		-2.50	-0.08	-2.51	-1.95
Brazil		-1.24	-0.16	-1.39	-0.05
Latin America		-3.67	0.07	-3.46	0.78

Table 6.1. (continued)

Tree Crop Net Trade ($ billions, 1985)				
Africa	0.00	-0.23	-0.23	-0.28
Low Income Asia	0.00	-0.03	-0.03	-0.33
Brazil	0.03	-0.32	-0.29	-0.45
Latin America	0.02	0.64	0.67	1.28
Tree Crop Tax Revenue ($ billions, 1985)				
Africa	0.00	-0.11	-0.11	-0.11
Low Income Asia	0.00	0.00	0.00	0.00
Brazil	0.00	-0.16	-0.16	-0.17
Latin America	0.01	-0.52	-0.51	-0.26

Table 6A.1. **Empirical Estimates of Demand and Supply Elasticities for Exports**

	Demand		Supply
	Price	Income	
Coffee			
Karunasekera (1984, Annex Table 2)	-0.15 to -0.31		0.33 to 1.28
Mabbs-Zeno and Krissoff (1990:188)	-0.3		n.a.
RUNS	-0.33	0.6	0.35
Cocoa			
Karunasekera (1984, Annex Table 2)	-0.11 to -0.33		0.34 to 1.0
Mabbs-Zeno and Krissoff (1990:188)	-0.7		n.a.
Panagariya and Schiff (1990a, Table 1)	-0.28 to -3.0[a]		
RUNS	-0.27	0.6	0.35 to 0.37
Tea			
Karunasekera (1984, Annex Table 2)	-0.2 to -0.5		0.16 to 0.72
Mabbs-Zeno and Krissoff (1990: 188)	-0.6		n.a.
RUNS	-0.14	0.5	0.24 to 0.39

a. Country based estimates rather than world.

n.a. Not available.

Chapter 7

Asia

Introduction

This chapter will focus on China and India, the two countries having the largest populations and greatest food needs. Both of these countries are currently undergoing significant transformation. In China, there is strong internal growth generated by high investment and major trade links with the rest of the world, while in the case of India, internal reform is closely associated with trade reform. Both countries have tended to tax agriculture and protect industry. India, however, has provided significant input subsidies to agriculture which dampens the taxation effect. India's manufacturing tariffs have tended to be much higher than China's. This is also reflected in a low degree of openness, with exports representing less than 7 per cent of India's GDP. Exports represent 10 per cent of China's GDP.

China

By the sheer size of its population, China plays an important role in world agriculture, even if its net agricultural trade is small. Moreover, though the net reproduction rate has decreased recently, China's population will grow by about 1.4 per cent per annum through the rest of this decade, increasing its food needs and further influencing world agricultural markets. Recent reforms of the Chinese economy and a reduction in international tensions in the Far East have led to rapid growth of the Chinese economy. If this rapid growth continues at its current pace, there will be a greater than proportional increase in the demand for food, particularly of the relatively income-elastic commodities such as meat. This will add to the growing food demands of China.

China: From the Present to the Future

Despite its huge population, China in 1985 accounted for only 2.5 per cent of world GDP (or roughly $290 per capita)[1]. In the same year, it accounted for 22 per cent of the world's population. Its growth rate, however, has been spectacular over the last few years, with real growth of about 6 to 7 per cent. For the period 1990-2002, we are using a real GDP growth rate assumption of 6.6 per cent per annum. The population growth rate is assumed to be 1.4 per cent per annum, leading to an increase in per capita income of 5.2 per cent. This would roughly double China's share of world GDP, to about 4.8 per cent.

Like many developing countries, production and income are not evenly divided between rural and urban activities. In 1985, agriculture accounted for 40 per cent of Chinese GDP and 71 per cent of the total labour force. This accounts for a rural-to-urban income parity index of 30 per cent (i.e. rural per capita incomes are only 30 per cent of urban per capita incomes). The rural-urban income gap is reduced somewhat by the year 2002, mainly through rural-to-urban migration. Urban GDP is assumed to grow by over 7 per cent, while rural GDP increases by 5 per cent. However, rural labour grows much more slowly than urban labour. The continuing income gap between the rural and urban sectors causes rural labourers to migrate to better paying jobs in the rapidly growing urban sector.

In 1985, exports represented about 9.2 per cent of GDP, while imports were roughly 13.9 per cent. Agricultural exports amounted to only 10 per cent of the total value of exports, and agricultural imports were only 3.8 per cent of total imports. The aggregate trade balance in 1985 was negative, but the agricultural trade balance was slightly positive. The largest market for Chinese manufacturing exports were Far East Asia, the United States, Japan, the EC, and Eastern and Central Europe. About 45 per cent of Chinese manufacturing imports originated in Far East Asia, with the United States, Japan, and the EC providing the bulk of the remaining imports.

Table 7.1 presents supply and demand trends for the agricultural commodities. The demand trend incorporates both intermediate demand (seed and feed) and household demand (and changes in stocks). The difference between the supply and demand trends will determine changes in the self-sufficiency ratios. While China is basically self-sufficient in the 1985 base year, if the supply and demand trends continue, China will see a strong shift into livestock production (both meat and dairy products), with a significant import requirement for feed (coarse grains and oil meal), and a requirement for rice, wheat and other food imports for household consumption.

The main remaining component of the base simulation is the level of price intervention in the Chinese economy. In agriculture, on average, domestic prices were lower than world prices. This implies that imports were subsidised and exports were taxed, and suggests that agricultural production was in effect taxed. The average level of taxation was about 35 per cent, though there are variations across sectors. The highest level of taxation occurs in the rice sector, with lower levels in wheat, coarse grains, and vegetable oils. Livestock is also taxed, particularly other meats, which is a very large part of the total livestock sector. Agricultural input subsidies are very low, with the sugar sector receiving the only significant amount of input subsidy. Finally, the average level of non-agricultural import tariffs is 41 per cent[2]. The agricultural taxation and non-agricultural import tariffs result in significant protection of the urban economy.

Reform, Growth, and Capital Transfers

In this section, we focus on alternative scenarios, where we modify trade policy and growth rates. The first subsection will discuss the effects of partial and complete global trade reform. We will also present the results of unilateral price reform in China, and its effect on the global economy. In the second subsection we will analyse the consequences of higher growth in the OECD economies and how this affects growth in China.

Trade Reform

As shown above, partial trade reform will lead to an increase in world prices for most agricultural commodities. This is a consequence of a removal of heavy agricultural protection amongst the large agricultural-producing OECD countries. As producer prices decrease, supply decreases, leading to a rise in the world price. The main exceptions to this rule include rice, coffee, and cocoa. Rice production is taxed heavily in some major producing countries, notably China. As the level of taxation is reduced, this increases producer incentives, leading to a rise in production. Moreover, demand will fall as consumer subsidies are reduced. Other meats and other food in general are not protected. A drop in the world price of these aggregate commodities is generated by a drop in demand as consumers substitute into other food commodities, whose domestic price tends to fall.

The consequences for China are very beneficial. China may expect to see a real income gain of about 4.3 per cent per year by the year 2002, or roughly $50 billion (1985 dollars). The largest gains accrue to the rural sector, where farm incomes increase significantly from higher producer prices, and there is a drop in the price of manufactured goods. Since poverty tends to be concentrated in the rural areas, this has favourable consequences for income distribution in China. The gains in the urban sector are smaller. Higher domestic food prices lead to a welfare loss which is partly compensated by a decrease in import prices as tariffs are reduced. The higher rural incomes generate demand for urban goods, both for household consumption and increased investment in farm equipment and other rural investment goods. These two effects are enough to generate growth in the Chinese urban sector. China also experiences a significant gain in its terms of trade. It is a large importer of rice and other food in the year 2002 in the base simulation, and both commodities will decrease in price under the partial reform scenario. It also is a significant exporter of coarse grains and meat, whose prices will increase.

The partial reform scenario improves China's agricultural trade position. An increase in supply and a decrease in demand for many commodities lead to an improvement in the self-sufficiency ratios (see Table 7.2). The sectoral self-sufficiency rates mask the aggregate effect, but the overall agricultural net trade will improve by $32 billion (1985 dollars).

Full multilateral trade reform results in change going in the same direction as partial reform, simply magnifying the movement of prices and welfare. The income gains for China are projected to be about 6.5 per cent, or $76 billion (1985 dollars). All the gains accrue to the rural sector, as the urban sector actually suffers a loss in welfare. The dramatically higher rural incomes, particularly compared to urban incomes, significantly decreases the rural-to-urban labour migration. This leads to a smaller labour force, and reduced urban savings leads to a smaller capital stock as well. (Note, this is compared to the base simulation, and both urban labour and capital stock have an overall positive growth rate.) In trade, China once again sees an increase in self-sufficiency rates, and in some cases dramatic improvements. For example, China becomes self-sufficient in rice. The larger losses will occur in coffee and tea, the former, however, being a relatively minor crop. In the aggregate, China will become a net agricultural exporter.

The final trade reform simulation concerns China alone. In this simulation, we eliminate all Chinese price distortion measures, agricultural and non-agricultural, as well as agricultural input subsidies. Unilateral Chinese trade reform could have a significant potential impact on world agricultural markets. Virtually all food commodity prices decrease. As the government reduces agricultural taxation, Chinese farmers increase production, leading to higher world supply and therefore, lower world prices. The reduction in prices tends to be highest in commodities that are the most highly taxed, for example, rice and beef.

The real income gain in China is an impressive 4 per cent per annum by the year 2002 ($46 billion, 1985 dollars). Many other regions gain. The food-importing regions gain from a positive terms of trade shock. The OECD countries gain in general, mainly because the drop in world prices leads to a *de facto* drop in protection (since we assume perfect price transmission). The lone exception among the OECD regions is Australia/New Zealand, where the price wedges are very low, and the lower food prices are detrimental to the terms of trade. Another source of growth for many regions is that lower food prices reduce the consumer price index, leading to a reduction of wage pressures. This effectively reduces unemployment and leads to an increase in urban output. The negative side of this simulation is that, except for China, the rural sectors suffer a significant drop in real income induced by the drop in producer prices. While the global and regional gains would be more than sufficient to offset the losses in the rural sector, mechanisms need to be implemented which would enable farmers to benefit from reduced protection. In this sense, a global trade reform would be much more beneficial to the rural sector, in China and most other regions of the world, except for the highly protected OECD countries.

Unilateral reform leads to higher levels of self-sufficiency, but not as much as under full multilateral reform. While the rise in domestic prices increases production and reduces demand, this phenomenon is dampened by lower world agricultural prices (rather than higher in the case of full multilateral liberalisation). Nonetheless, the higher supply should lead to a positive net aggregate agricultural trade.

To conclude, these three reform scenarios all lead to significant positive gains for the Chinese economy. In particular, the rural sector achieves an impressive real income gain which reduces rural-urban income disparity. All three reforms lead to an improvement in the agricultural trade balance. In the case of both multilateral and unilateral full trade reform, China could even be a net agricultural exporter by 2002.

The last simulation, unilateral trade reform, reflects the weight of the Chinese economy on world agricultural markets. Complete price reform in China will have significant consequences for world agricultural prices. Finally, multilateral trade reform is more beneficial than unilateral trade reform for the rural sectors of the developing countries.

Higher Growth of the OECD Countries

The locomotive effect of higher growth of the OECD countries is limited. GDP in the low income regions is less than 1 per cent higher in the year 2002 (compared to the base simulation), as compared to 19 per cent for the OECD countries themselves. In China, the negative effects in the urban sector, slightly outweigh the positive effects in the rural sector. In the middle and high income developing economies, GDP is 1.4 to 2.1 per cent higher in the year 2002 than in the base simulation. The welfare figures are more positive.

The transmission effects are multiple. In the first place, higher incomes in the OECD countries lead to higher demand and therefore, higher prices. Food prices in particular increase by 5 to 6 per cent, and import prices in the OECD countries for non-food commodities will also increase. The higher food prices will benefit all developing countries which are net food exporters. The higher manufacturing import prices will benefit all regions which sell a large share of their exports in the OECD countries.

In virtually all regions, farmers are better off because the higher world prices are passed through directly to higher farm gate prices. The effects on the urban economy are less clear. Higher food prices hurt urban consumers and could lead to wage pressures, possibly aggravating unemployment in those regions with imperfect labour markets. On the other hand, higher rural incomes lead to less migration pressure, reducing labour supply in the urban economy, possibly relieving labour market pressures. In the case of China, a decrease of migration would tend to lower urban GDP since no unemployment is assumed in China. Higher rural incomes leads to an increase in demand for urban products. Finally, those regions with the strongest trade links to the OECD countries, for example, the Far East and parts of Latin America, tend to do well from higher import demand.

China does not benefit from higher growth in OECD countries. While the rural sector benefits from higher income, the country as a whole suffers from a higher food import bill, and urban consumers are particularly hard hit. The real wage in the urban sector suffers a decline of 1.7 per cent. Exports, in the base year, account for only 9 per cent of total GDP, with roughly 50 per cent sold in the OECD countries. The increase in trade only has a small effect on China's GDP.

Conclusion

No one can have any doubt about the importance of the Chinese economy in the world today and in the future. While its share of world GDP is still small, it is likely to double in the next decade, and a need to feed over 1.3 billion persons by the year 2002 will make China an important factor in world agricultural markets.

In all three cases of price reform, the poorer, rural sector of China, markedly increases its well-being, and China in the aggregate does better. For the rural poor, multilateral trade reform is more beneficial than unilateral trade reform. The unilateral trade liberalisation gives an indication of the importance of China in world agricultural markets. The world as a whole would be better off with multilateral trade liberalisation. The overall gains achieved can easily compensate the small group of countries which are hurt by higher food prices.

Higher growth in the OECD countries does not necessarily entail significantly higher growth in the rest of the world. While higher demand leads to higher food and import prices, the higher food prices benefit rural but not urban incomes. In the case of China, with relatively low import penetration shares, higher import demand is not enough to compensate for higher food prices, though there is an improvement in the rural-urban income parity index.

Under our base assumptions about demand and supply growth, China is likely to become a significant food importer, particularly if there is no change in internal Chinese price policies and no change in the trade policies of other regions, particularly of the OECD countries. This section has not dealt with the important issue of increasing technological progress, but it has shown that reform of trade policies is an important component of achieving food self-sufficiency in China.

India

India's role in the world economy is similar in significance to China's, particularly in terms of population and nutritional needs. In 1985, India's population represented 16 per cent of the world's population, below China's share of 22 per cent. However, it is expected to have a higher population growth rate than China, which will increase its share of world population by the year 2002 to roughly 1 billion people, while China is expected to have a population of over 1.3 billion.

Current forecasts are for quite strong Indian growth, with an expected average per annum increase of 4.7 per cent, which amounts to 3 per cent per annum per capita. This is lower than the growth forecasts for some other Asian economies, including China, but is better than many other developing regions or the OECD countries. India's share of global GDP will increase from 1.8 per cent to 2.4 per cent.

Growth in agricultural output has been steady, if not spectacular. Reliance on imports has decreased, despite population pressures[3]. While the Green Revolution ushered in a new era, it apparently had little effect on overall growth. What it did was to modify the source of growth, away from expansion of areas under production, towards higher yields. Another important characteristic of Indian agriculture is that there are large differences in yields and output across regions. Certain regions have benefited more from the Green Revolution than others, partly for agroclimatic reasons, but also due to the better introduction of the new varieties and new technologies, such as irrigation. This has had impacts on income distribution as the more productive regions have been able to market their surplus.

The role of government in agricultural production takes the form of input subsidies, mainly for fertilizers, irrigation, and electricity. The subsidies for some of the more significant crops vary from 11 to 31 per cent. Estimates of the domestic-to-world agricultural price wedge indicate that domestic prices are lower than world prices, implying that agriculture is taxed. Moreover, given the high level of non-agricultural import tariffs, the Indian government has provided significant protection to non-agricultural production, leading to a large negative bias in the rural-to-urban terms of trade.

Trade Reform

Multilateral Partial Trade Reform

Given the base trend assumptions and the demand elasticities in the model, in the final year of the base simulation India is close to self-sufficiency in the aggregate, with an aggregate self-sufficiency ratio of 0.99. The disaggregated data depict wide variations from this overall self-sufficiency. In crops, the self-sufficiency ratio is 1.09, but India is expected to import wheat, coarse grains, and vegetable oils. India will have an exportable surplus in rice and sugar. In all livestock sectors, India will be a significant exporter, and the overall self-sufficiency ratio is 1.18. The same is also true in tree crops, though there is a significant slow down in tea production which could lead to imports.

These self-sufficiency ratios suggest what will occur to India under partial multilateral trade reform. Except for livestock, India will suffer from a negative terms-of-trade shock since it exports agricultural commodities which fall in price, and imports commodities which increase in price. The livestock sector looks more promising since India has a significant surplus, particularly in dairy products, and the world price of livestock products increases under partial trade reform. The overall terms-of-trade shock is a positive 3.4 per cent.

The domestic effects are not too encouraging. Rural GDP decreases despite the increase in aggregate producer prices. First, there is a reduction in input subsidies, raising the cost of production. Second, the increase in producer prices is not uniform, in particular, the world price of rice, tree crops and other food decline. Third, domestic urban demand decreases because urban food prices increase and this leads to a substitution out of food into other commodities. The substitution effect into non-agricultural goods is strengthened by a 30 per cent drop in manufacturing tariffs. Simultaneously, urban income decreases due to a rise in unemployment and a decline in the price of urban factors as the urban sector is forced to devalue because of the new competition from the cheaper imports. Therefore, agricultural demand decreases from a substitution effect and an income effect. Overall, this implies a small gain in rural welfare which is, in part, offset by a small loss in urban welfare, summing to only a small gain in total welfare of about 0.2 per cent of the total base GDP in the year 2002. Given the closure rule, household taxes increase to meet the government budget deficit target. Government revenues are bound to decline with the reduction in agricultural export taxes and non-agricultural import tariffs.

Complete Multilateral Trade Reform

The changes in world prices are more pronounced under full trade liberalisation and this tends to amplify the changes in other variables. In the case of India, which is both an importer and exporter, when the world prices go in opposite directions some of the sectoral effects may cancel each other in the aggregate. However, there is a very significant positive change in the terms of trade of 13.9 per cent. The gains in the terms of trade will be particularly significant in sugar, beef, and dairy products, which India exports and whose world price increases markedly. The elimination of import tariffs could put significant pressure on the trade balance but, in part, this will be offset by the much higher prices for India's agricultural exports.

Rural GDP (at factor cost) goes up by 1.5 per cent, which is less than in some other developing countries, but India has a higher initial level of input subsidies than many other countries, and rice, which is a significant part of Indian agriculture, goes down in price. The increase in the urban GDP is more significant. The elimination of unemployment provides a boost to the urban economy. While the elimination of import tariffs causes a readjustment of production in the urban sector, it also benefits the cost side since the price of imported intermediates and investment goods will decrease. The overall increase in urban GDP is 4.3 per cent. Real incomes increase more in the rural sector than in the urban sector. The share of sugar and livestock products in the rural consumer budget is low, and these are the goods whose price increases the most. Welfare in both the rural and urban sectors goes up, with a total welfare gain of $42 billion, or about 6.4 per cent of the base simulation GDP in the year 2002.

Unilateral Reform

In this section we describe the results of unilateral reform in India which incorporates trade reform, elimination of agricultural import subsidies, and removal of labour market distortions. The largest share of the gains occurs in the rural economy, indicating the extent to which agriculture in India has been taxed. Rural real incomes increase by 18 per cent, while urban real incomes decline by 1 per cent. The total increase in real income is 4.5 per cent. Note that in both rural and urban sectors, the GDP (at factor cost) increases, but this reflects a statistical calculation which does not take into account relevant price changes. The increase in the domestic producer price, from the removal of the negative price wedge, provides a significant boost to farmers. While farmers lose their input subsidies, they are partially compensated by the reduction in manufacturing tariffs, which not only reduces the price of imports but will also reduce the price of competing domestic goods. The urban economy does not fare as well. The increased competition from imports, with higher food prices, is only partially compensated by the reduction in import prices and the increase in employment. The overall direct tax rate also increases, proportionally more in the urban sector, in order to compensate for the loss of government revenues from import tariffs and export taxes.

Growth of OECD Countries

At the world level, higher growth of the OECD countries implies higher world prices from a demand pull effect. As seen earlier, agricultural prices could rise from 5 per cent to 10 per cent, and there will also be rises in manufactured goods as well. The rise in world prices leads to a 3.9 per cent improvement, in the aggregate, in India's terms of trade. Overall, both the rural and urban economies benefit in a similar manner. The rural economy benefits from higher demand and higher prices. The urban economy could suffer from higher food prices, leading to higher wage demands, but an increase in urban export volume increases demand for urban labour, leading to a small decrease in urban unemployment. The welfare gains are not spectacular. The rural sector witnesses a gain in real income of 0.3 per cent, while the urban economy benefits from a rise of 0.5 per cent. Note that in the base simulation exports represent only 5 per cent and imports 6.9 per cent, of total GDP. These are small shares, and moreover only 50 per cent of manufacturing exports go to the OECD countries. The locomotive effect from higher growth of OECD countries to higher developing country growth is not simply translated by a higher volume of trade. Trade's counterpart, financial transfers play a significant role which is not modeled in the RUNS context. Furthermore, higher growth in the OECD countries, generated by technological innovation, should lead to higher productivity growth in the non-OECD regions as well.

Higher Levels of Foreign Savings

In this experiment, foreign net transfers to India were increased by $12 billion in each year starting in 1993. In approximate terms, this corresponds to 25 per cent of India's import bill in the base simulation in 2002, or 1.8 per cent of total GDP (at factor cost). As expected, this would be very beneficial to India. Real income increases by 6 per cent in 2002, with a higher long-term effect than short-term effect as the increasing capital inflows take time to be transformed into physical capital. The urban capital stock is 10 per cent higher in the year 2002 than in the base simulation. The consequences for the rural economy are negative. Both real rural income and rural GDP decline. The largest share of the net new transfers goes to urban investment, leading to an increase in urban capital and an increase in the demand for labour. This effectively reduces unemployment to near zero, particularly since this simulation has near negligible effects on the food price. As urban incomes increase, migration increases, leading to a decline in rural employment and rural income.

Unfortunately, this simulation leads to a net global loss, though the important losses are concentrated in the OECD countries. There are two possible explanations for this global loss. As there is no investment function in the base version of the model, there is no system for an efficient global allocation of investment funds. Even within each region, investment funds are divided between rural and urban investment based on fixed shares, i.e. investment does not respond to differences in rates of return. The second reason for the overall global loss is that the simulations are undertaken in a second best situation, particularly with respect to the labour market closure.

Transferring the entire amount of new resources to rural investment, rather than splitting it between both rural and urban investment, does not help rural welfare. Quite the contrary. Rural investment, particularly in India, will be spent almost entirely on farm equipment, pumps, and generators. This has two effects. It increases the final demand of urban goods and it increases the stock of farm equipment which can be substituted for labour. Therefore, labour demand in the rural sector decreases, in volume and value, and the return on land will also decrease. It has only small effects on agricultural prices, which increase slightly from an increase in urban demand. Urban labour demand goes up significantly, enough to pull in new migrants and simultaneously reduce unemployment to a low level. Overall, the economy gains in real income by 8.9 per cent, but all of the increase is in the urban sector, while the rural sector suffers a decline. This does not mean that rural investment is unprofitable, but rather that increasing the rural rate of return requires reducing taxation on the farming sector.

Conclusion

Trade reform, though important for India, will not produce tremendous benefits in the short run. India is a fairly closed economy, with imports representing less than 7 per cent of GDP in 2002 in the base simulation[4]. However, trade reform is important to reducing poverty in India which is concentrated in the rural sector. The rural sector is heavily taxed, directly by depressed producer prices and indirectly by high protection in the urban sector. Furthermore, a reform of the urban labour market would provide a significant boost to the Indian economy. Growth in OECD countries provides only small benefits for India, in part, because of the low degree of openness of the Indian economy. An increase in foreign capital flows would be very beneficial, particularly to the urban sector. The increase in demand for investment goods would virtually eliminate urban unemployment and has significant multiplier effects. The reverse is true in the rural sector. Increased investment in the rural sector tends to lower rural labour demand, leading to increased migration and lower wages. Elimination of the double taxation of agriculture is a first and necessary step for improving Indian incomes in both the rural and urban sectors, and for improving income distribution.

Notes and References

1. Unless otherwise stated, all dollar value amounts are in 1985 US dollars.
2. Excluding tariffs on services.
3. See Subramanian (1992) for a more thorough analysis of Indian agriculture.
4. Note, we assume that all import barriers are measured by tariff equivalents. Removal of import quotas could have a much more significant impact than removal of tariffs.

Table 7.1. **Trends and Self-Sufficiency Rates in Base Simulation in China**

	Supply Trend 1990-2002	Demand Trend 1990-2002	Self-Sufficiency 1985	Self-Sufficiency 2002
Wheat	3.6	4.6	0.94	0.73
Rice	3.9	4.5	1.01	0.89
Coarse Grains	4.0	2.7	1.09	1.30
Sugar	7.7	5.3	0.77	1.03
Beef, Veal, & Sheep	7.6	6.1	1.04	2.67
Other Meats	6.5	7.2	1.01	1.08
Coffee	10.2	6.4	0.96	1.62
Cocoa	–	7.5	–	–
Tea	7.6	8.9	1.44	1.50
Vegetable Oils	5.1	6.9	1.04	0.65
Dairy Products	4.2	4.9	0.96	1.13
Other Food	3.5	4.7	1.00	0.75
Wool	3.1	4.3	0.60	0.63
Cotton	4.8	6.0	1.07	1.11
Other Agriculture	5.9	5.1	1.00	1.19
Food Crops	3.9	–	1.00	0.87
Food Livestock	6.6	–	1.01	1.23
Population	1.4	–	–	–
Total Labour	2.2	–	–	–
Total GDP	6.6	–	–	–

Table 7.2. **Self-Sufficiency Rates in China**
(2002)

	Base Simulation	Partial Multilateral Liberalisation	Full Multilateral Liberalisation	Full Unilateral Liberalisation
Wheat	0.73	0.73	0.81	0.72
Rice	0.89	0.93	1.05	0.99
Coarse Grains	1.30	1.27	1.27	1.20
Sugar	1.03	1.03	1.27	0.89
Beef, Veal, & Sheep	2.67	2.70	3.12	2.76
Other Meats	1.08	1.15	1.37	1.29
Coffee	1.62	1.28	0.55	1.16
Cocoa	–	–	–	–
Tea	1.50	1.35	1.18	1.23
Vegetable Oils	0.65	0.66	0.73	0.64
Dairy Products	1.13	1.07	1.21	0.86
Other Food	0.75	0.79	0.88	0.95
Wool	0.63	0.57	0.50	0.52
Cotton	1.11	1.05	0.98	1.02
Other Agriculture	1.19	1.12	1.06	1.04

Chapter 8

Post-Soviet Agriculture

Introduction

Over the last five years, Eastern Europe and the USSR have emerged from decades of central planning and relative isolation from world markets. These regions are undertaking massive changes in market and institutional structures, and opening up their economies to the rules and rigours of the world markets.

While the changes occurring in Eastern Europe and the former USSR will in the long run have a significant impact on many different sectors, in the short and medium term, the most significant impact is likely to be in the agricultural sector. Whether the former USSR is going to continue to be a food importer, especially of grain, or will become an exporter once the structural adjustment is absorbed, will have a tremendous impact on world food prices, and the relations between the major food exporters. At the moment, we are witnessing a collapse of agriculture in the former Soviet Union, with both the downstream and upstream activities associated with agriculture showing signs of paralysis. This has led to large demands for food imports, straining the region's tight foreign exchange reserves. At the same time, farmers and consumers have benefited from large subsidies, aggravating the government's finances and inflation.

This chapter will attempt to shed some light on the future of agriculture in the former Soviet Union and its impact on world markets. Using RUNS, we will look at the impacts of several different scenarios on world prices and world trade. First and foremost is price liberalisation. In some respects, this is the easiest reform since it requires little in terms of investment and other changes in production. The next scenario incorporates the elimination of waste. This will necessitate a longer-term economic strategy, including investments in grain storage, improved transportation, and other similar investments. The final scenario, simulates improvements in agricultural productivity. This will also take time as investments need to be made in equipment, land, and human capital, and it will also require changes in property rights and other institutional arrangements. However, productivity improvements will only be efficient if both the pricing mechanism and the necessary upstream and downstream activities are in place and working.

Because of the importance of consumer subsidies in the former Soviet Union, the concept of consumer subsidy equivalent (CSE) has been introduced specifically in this region. (In many regions, there is no significant wedge between the producer price and the consumer price. If a producer is taxed, the consumer is subsidised. If a producer is protected, the consumer is taxed.) In the case of the former Soviet Union, the price wedge between the producer price and the consumer price can be significant, and this has important ramifications for the deficit. The results of the simulations in this chapter should be compared to the simulations in Chapter 3, i.e. the base version of the model without unemployment.

Background

We will sketch some highlights of the role of agriculture in the former Soviet Union (FSU) in the past and today. For a more complete description of the FSU economy, including agriculture, see OECD (1991b), and the joint IMF, IBRD, EBRD and OECD study (1991). Note that most data, even volume statistics, are subject to considerable uncertainty. The former Soviet authorities were not always accurate when presenting volume statistics, and value-based statistics are even less reliable, given the complex price system in the former Soviet Union and the inadequacy of exchange rates for transforming ruble amounts to hard currency values.

Agriculture in the Aggregate. Agriculture in the former Soviet Union is a more important part of the economy than in the market-based industrialised countries. Agriculture's share of GDP is around 15 per cent, and the total agro-food complex has a 30 per cent share of GDP. In the OECD countries, agriculture's share of GDP is less than 5 per cent. These shares are also reflected in the distribution of labour. Over 16 per cent of FSU labour is employed in agriculture. The consumer food budget share is around 35 per cent, while the comparable figure for the industrialised countries is 15 per cent.

Production. Agricultural production is heavily weighted towards livestock, with meat and milk production representing up to 48 per cent of total agricultural output (in value). The high level of livestock production, along with inefficient feeding mechanisms, has led to the high levels of feed imports. Grain and oil seed production represent another 15 per cent of total agricultural production.

Trade. Despite large investments in the rural sector, food production in the former Soviet Union has stagnated, leading to significant agricultural imports. Between 1985 and 1989, the average level of imports was $17 billion, of which 20-33 per cent was for grains, and another 20-25 per cent was for sugar imports. Exports of agricultural products are insignificant, the only exported commodity being cotton.

Prices. There is no doubt that until the most recent moves to liberalise prices, food consumption has been heavily subsidised in the former Soviet Union. While aid to production has been significant, a move to liberalise farm gate prices could lead either to a decline or rise in production, depending on the base assumption of the value of the ruble. Based on the official exchange rate, the FSU farm gate prices have been significantly higher than world (reference) prices. If the black market exchange rate is used, the FSU farm gate prices are significantly lower than the world reference price[1]. Table 8.1 provides an indication of the levels of producer and consumer subsidies/taxes for 1986-90 under two different exchange rates. Using either exchange rate, food consumption in general is heavily subsidised. The lower the value of the ruble (i.e. the higher the ruble/$ exchange rate), the higher is the consumer subsidy. The average subsidy rate in 1986 is 23 per cent under the 1.91 Rb/$ exchange rate, and is 41 per cent at the higher exchange rate. Producer incentives are either positive or negative depending on the exchange rate. At an exchange rate of 1.91 rubles per dollar, the production of almost all commodities is subsidised (the tariff equivalent is positive) in 1986 and 1987, wheat being a key exception. In 1990, wheat is no longer taxed, but the other feed crops, coarse grains and oil seeds, are taxed. The aggregate tariff equivalent (production-weighted) drops from 16.4 per cent in 1986 to 2.3 per cent in 1990. At a rate of 2.5 Rb/$, production of many commodities is taxed, and the overall tax rate is 11 per cent in 1986, falling to 22 per cent in 1990. As the table indicates, the value of the ruble is a key component of the analysis.

Simulations

Price Reform

The first reform scenario simulates an alignment of the FSU domestic prices with world prices, and the removal of input subsidies in agricultural production, i.e. a unilateral full liberalisation in the FSU. This would appear to be the easiest reform to implement, and its implementation is a necessary condition for current and future production efficiency. Price reform is also a necessary condition for dealing with the two huge deficits: the government fiscal deficit and the current account balance.

Table 8.2 indicates the change in world agricultural prices. In general, all world prices drop, with fairly significant falls in the price of beef and dairy products, respectively -8.6 per cent and -3.7 per cent. The drop in world prices derives from a significant fall in FSU consumption. The removal of large consumer subsidies in the meat and dairy sector results in a large increase in the consumer price leading to a reduction in demand. The estimated levels of distortions at the production level are relatively small, leading to only marginal changes in domestic production. Imports of these products bear the brunt of the reduction in demand.

Sugar is the only commodity experiencing a large rise in world price. Domestic production is protected and consumption is taxed. Liberalisation leads to a reduction in the producer price, i.e. a drop in production, and a reduction in the consumer price, i.e. an increase in consumption. Together, these two effects lead to a rise in the world price of sugar. Wheat presents a different picture. Production is protected and consumption is subsidised. Liberalisation therefore leads to a relatively neutral effect on the world price, with a small rise of 0.3 per cent.

Total net agricultural imports in the former Soviet Union decrease in value by $24 billion[2] in 2002, the final year of the simulation. Of this drop, the OECD countries absorb a loss in total net agricultural exports of $10 billion, Eastern Europe a drop of $4 billion, Latin America a drop of $4 billion, and the remainder is allocated to the other regions. The bulk of the drop in FSU imports is represented by meat and dairy products. The largest drop in meat exports will be absorbed by the United States and the EC. The decrease in agricultural imports in the former Soviet Union, releases pressure on the balance of payments, leading to a significant rise in imports of manufactured and capital goods[3]. Table 8.4 represents the self-sufficiency ratios for the former Soviet Union in the base scenario, and for all the simulations which depend on the low exchange rate (1.91 Rb/$)[4]. The ratios increase significantly under price liberalisation for a few key commodities, particularly for coarse grains, beef, and vegetable oils.

Overall, price reform in the former Soviet Union is very beneficial. Table 8.3 presents the income gains for all regions. The former Soviet Union experiences an increase in income of 2.4 per cent in the year 2002. The total gains are much higher if they were added up over the period 1993-2002, and included the discounted benefits accruing after 2002. The static gains arise from an increase in allocative efficiency from the removal of price distortions. The dynamic gains accrue from the significant increase in total domestic savings, hence investment, and therefore a large increase in the capital stock. In the year 2002, the capital stock is 20 per cent greater than in the base simulation.

The rest of the world also benefits, although the distribution of the income gains is uneven. Overall, the OECD countries benefit quite significantly, with a rise in income in the year 2002 of 0.2 per cent. The reduction in world agricultural prices, while detrimental to farmers and agricultural exports, leads to a reduction in farm subsidies, an increase in domestic investment, and an increase in urban production. The only OECD region to suffer a loss is Australia/New Zealand, which is a major agricultural exporter experiencing a significant decline in world prices. This region also has the lowest level of agricultural protection, and therefore does not reap any significant benefit from the reduction in government subsidy expenditures.

Amongst the developing regions, gains and losses vary between -0.3 per cent and 0.2 per cent. The larger losers are the Latin American countries which are significant agricultural exporters. All food-importing countries will gain from a drop in world agricultural prices.

Price Reform Revisited

As mentioned earlier, there is a great deal of uncertainty concerning the appropriate exchange rate used to convert the world's agricultural reference prices into rubles. This obviously affects the price wedges used in simulating reform in the former Soviet Union. Similar to prior papers[5] analysing agricultural price reform, we have undertaken a sensitivity simulation using a different ruble exchange rate assumption. The original exchange rate was 1.91 Rb/$. In the alternative scenario, we have used an exchange rate of 2.5 Rb/$[6]. Compared to the previous simulation, under the higher exchange rate, producers in general will be less protected (or taxed more), and consumers will be subsidised more.

Under the assumption of an exchange rate of 2.5 Rb/$, price reform in the former Soviet Union leads to larger decreases in world prices, mostly due to the influence of a marked reduction in domestic consumption. As above, production in the former Soviet Union will increase as farmers benefit from an increase in the farm gate price. The combination of the increase in domestic production and decline in consumption leads to a higher decline in imports than earlier. In other words, the choice of the ruble exchange rate does not change the overall picture of an increase in domestic production and a decline in consumption, it will only affect the magnitude of these movements.

There is a much more significant improvement in income in the former Soviet Union, with an increase of close to 6 per cent in the year 2002. The higher distortions in the original period lead to higher static gains. The dynamic gains are not as significant, and urban capital increases by 24 per cent in the year 2002. Under the first scenario, capital was already 20 per cent greater under reform. In the other regions, by and large, the income gains and/or losses are mostly amplified.

Removal of Distribution and Processing Inefficiencies

There have been various estimates of processing and distribution losses in the downstream agro-industrial sector. The problems include poor harvesting techniques, inadequate storage, poor transportation and distribution networks, and an inefficient food-processing sector. The estimates of loss vary from 20 to 30 per cent of total harvest, depending on the region and commodity. We have simulated this **waste** by throwing away 20 per cent of domestic agricultural production for all commodities in the base simulation. This is similar to adding to stocks; producers are paid for their production, however 20 per cent of the production simply does not enter the demand stream. The main consequence of this phenomenon is a transfer of resources from the government to farmers, and the government does not receive any revenue since this share of the production goes unsold.

In the reform simulation, we remove this waste of agricultural production starting in the year 1993. We decrease waste by 33 per cent in 1993, another third in 1996, and the final third in 1999, so that by the year 2002, all waste is eliminated. The elimination of the waste is on top of the price reform which occurs in 1993 (under the exchange rate of 1.91 Rb/$). We do not model the increase in efficiency *per se*. While improving labour productivity is one feature of the reform process, increasing efficiency will require an increase in capital investment as well. It may not necessarily require a significant increase in investment, but possibly a better spatial reallocation of crops and the processing plants. The concentration of the processing sector in urban areas increases the transportation losses of perishable commodities.

To the extent that the former Soviet Union is a large agricultural producer, even if it has not attained self-sufficiency, a *de facto* increase in total world supply emerging from the removal of waste, leads to fairly large decreases in world agricultural prices, above and beyond those from simply removing domestic price distortions. Simultaneously, the increase in total domestic supply further reduces the pressure to import agricultural commodities. In the aggregate, net agricultural imports fall to $3.3 billion in the year 2002, a drop from the initial base of $75 billion. Imports in all agricultural sectors drop, the hardest hit being the beef sector. In dairy products, the former Soviet Union switches from being a net importer to a net exporter. We should be somewhat cautious about these results since we have applied a uniform level of waste of 20 per cent. Certain studies have shown that cereal waste is as high as 35 per cent, and waste in the livestock and dairy sector is around 11-12 per cent[7]. Given the low levels of imports of cereals in this simulation, the former Soviet Union could easily be a net exporter of cereals with a higher initial level of waste. The self-sufficiency ratios in Table 8.4 clearly indicate the vast improvement in the agricultural trade balance.

The consequences of this scenario on trade with the rest of the world is obvious. The value of net agricultural exports from the OECD countries drops by $33 billion in the year 2002, in Latin America by $8 billion, and in Eastern Europe $13 billion. The hardest hit sector will be livestock.

The gain in income in 2002 more than doubles, reaching a level of 5.1 per cent in the former Soviet Union. There are significant dynamic gains as the losses incurred by the government are reduced, leading to higher investment levels and therefore an increase in the capital stock. In 2002, the urban capital stock is a full 32 per cent greater than in the base simulation. The OECD countries continue to benefit from reform in the former Soviet Union. Paradoxically, the reduction in food exports reduces pressure on government budgets, leading to an increase in investment and growth. To be sure, the model assumes that the reduction in world prices is fully transmitted to the domestic economy. If regions decide to insulate producers from the fall in world prices, this could aggravate the cost of government intervention.

Productivity Improvements

In this simulation, we provide an exogenous shock to the agricultural productivity trends. We have assumed that the change in the production possibility frontier will be the hardest change to achieve in the reform process. It requires investment in farm management techniques, investment in human capital, improvement of the equipment stock, and improvement in rural infrastructure including, for example, rehabilitation of irrigation pumps and canals. On a regional and national level, it will require a rethinking of cropping patterns. For the purposes of this simulation, we have augmented the exogenous productivity factor by 1 per cent each year in each sector, starting in 1996[8]. The productivity improvement is added to the two previous reforms, price and elimination of waste. In other words, these three reforms are cumulative.

Since the increase in productivity leads to an increase in FSU agricultural supply, world prices decrease even further. Net FSU imports decline even more, although this is somewhat tempered by an increase in domestic consumption. The decrease in world prices (compared to the previous simulation), leads to an expansion of consumption. The overall value of agricultural net trade changes from a negative $3.3 billion, to a positive net export of $18 billion, mainly composed of dairy products, oil seeds, and other foods.

Total income increases by 7.8 per cent in 2002 in the former Soviet Union. Here the gains accrue largely to rural GDP, as the effects on savings and investment are not significant. In the OECD countries, there are again relative increases in income, largely due to reduced export subsidies and lower world prices.

Conclusions

The weight of FSU agriculture in the world economy is significant. With or without self-sufficiency, FSU production and consumption shares will affect world agricultural markets. The ability of the FSU economy to reform itself is still in doubt, and the pace of reforms, if they occur, is also uncertain.

A critical factor for the future of post-Soviet agriculture will be the relations among the newly independent republics of the former Soviet Union. The RUNS model does not incorporate the new republics as separate entities and therefore we can only speculate about the consequences of the division of the former Soviet state. To date, there is an inclination among most republics to retain free trade among these republics, with no internal barriers and a common external tariff structure. However, it is clear that the elimination of the command economy, local control over production, and the free movement of goods, services and capital are unlikely to replicate the pre-reform production and trade patterns. The old system led to regional overspecialisation and, by and large, did not necessarily reflect regional comparative advantage (not to mention the environmental consequences in certain regions). In the short run, we might expect a decline in production, *ceteris paribus*, as regions undertake new investments and restructure production. In the medium run, we would expect gains in productivity as each region, faced with market prices, captures the benefits of comparative advantage.

Using the RUNS model, we have attempted to show the likely consequences for the former Soviet Union and the world economy of several steps towards agricultural reform. In sequence, we have looked at price reform, improving supply management, and increasing agricultural productivity. All three steps lead to sizable increases in income in the FSU economy. In the aggregate, these reforms are also very beneficial to the OECD countries, leading to a *de facto* price liberalisation in the OECD countries. The benefits for the developing countries are mixed. The large food exporters lose as world prices decrease, while the food-importing countries benefit from an increase in the terms of trade.

Notes and References

1. As an example of the crucial role of the exchange rate, let the world price (of an undefined commodity) be equal to \$100. If the farm gate price is 150 rubles, and the official exchange rate is 1 ruble per dollar (Rb/\$), then the domestic to world price ratio is 1.5. Price liberalisation implies a reduction of the farm gate price to 100 rubles, thereby leading to a decline in production, *ceteris paribus*. If the black market rate is 10 rubles per dollar, then the price ratio is 0.15. An alignment of the farm gate price to the world price implies a farm gate price of 1 000 rubles, which could lead to a significant increase in output. In any modelling exercise, the value of the ruble becomes a critical issue.
2. All monetary amounts are evaluated in 1992 US dollars.
3. The relaxation of the balance-of-payments constraint is further aided by a reduction in the price of manufactured imports. As significant regions of the rest of the world reduce agricultural exports, they are required to reduce the price of their manufactured exports in order to meet their balance-of-payments constraint.
4. Table 8.4 presents two different definitions of the self-sufficiency ratios. The top table includes changes in stock and waste in the denominator, i.e. they are considered as part of total demand. The lower part does not include these components and they are indicative of the potential gains from the elimination of waste.
5. See Liefert *et al.* for example.
6. Liefert *et al.* have a lengthy discussion concerning the appropriate exchange rate. While using their same assumptions, we could use a higher exchange rate. In 1986, the average black market rate was 4 Rb/\$, and this increased steadily to 10 Rb/\$ by 1989, and was well over 100 Rb/\$ by mid-1992 (see Cowitt).
7. *Source*: OECD (1991) and authors' own calculations.
8. If the base productivity factor is 1 per cent, in this simulation it becomes 2 per cent. We did not change the productivity of the urban sector.

Table 8.1. **Agricultural Input Subsidies and Producer and Consumer Price Wedges**

Agricultural Input Subsidies

	1986	1987	1990
Wheat	13.9%	16.1%	1.5%
Rice	40.8%	41.4%	20.1%
Coarse Grains	24.1%	22.9%	10.0%
Beef, Veal, & Sheep	14.5%	13.7%	7.5%
Other Meats	5.2%	4.9%	3.0%
Oils	7.9%	6.6%	2.3%
Dairy Products	14.1%	13.9%	6.9%
Cotton	31.9%	34.4%	17.8%
Total	14.1%	13.8%	6.1%

Price Wedges — Exchange Rate = 1.91 Rb/$

	Producer			Consumer
	1986	1987	1990	1986
Wheat	-32.2%	-15.2%	35.7%	-39.7%
Rice	132.7%	87.1%	80.0%	0.0%
Coarse Grains	-2.0%	28.0%	-10.4%	-10.9%
Sugar	79.1%	115.1%	27.7%	60.2%
Beef, Veal, & Sheep	20.1%	1.7%	-4.6%	-45.0%
Other Meats	33.8%	22.9%	-2.2%	-3.3%
Oils	9.8%	28.3%	-14.1%	-38.3%
Dairy Products	25.2%	8.4%	0.8%	-27.1%
Cotton	43.4%	6.5%	-6.5%	-19.4%
Total	16.4%	12.6%	2.3%	-23.2%

Price Wedges — Exchange Rate = 2.5 Rb/$

	Producer			Consumer
	1986	1987	1990	1986
Wheat	-48.2%	-35.2%	3.7%	-53.9%
Rice	77.8%	43.0%	37.5%	0.0%
Coarse Grains	-25.1%	-2.2%	-31.6%	-31.9%
Sugar	36.8%	64.3%	-2.5%	22.4%
Beef, Veal, & Sheep	-8.3%	-22.3%	-27.1%	-58.0%
Other Meats	2.2%	-6.1%	-25.2%	-26.1%
Oils	-16.1%	-2.0%	-34.4%	-52.9%
Dairy Products	-4.3%	-17.2%	-23.0%	-44.3%
Cotton	9.6%	-18.6%	-28.6%	-38.5%
Total	-11.1%	-13.9%	-21.9%	-41.4%

Table 8.2. **Changes in World Agricultural Prices**
(per cent change in year 2002 compared to the base simulation)

	PLIB1	PLIB2	PLIB +WASTE	PLIB1 +WASTE +PROD
Wheat	0.3	-1.5	-3.0	-4.6
Rice	-0.1	-0.7	-2.4	-3.4
Coarse Grains	-2.1	-5.1	-6.5	-8.8
Sugar	5.2	3.1	4.2	3.8
Beef, Veal, & Sheep	-8.6	-12.7	-11.3	-12.3
Other Meats	-0.5	-2.7	-2.9	-3.8
Coffee	-0.3	-0.6	-2.0	-2.8
Cocoa	-0.2	-0.2	-1.5	-2.0
Oils	-1.3	-2.5	-3.7	-4.9
Dairy Products	-3.7	-6.3	-11.9	-15.1
Other Food Products	-0.1	0.1	-2.8-	4.1
Wool	0.4	1.1	-5.3	-7.8
Cotton	0.3	-2.8	-3.9	-5.8
Other Agriculture	-0.3	-0.6	-3.5	-4.8

Table 8.3. **Changes in Income as a Percentage of the Base Simulation GDP**
(per cent change in year 2002)

	PLIB1	PLIB2	PLIB1 +WASTE	PLIB1 +WASTE +PROD
Asia	0.0	-0.1	-0.1	-0.1
Africa	0.0	0.1	0.0	-0.1
North Africa, Middle East	0.1	0.2	0.3	0.3
Latin America	-0.2	-0.4	-0.4	-0.4
OECD	0.2	0.3	0.3	0.4
Eastern Europe	0.8	1.1	1.1	1.2
Former Soviet Union	2.4	6.0	5.1	7.8
Total	0.2	0.5	0.5	0.6

a. The simulation acronyms refer to:
PLIB1 — price liberalisation starting in 1993 under an exchange rate of 1.91Rb/$.
PLIB2 — price liberalisation starting in 1993 under an exchange rate of 2.5Rb/$.
WASTE — PLIB1 plus the gradual reduction of waste starting in 1993.
PROD — PLIB1 plus WASTE plus a gradual improvement in productivity starting in 1996.

b. The income measure was described in Chapter 2.

Table 8.4. **Self-Sufficiency Ratios**

Ratio of Supply to Total Demand (**including** stock changes and waste)

	BASE 1990	BASE 2002	PLIB1 2002	PLIB1 +WASTE 2002	PLIB1 +WASTE +PROD 2002
Wheat	0.91	0.82	0.76	0.83	0.89
Rice	0.69	1.29	1.03	1.23	1.32
Coarse Grains	0.74	0.77	0.83	0.91	0.99
Sugar	0.72	0.58	0.36	0.33	0.34
Beef, Veal, & Sheep	0.63	0.67	0.90	0.95	0.96
Other Meats	0.73	0.79	0.77	0.79	0.81
Coffee	0.00	0.00	0.00	0.00	0.00
Cocoa	0.00	0.00	0.00	0.00	0.00
Tea	0.53	0.74	0.71	0.75	0.78
Oils	1.12	0.99	1.21	1.41	1.48
Dairy Products	0.86	0.88	0.91	1.04	1.10
Other Food Products	1.06	1.03	1.01	1.16	1.22
Wool	0.75	0.83	0.82	0.90	0.95
Cotton	1.04	1.03	1.00	1.13	1.19
Other Agriculture	0.73	0.87	0.85	0.96	1.00

Ratio of Supply to Total Demand (**excluding** stock changes and waste)

	BASE 1990	BASE 2002	PLIB1 2002	PLIB1 +WASTE 2002	PLIB1 +WASTE +PROD 2002
Wheat	1.11	0.99	0.89	0.83	0.89
Rice	0.80	1.73	1.30	1.23	1.32
Coarse Grains	0.87	0.91	0.99	0.91	0.99
Sugar	0.84	0.65	0.39	0.33	0.34
Beef, Veal, & Sheep	0.72	0.77	1.10	0.95	0.96
Other Meats	0.86	0.94	0.91	0.79	0.81
Coffee	0.00	0.00	0.00	0.00	0.00
Cocoa	0.00	0.00	0.00	0.00	0.00
Tea	0.59	0.87	0.83	0.75	0.78
Oils	1.45	1.23	1.60	1.41	1.48
Dairy Products	1.04	1.06	1.12	1.04	1.10
Other Food Products	1.34	1.30	1.27	1.16	1.22
Wool	0.88	1.00	0.98	0.90	0.95
Cotton	1.32	1.30	1.25	1.13	1.19
Other Agriculture	0.85	1.05	1.03	0.96	1.00

Chapter 9

Trade Liberalisation and Technical Change[1]

Introduction

Even before the Uruguay Round of trade talks under the GATT had started, economists were estimating the likely consequences of liberalisation of international agricultural markets (Valdés and Zietz, 1980). In this, and other studies of price liberalisation, the usual procedure to assess the implication of trade liberalisation has been to assume a change in current policies and trace through the consequences for welfare, world prices, trade and other variables of interest.

Anderson and Tyers (1990) have argued that this ignores a number of features which are likely to influence the assessment of the consequences of this process, specially the implications for developing countries. One such feature is the dynamic effects of price-induced technological change, an issue which has been raised in a number of recent papers (Roe and Pardey, Alston and Pardey, Fulginiti and Perrin). Anderson and Tyers employed a partial equilibrium model of world food markets, with full price transmission, to assess the impact of food policy liberalisation by OECD countries. They show that, due to this policy change, the annual welfare gain of developing countries will increase from $1 billion to $12 billion when price-induced increases in productivity are taken into account.

In this chapter, the implications of trade liberalisation are simulated, incorporating induced technological change in agriculture into the RUNS model. A partial equilibrium framework is not adequate for the analysis of trade liberalisation, much less for the problem at hand. Hertel (1990) argues that partial equilibrium models, where the production possibilities frontier for agriculture is fixed, cannot account for the resource shifts across sectors that will follow the changes in the terms of trade of agriculture relative to non-agriculture. This critique is, *a fortiori*, applicable to the case of price-induced changes in productivity, where changes in factor proportions in agriculture and in the non-agricultural sector are likely to be a central part of the analysis.

The rest of this chapter is organised as follows: first, there is a brief overview of the literature dealing with the relationship between productivity and prices, then the general characteristics of the experiments performed with the RUNS model are presented, after which the results of partial agricultural liberalisation in the OECD countries are presented. This is followed by the results of partial agricultural liberalisation in all countries and finally there are some concluding comments.

Technical Change and Price Distortions

The model of induced technical change (Hayami and Ruttan, 1971 and 1985) has taught economists to think about technology as an endogenous variable that responds to economic incentives. While relative factor prices (or relative factor scarcities) play the central role in this theory, many economists, including Ruttan (1982), suggest that product prices are also an important determinant of the allocation of resources to agricultural research. This indeed seems to be a generally held view, as Alston and Pardey (1991) have argued. However, one conclusion of the analysis of Alston and Pardey (p. 33), which is based on a political economy model, indicates two benchmark scenarios: "Low rates of public sector investment in research are likely to be found where the government perceives a high opportunity cost of government revenues. These will be places where agricultural production is taxed, a policy that both reflects that perception and indirectly diminishes the private and public sector incentives to invest in agricultural R&D. On the other hand, cheap food policies might also involve implicit taxes on agricultural producers and these might coincide with a greater propensity for public sector research. While the weight of the analysis favours a positive relationship between the rate of protection and the size of the research budget, the opposite cannot be ruled out."

The argument that private incentives to invest in research are lower when agriculture is taxed, is based on the fact that taxation reduces producers' gains from supply shifts due to research. This result, obtained from welfare economic analysis, puts the weight of a producer's decision on a comparison of gains under two hypothetical situations: the after research situation with tax and the after research situation without tax. Earlier literature, on the other hand, has emphasized the role of "stress" (that is, negative or falling profits) as a factor influencing the adoption of technology (see de Janvry, 1973). The driving force here is a comparison between actual profitability and (expected) profitability with research under the current policy regime. In places where agriculture is heavily taxed, the stress factor may very well be a major incentive for adopting technology and the argument can be easily extended to include incentives to support research or to lobby for increased government funded research. Lobbying for increased government support for research may be a good strategy for agricultural producer groups where agriculture is mainly taxed indirectly, like when the exchange rate is overvalued.

Nonetheless, the qualitative arguments of Alston and Pardey lend support to the hypothesis of a positive association between the allocation of resources to research and protection. Empirical results are scarce to date. The econometric effort of Alston and Pardey is perhaps the first attempt to test the existence and direction of the link between price and allocation of resources to research. However, the negative coefficient between rates of protection and research funding found in their study (somewhat to their surprise, it seems), although intriguing, cannot yet be taken as a definite answer to the question.

Fulginiti and Perrin (1991) have directly estimated the relationship between prices and productivity. A production function with variable elasticities of production is estimated with cross-section/time-series data from 18 developing countries[2]. The elasticities of production depend on price variables (output and input), research expenditures and input quality. The estimated elasticity of productivity with respect to price for the entire sample is 0.13, although there is large variability across country-specific estimates. A complete elimination of agricultural trade wedges leads to an average price increase of 58 per cent and a corresponding increase in productivity of 26 per cent. In this experiment, since research expenditures were not allowed to change in response to prices, these figures, as Alston and Pardey have suggested, indicate only intermediate-run responses, mostly reflecting the decision of farmers to adopt existing technologies.

The informed "vote" of the profession tends to support the more radical view that higher prices lead to increased expenditures in research and productivity. In this case it would be unclear how the developing countries will be affected since it is not only the simultaneity between price and productivity that is relevant, but also indirect effects through the government budget. In many developing countries, especially the poorer ones, liberalisation of agricultural trade will affect government revenues and, as a result, public expenditure on research and development related to agriculture. An assessment of the magnitude of all these effects is a necessary step for evaluating of the impact of trade liberalisation. However, econometric evidence on the link between agricultural pricing policies and allocation of resources to research is very scarce to date. In consequence, here we do not fully model all the ramifications of technological change, leaving aside the link between liberalisation, government revenue and government expenditures on research and development.

The implied productivity changes estimated by Fulginiti and Perrin do not account for the fact that if the 18 developing countries in their sample reduce protection simultaneously, the world price will be affected and this, in turn, will affect the estimated productivity changes. This may be relevant for the assessing the outcome of the Uruguay Round. This chapter incorporates the response of productivity to price changes into the RUNS model to evaluate how this mechanism affects the outcome of agricultural policy reforms.

Characteristics of the Experiments

It is assumed that productivity responds to prices with a lag of two periods (in the RUNS model, from 1987, one period is equal to three years). This is consistent with Fulginiti and Perrin who have used a five-year moving average of past prices in their study. The elasticities of productivity with respect to price changes are, for the most part, adopted from Fulginiti and Perrin. While the countries included in their study cover most of the regions in the RUNS model, there is not an one-to-one mapping. Most of the elasticities shown in Table 9.1 are regional averages computed from country estimates in Fulginiti and Perrin. We assigned the 18-country mean to OECD regions and South Africa. For the European Economies in Transition we adopted the same elasticity as for

Latin America, and for the Commonwealth of Independent States we assumed an elasticity of zero. Sensitivity analysis shows how the results change with different responses of productivity to prices.

The simulations are based on the supposition that partial liberalisation of agricultural trade is achieved in 1993. The model is solved until the year 2002 and the effects of technological change do not start affecting the results until 1999. The effect is such that, for example, in the case of Low Income Asia, *ceteris paribus*, a 1 per cent increase (decrease) in a producer price, in terms of the baseline, will induce supply to increase (decrease) by 0.256 per cent more (less) than without technical change (Table 9.1). The production function parameters g of the RUNS model for 1999 and 2002 were modified to obtain such an effect. Equation (2.1) is modified to endogenise productivity parameters:

$$S_{it} = (1 + e_i\,[\,(p^{*}_{i,t-2} - p^{B}_{i,t-2})/p^{B}_{i,t-2}\,])\,(1+\gamma_{it})^{t}\;\alpha_i\;(p^{*}_{it} - c_i)^{\beta} \quad (9.1)$$

where e, p^*, p^B are respectively the productivity elasticities, the equilibrium relative prices in the current and base simulations. Thus when the elasticity equals zero, this mechanism is not operating.

The implications of technical change are evaluated by comparing the baseline scenario, in 2002, to simulation results with and without technical change. However, this needs to be interpreted with care due to the fact that by 2002 the shock introduced with liberalisation without technical change will have probably exerted most of its effects in the model. On the other hand, liberalisation with technical change will be affecting the results only for the second period. Since there are frictions in the RUNS model that impede instantaneous intersectoral factor movements, we are probably underestimating the full implications of technological change.

Partial Agricultural Liberalisation in OECD Countries

This section analyses the impact of a 30 per cent reduction in support to agriculture in OECD regions. We concentrate on world price and welfare effects.

Price Changes

Table 9.2 gives the estimated world price changes in 2002 under three different sets of productivity elasticities. For comparison purposes, the results without endogenous technical change are also shown. We examine first the results in the third column of Table 9.2. For livestock commodities, except wool, world prices increase more in relation to the baseline when endogenous technical change is considered. This reflects mostly the response of OECD countries to the reduction in producer prices in this highly protected sector. Even though productivity responds positively in the rest of the world, this is not strong enough to compensate for the decline in productivity in OECD regions. In all OECD regions, except Australia and New Zealand, the contraction of the livestock sector is larger when endogenous technical change is considered. In Australia and New Zealand, the expansion of the sector is driven mostly by beef, sheep and veal and by wool, commodities which are lightly protected in that region. Since Australia and New Zealand are, by far, the largest exporters of wool, their response leads to a lower increase in price when endogenous technical change is taken into account.

For crops, the opposite takes place: the price of commodities which are directly affected by liberalisation increases more without induced technical change. Non-OECD countries expand production with endogenous technical change due to increased producer prices. For some commodities, a positive response of production and trade in the OECD countries is observed too. For example, production of oilseeds increases and demand for oilseeds for feed decreases in the United States because of the relatively lower protection levels of oilseeds and the contraction of livestock production. To a smaller degree, the same response is also seen for coarse grains in the United States.

A noticeable aspect of the price changes displayed in Table 9.2 is the increase in the relative prices of beef and (in particular) dairy products in relation to coarse grains and oilseeds. Endogenous technical change causes a larger increase in relative prices of livestock. This is accompanied by increased migration of livestock production from the OECD countries to the developing regions. The percentage changes, from the baseline, in the self-sufficiency ratio (i.e. the ratio of domestic production to domestic consumption) for dairy products in the Low Income countries is 3.9 without technical change and 9 with technical change. The corresponding figures for the Middle Income countries are 4.5 per cent and 10.8 per cent. Significant changes in the trade share of Low and Middle Income countries are also noted. As livestock production moves South, production of oilseeds and coarse grains moves North, with the export share of Middle Income countries in oilseeds declining 18 per cent in relation to the no technical change scenario and that of the OECD regions increasing 16 per cent.

The relative magnitude of the elasticities of productivity with respect to prices is important in determining whether prices will increase more or less with endogenous technical change. Since empirical evidence on these elasticities is scarce, we consider two additional experiments to determine the sensitivity of the results (prices and welfare) to the values of these elasticities: (i) the elasticity in the OECD regions is reduced to 0.20 (called experiment B) and (ii) the elasticity for all countries is set at 0.359 (the sample average in Fulginiti and Perrin) (experiment C).

In experiment B, due to the lower elasticity in OECD regions, productivity in these regions is not reduced as much as before and world prices increase less with endogenous technical change considered. Moreover, price increases are lower than in the base case, except for oilseeds. As noted above, the strong response of production and exports of this commodity in the United States is a factor explaining the smaller price increase in the base case. This response, however, becomes weaker with the lower elasticity.

Similarly, world price increases are lower in experiment C. With productivity in all countries responding with equal strength to price changes, the response of the non-OECD countries carries a higher weight. In comparison to the base case, except in Africa, Nigeria, the Mediterranean and the Gulf regions, the elasticity of productivity with respect to prices has been increased in this experiment.

Welfare Changes

Welfare changes in 2002, are shown in Table 9.3 for groups of countries aggregated according to income level. Significant additional welfare gains to all developing countries can be attributable to endogenous technical change. Both urban and rural households are better off. In the Upper Income countries, however, the additional benefits are not sufficient to turn them into net gainers from trade liberalisation.

No significant changes in welfare are observed in the OECD region. Urban households gain in this region, offsetting the loss to rural households. Most OECD countries, however, are better off with endogenous technical change (the exceptions are Canada and the European Community). The world as a whole gains; the losses in OECD countries are more than compensated by the gains elsewhere. Sensitivity analysis with respect to the magnitude of the productivity elasticities suggests that the welfare results are robust (Table 9.4).

Partial Agricultural Liberalisation in All Countries

We now turn to a scenario in which both the developed and the developing countries reform their agricultural policies. As before, a reduction of 30 per cent in protection is considered. The results have already been discussed in Chapter 3. We focus on prices and welfare changes induced by endogenising the productivity parameters.

Price Changes

Endogenous technical change tends to reduce the magnitude of price increases (Table 9.5, column 4). The only exception is dairy products, for which the productivity decline caused by lower producer prices in the OECD countries and in some developing countries is not compensated by the productivity increase in the rest of the world.

As in the OECD countries' liberalisation scenario, developing countries will produce a higher proportion of livestock products, mainly beef and dairy products, when the effects of technological change are considered. This is reflected in changes in self-sufficiency ratios. For instance, for beef, veal and sheep the percentage change from the baseline in the Low Income countries is 1.7 without technical change and it is 5.3 with technical change. In the Middle Income countries, the corresponding percentages are 7.3 and 12. In the OECD countries, in turn, these changes are -4.8 per cent and -8.9 per cent respectively. A similar tendency is also seen in the case of dairy products.

It is interesting to observe that while the self-sufficiency ratio for coarse grains is practically constant in the Low Income countries, in the Middle Income countries, it is lower with technical change. The same, however, does not occur for oilseeds. For this commodity, the Low Income countries experience a decrease in the self-sufficiency ratio, but not the Middle Income countries. For the latter, the percentage changes in the self-sufficiency ratio are 7.59 without technical change and 10.31 per cent with technical change. In the OECD countries, the self-sufficiency ratio declines in relation to the baseline without technical change, but with technical change it is slightly higher than in the baseline.

When elasticities of productivity are changed, the price increases are, for the most part, smaller than in the base experiment (Table 9.5, columns B and C). In experiment B, this is due to the weaker response in the OECD countries to the declines in producer prices. In experiment C, however, where the response in OECD regions is unchanged from the base experiment, it reflects the fact that the elasticity in a number of other regions was increased in comparison to the base experiment[3].

Welfare Changes

Table 9.6 shows welfare changes for the year 2002, with percentages indicating changes in real income. The Middle and Upper Income developing countries and the OECD countries experience larger reductions in welfare in the rural sector when the effects of endogenous technical change are accounted for. These losses are not offset by the gains of urban households and the total welfare gain from liberalisation is reduced in the Upper Income and OECD regions. The welfare gains experienced by urban households in the Middle Income countries more than offset the losses of rural households. The Low Income developing countries are the big gainers. In this group China, which heavily taxes its agriculture, reaps the bulk of these gains.

Table 9.7 displays results of sensitivity analysis with respect to the values of productivity elasticities. The results are quite robust to these changes in elasticity. In experiment B, where the elasticity in the OECD countries is reduced to 0.2, the overall gain in welfare is slightly higher than in the previous case. Rural households in the Low Income developing countries gain slightly less, those in the Middle and Upper Income countries lose more, and there is no significant change in rural households' welfare in the upper income countries. Obviously rural households in the OECD countries experience smaller losses. Urban households gains are about the same in all regions. In experiment C, the losses to rural households are slightly higher than in experiment B, and the gain of the Low Income developing countries is bigger. The larger gain for these countries is a direct consequence of higher productivity elasticities adopted in the experiment. Urban consumers are better off in all countries.

Conclusions

This chapter considered the effects of allowing for induced technical change in assessing the consequences of trade liberalisation. The RUNS model was used to estimate the implications for prices of agricultural commodities and welfare. A direct link between changes in producer prices and productivity was introduced based on existing empirical results. Two liberalisation scenarios were considered: (i) 30 per cent reduction in agricultural support in the OECD countries and (ii) 30 per cent reduction in agricultural support in all countries.

Whether the rate of productivity growth will increase or decrease in a given country depends on what happens to producer prices. In the OECD countries' liberalisation scenario, quite clearly, the developing countries experience an acceleration of the rate of productivity growth and the opposite takes place in the OECD countries. In the global liberalisation scenario, however, the results are more difficult to interpret due to the fact that some commodities are taxed and others are protected.

Accounting for the effects of induced technical change leads to an increase in worldwide economic well-being. The OECD countries do not experience any additional gain from their liberalisation with technical change. The gains from global liberalisation for the OECD countries are diminished by technical change because lower producer prices reduce the rate of productivity growth in the region. The Upper Income region gains less with global liberalisation when induced technical change is taken into consideration.

These results indicate that the gains for most developing regions can be significantly enhanced in the event of a positive response of productivity to price changes. In practice, however, there are a number of impediments for the operation of this process in the developing countries, especially the poorest ones: lack of adequate infrastructure, deficiencies in information about existing technologies, and factor markets (mainly labour and land) that operate under regulations that weaken producers' responses to economic incentives. While the experiments included a lag of six years between the change in price and the consequent productivity change, for these gains to be realised policies to facilitate the process should be implemented. These policies require adequate infrastructure for efficient delivery of inputs (fertilizers) and outputs, rural extension services and elimination of distortions in the labour and land markets.

Notes and References

1. This chapter was written by Antonio Salazar P. Brandao, Marinos E. Tsigas, Dominique van der Mensbrugghe and Ian Goldin, and is based on "*Agricultural Productivity Growth and Trade Liberalization: A General Equilibrium Analysis*", mimeo OECD/World Bank, 10 June 1992.
2. Argentina, Brazil, Chile, Colombia, Dominican Republic, Egypt, Ghana, Côte d'Ivoire, Korea, Malaysia, Morocco, Pakistan, Philippines, Portugal, Sri Lanka, Thailand, Turkey and Zambia.
3. Note that prices of dairy products increase more in experiment C than in experiment B. Even though the difference is very small, it indicates that as the elasticity of productivity with respect to prices is increased in the OECD countries, the slow down in productivity there becomes a dominant element in determining the magnitude of price changes in these commodities.

Table 9.1. **Assumed Productivity Elasticities with Respect to Prices in the Base Experiments**

Regions	Elasticity
Low Income Asia, China, India	0.256
Upper Income Asia, Indonesia	0.172
Africa, Nigeria	0.805
South Africa and OECD	0.359
Maghreb	0.345
Mediterranean, Gulf	0.458
Latin America, Mexico, Eastern Europe	0.206
Brazil	0.515
Former Soviet Union	0.000

Table 9.2. **Impact of Agricultural Liberalisation in OECD Countries on World Prices**
(Percentage change in the year 2002 from the base simulation)

	NETC	WETC BASE	WETC B	WETC C
Wheat	4.2	3.9	3.2	3.0
Rice	1.9	1.5	1.0	0.9
Coarse Grains	2.5	1.2	1.2	1.2
Sugar	5.2	4.8	3.9	4.1
Beef, Veal & Sheep	4.5	5.1	3.9	4.3
Other Meats	2.0	2.5	1.8	2.0
Coffee	0.8	0.8	0.5	0.4
Cocoa	0.6	0.7	0.4	0.4
Tea	1.7	1.6	1.2	1.4
Vegetables Oils	3.4	2.1	2.2	1.7
Dairy Products	8.1	9.3	6.9	6.5
Other Food	0.6	0.8	0.6	0.7
Wool	1.8	1.1	1.0	0.8
Cotton	1.5	1.0	0.8	0.7
Other Agriculture	1.1	1.3	1.0	1.0

Note: NETC: No endogenous technical change.
WETC: With endogenous technical change.
Experiment B: OECD productivity elasticity reduced to 0.20.
Experiment C: All productivity elasticities equal to 0.359.

Table 9.3. **Impact of Agricultural Liberalisation in OECD Countries on Welfare**
(Percentage change in the year 2002 from the base simulation in real income)

Regions	Rural Households		Urban Households		All Households	
	NETC	WETC	NETC	WETC	NETC	WETC
Low Income	0.3	0.5	-0.2	0.2	0.1	0.7
Middle Income	0.3	0.5	-0.2	0.2	0.2	0.6
Upper Income	0.2	0.4	-0.5	-0.5	-0.2	-0.1
OECD	-0.6	-0.8	1.1	1.2	0.5	0.5
World	-0.3	-0.3	0.6	0.8	0.3	0.5

Table 9.4. **Sensitivity Analysis for Liberalisation in OECD Countries**
(Percentage change in the year 2002 from the base simulation in real income)

Regions	Experiment B			Experiment C		
	Rural Households	Urban Households	All Households	Rural Households	Urban Households	All Households
Low Income	0.5	0.2	0.6	0.5	0.3	0.7
Middle Income	0.4	0.2	0.6	0.4	0.2	0.7
Upper Income	0.3	-0.4	-0.1	0.4	-0.4	-0.1
OECD	-0.8	1.2	0.5	-0.8	1.3	0.5
World	-0.4	0.8	0.5	-0.4	0.9	0.5

Note: Experiment B: OECD productivity elasticity reduced to 0.20.
Experiment C: All productivity elasticities equal to 0.359.

Table 9.5. **Impact of Global Agricultural Liberalisation on World Prices**
(Percentage change in the year 2002 from the base simulation)

	NETC	WETC BASE	WETC B	WETC C
Wheat	5.9	4.3	3.8	3.5
Rice	-1.9	-5.4	-6.0	-7.5
Coarse Grains	3.6	2.0	1.9	1.4
Sugar	10.2	9.6	8.9	8.8
Beef, Veal & Sheep	4.7	4.1	2.8	2.9
Other Meats	1.0	0.5	-0.2	-0.6
Coffee	-6.1	-6.5	-6.8	-10.3
Cocoa	-4.0	-6.1	-6.4	-5.5
Tea	3.0	2.5	2.0	2.6
Vegetable Oils	4.1	3.2	3.3	2.6
Dairy Products	7.2	8.4	5.9	6.0
Other Food Products	-1.7	-1.1	-1.5	-1.6
Wool	3.2	2.5	2.5	2.1
Cotton	3.7	1.1	1.0	1.0
Other Agriculture	5.9	5.9	5.7	5.8

Note: NETC: No endogenous technical change.
WETC: With endogenous technical change.
Experiment B: OECD productivity elasticity reduced to 0.20.
Experiment C: All productivity elasticities equal to 0.359.

Table 9.6. **Impact of Global Agricultural Liberalisation on Welfare**
(Percentage change in the year 2002 from the base simulation in real income)

Regions	Rural Households		Urban Households		All Households	
	NETC	WETC	NETC	WETC	NETC	WETC
Low Income	1.1	2.0	-0.1	1.4	1.0	3.4
Middle Income	0.0	-0.1	0.5	1.1	0.4	1.0
Upper Income	-1.4	-2.0	2.5	3.0	1.1	1.0
OECD	-0.7	-0.9	1.1	1.3	0.5	0.4
World	-0.4	-0.5	1.0	1.3	0.6	0.8

Table 9.7. **Sensitivity Analysis**
(Percentage change in the year 2002 from the base simulation in real income)

Regions	Experiment B			Experiment C		
	Rural Households	Urban Households	All Households	Rural Households	Urban Households	All Households
Low Income	1.9	1.4	3.3	2.2	2.0	4.3
Middle Income	-0.2	1.1	0.9	-0.2	1.2	1.0
Upper Income	-2.0	3.1	1.0	-2.2	3.3	1.1
OECD	-0.8	1.3	0.5	-0.9	1.4	0.5
World	-0.5	1.4	0.9	-0.6	1.5	1.0

Note: Experiment B: OECD productivity elasticity reduced to 0.20.
Experiment C: All productivity elasticities equal to 0.359.

Chapter 10

Conclusions

The potential gains from freer trade has been one of the factors that has motivated the international community to seek more liberalised trade and broaden the coverage of the GATT. The simulations from the RUNS model has shown that the gains from even the liberalisation of a relatively minor contributor to most countries' GDP — agriculture — can produce benefits on the order of hundreds of billions of dollars. Full agricultural trade liberalisation, meaning the elimination of all interventions from tariffs to subsidies, could add $430 billion to global annual income. Of this sum, $250 billion would accrue to OECD countries and $180 billion to the rest of the world. Expanding the liberalisation to products where tariffs are already low, such as manufactured products, can produce even more gains. These are conservatively estimated as over $10 billion by the RUNS simulations. Manufacturing liberalisation — defined as the removal of only manufactured good tariffs — would add about $20 billion to the gains from agricultural liberalisation.

Partial liberalisation, such as that negotiated in the Uruguay Round, would produce significant gains. The removal of 30 per cent of the tariffs and subsidies for agriculture could yield gains of $190 billion, with the OECD countries accounting for $120 billion of the net gains and developing and formerly centrally planned countries benefitting by $70 billion. An additional 30 per cent liberalisation of manufactured products produces $23 billion more income, with the OECD countries gaining about 64 per cent of the extra benefit derived from manufacturing liberalisation.

The liberalisation of services and the removal of non-tariff barriers was not examined in the RUNS simulations. Such liberalisation would undoubtedly add to the income and growth dividend, yielding additional benefits which may even match those derived from our modelling exercises. While lack of data and difficulties associated with the conversion of non-tariff barriers to tariff equivalents has prevented the RUNS from modelling these impediments to trade, the incorporation of these elements is on the research agenda. Modelling exercises are nevertheless still likely to underestimate the gains from freer trade, as they do not take into account the intangibles: increased competition, greater international transfer of technology and business practices, which could conceivably bring the balance towards or perhaps beyond the trillion dollar mark — that is, beyond the GDP of all low income countries, including India and China. While the RUNS model has clearly highlighted the scale of the gains, its estimate that $450 billion would be derived from liberalisation is conservative, as it covers only the reduction of manufacturing and agricultural tariffs.

Naturally, there would be losers as well as gainers from trade liberalisation. Those producers that have been sheltered from competition by trade barriers and have received input subsidies would lose from their elimination, although indirectly there would be compensatory gains from reform elsewhere. Food importers would also suffer as a result of the higher prices projected for a number of cereals. However, improvement of internal and external terms of trade would benefit even those producers no longer benefiting from direct protection and subsidies.

For the losers, the aggregate level of losses are small compared to the gains. For example, the total losses from full agricultural liberalisation would be $21 billion, with most of this impact falling on farmers in OECD countries, although even they, as a result of productivity and overall economic growth, are expected to be better off in 2002 than today. From partial liberalisation, the losses are small, $2 billion, which is a small fraction of the current $300 billion in subsidies given to producers in OECD countries. Domestic direct income support could easily compensate for these relatively minor losses. Moreover, in some regions, if manufactured trade also was liberalised, this could fully compensate rural producers from the losses of agricultural trade liberalisation. For example, global agricultural trade liberalisation would reduce African rural incomes even though the countries as a whole would gain. The loss of subsidies and the fall of export prices of tree crops would contribute to lower rural income. The beneficiaries would be urban consumers who would have lower food prices as domestic protection is reduced. However, full liberalisation of both agricultural and non-agricultural trade results in aggregate real income increases of about 6 per cent compared to the base run and gains in rural value added (except in South Africa, where the (white) farmers have benefitted from subsidies) as the secondary effects of improved terms of trade benefit rural producers.

Another important potential outcome of agricultural trade liberalisation captured by the RUNS model is the impact of endogenous technological change on developing countries. Adding price-induced technological change benefits rural producers in developing countries — increasing the gains from agricultural trade liberalisation by about 40 per cent. However, since producer prices in the OECD countries are lower, the effect of agricultural trade liberalisation is to lower technological progress in these countries, in effect, transferring the productivity gains to developing countries. Despite increased losses in some of the OECD countries from the movement of technological gains from developed to developing countries, the world as a whole is better off, with the losses of rural households in the OECD countries more than offset by the gains elsewhere.

Besides demonstrating the enormous gains from freer trade, the RUNS model has also shown the substantial impact that liberalisation in the former Soviet Union could have on agricultural markets. Unilateral full price liberalisation and removal of input subsidies in the FSU would cause a fall in most world agricultural prices. The removal of the large consumer subsidies results, in particular, in a decline of meat and dairy product consumption while the elimination of producer distortion leads to only minor changes in domestic production. From the base run, imports into the FSU fall by about $24 billion as a result of domestic liberalisation. When the elimination of processing and distribution losses is added to the initial liberalisation exercise, imports decline further, to about $3 billion. Conceivably, therefore, with domestic productivity increases the former Soviet Union could become an exporter. However, these scenarios would change dramatically if the reforms result in a recovery of overall income growth and hence in food consumption. OECD country and developing country exporters of food products for this reason alone have a strong interest in the recovery of income growth in the FSU. Foreign assistance to the FSU is, in essence, an excellent policy for promoting agricultural exports of OECD countries.

Many developing countries have learned from hard experience that they cannot afford subsidies and distortions. Trade liberalisation, especially in the reduction of the coverage of quantitative restrictions, has been widespread in developing countries, with 60 countries lowering barriers to imports (In ten years, a World Bank index of trade openness has increased by 120 per cent).[1] Their future depends on a standardized system of international trade like that being offered by the Uruguay Round of the GATT. This book has shown that industrial countries can make a substantial contribution to their own, and equally significantly, to developing country and global development by following through on their Punta del Este commitment to "halt and reverse protectionism and to remove distortions to trade". The dismal alternative is to leave in place a world trading system that violates the principles of the market system which they profess and under which the OECD economies have prospered. This would deprive their citizens and those of non-OECD countries of potential higher employment and income — in reality, the prospects for full economic development, and with it, greater social harmony.

Note

1. See "Global Economic Prospects and the Developing Countries", April 1992, World Bank, Washington, D.C.

Bibliography

ADELMAN, I., J.-M. BURNIAUX and J. WAELBROECK (1989), "Agricultural Development-led Industrialisation in a Global Perspective", in Williamson and Panchamuki, (eds), *The Balance between Industry and Agriculture in Economic Development*, Macmillan Press in association with the International Economic Association.

ADELMAN, I. and S. ROBINSON (1978), *Income Distribution Policies in Developing Countries: A Case Study for Korea*, Oxford University Press, Oxford.

AKIYAMA, T. and D. LARSON (1989), "Recent Trends and Prospects for Agricultural Commodity Exports in Sub-Saharan Africa", *Working Paper 348*, World Bank, Washington, D.C.

AKIYAMA, T. (1988), "Cocoa and Coffee Pricing Policies in Côte d'Ivoire," PRE *Working Paper No. 64*, International Economics Department, World Bank, August, Washington, D.C.

ALSTON, J.M. and P.G. PARDEY (1991), "Technical Change, Constraints and Incentives: The Damaging Consequences of Getting Policies Wrong", paper presented at the conference on "Agricultural Technology: Current Policy Issues for the International Community and the World Bank", Airlie House, 21-23 October, Virginia.

ANDERSON, K. and R. BLACKHURST (eds) (1992), *The Greening of World Trade Issues*, Harvester, London.

ANDERSON, K. and R. TYERS (1990), "How Developing Countries Could Gain from Agricultural Trade Liberalization in the Uruguay Round", in Goldin and Knudsen, (eds) *Agricultural Trade Liberalization: Implications for Developing Countries*, OECD, Paris and World Bank, Washington, D.C.

ARMINGTON, P. (1969), "A Theory of Demand for Products Distinguished by Place of Production," *IMF Staff Papers*, Vol. 16, pp. 159-78.

ARMINGTON, P. (1991), "A Macro-closure Rule for RUNS", mimeo, IECAP, World Bank, July, Washington, D.C.

ARTUS, P., E. BLEUZE , F. LEGROS and J.P. NICOLAÏ (1989), "Epargne des ménages en France et fiscalité (1970-1988)", paper prepared for the AEA Colloquium on Modelling Fiscal Policy, 30 November-1 December, Rome.

BALASSA, B. (1971), *The Structure of Protection in Developing Countries*, The Johns Hopkins University Press, Baltimore.

BALASSA, B. (1987), "The Adding-Up Problem", mimeo, printed in 1989, *Banca Nazionale del Lavoro Quarterly Review*, No. 168, March.

BALASSA, B. (1990), "Incentive Policies and Export Performance in Sub-Saharan Africa", *World Development,* 18, 3, pp. 383-391.

BALLARD, C. (1990), "Marginal Welfare Cost Calculations", *Journal of Public Economics*, 41:263-76.

BANURI, T. (1991), *Economic Liberalisation: No Panacea*, Clarendon Press, Oxford.

BARRO, Robert J. and Herschel I. GROSSMAN (1971), "A General Disequilibrium Model of Income and Employment", *American Economic Review*, 61, 82-93.

BARRO, Robert J. and Herschel I. GROSSMAN (1976), *Money, Employment and Inflation*, Cambridge University Press, London.

BATEMAN, M.J. *et al.* (1990), "Ghana's Cocoa Pricing Policy", *Working Paper WPS* 429, World Bank, Washington, D.C.

BERTHÉLEMY, J.C. and C. MORRISSON (1989), *Agricultural Development in Africa and the Supply of Manufactured Goods*, OECD Development Centre Studies, Paris.

BHALLA, S. (1991), "Sri Lanka", in A.O. Krueger, M. Schiff and A. Valdés (eds), *The Political Economy of Agricultural Pricing Policy*, World Bank, Washington, D.C.

BHAGWATI, J.M. (1978a), *Anatomy and Consequences of Exchange Control Regimes*, Ballinger/NBER, Cambridge.

BHAGWATI, J.N. (1978b), *Foreign Trade Regimes and Economic Development: Anatomy and Consequences of Exchange Control Regimes*, Ballinger/NBER, Cambridge.

BHAGWATI, J.N. (1988), "Export-promoting Trade Strategy: Issues and Evidence", *World Bank Research Observer*, Vol. 3, No. 1, pp. 27-57.

BINSWANGER, H.P. and V.W. RUTTAN (1978), *Induced Innovation: Technology, Institutions and Development*, The Johns Hopkins University Press, Baltimore.

BLANDFORD, D. (1990), "The Costs of Agricultural Protection and the Difference Free Trade Would Make", in F. Sanderson (ed.), *Agricultural Protectionism in the Industrial World*, Resources for the Future, Washington, D.C.

BOVENBERG, L. (1989), "The Integration of Macro and Micro Relations in Dynamic Policy Models: The Case of Saving and Investment Behaviour", International Institute of Public Finance, 45th Congress, 28-31 August, Buenos Aires.

BRANDÃO, A.S.P., T.W. HERTEL and A. CAMPOS (1991), "The Implications of International Trade Liberalization for Brazilian Agriculture: A General Equilibrium Analysis", AGRAP, World Bank, Washington, D.C.

BRANDÃO, A., M. TSIGAS, D. VAN DER MENSBRUGGHE and I. GOLDIN (1992), "Agricultural Productivity Growth and Trade Liberalisation: A General Equilibrium Approach", paper presented at a joint OECD Development Centre/World Bank Workshop, 5-7 February, Washington, D.C.

BROWN, D.K. (1987), "Tariffs, the Terms of Trade and Natural Product Differentiation," *The Journal of Policy Modeling*, (Autumn), pp. 503-526.

BROWN, M. and I. GOLDIN (1992), *The Future of Agriculture: Developing Country Implications*, OECD Development Centre Studies, Paris.

BURINGH, P., H.D.J. VAN HEEMST and G.J. STARING (1975), *Computation of the Absolute Maximum Food Production of the World*, Agricultural University of Wageningen.

BURNIAUX, J.-M. (1987), *Le Radeau de la Méduse : Analyse des dilemmes alimentaires*, Economica, Paris.

BURNIAUX, J.-M., F. DELORME, I. LIENERT and J. MARTIN (1990), "WALRAS — A Multi-Sector, Multi-Country Applied General Equilibrium Model for Quantifying the Economy-Wide Effects of Agricultural Policies", *OECD Economic Studies*, No. 13, pp. 69-102, Paris.

BURNIAUX, J.-M., D. VAN DER MENSBRUGGHE and J. WAELBROECK (1990), "The Food Gap of the Developing World: A General Equilibrium Modelling Approach", in Goldin and Knudsen (eds), *Agricultural Trade Liberalization: Implications for Developing Countries*, OECD, Paris and World Bank, Washington, D.C.

BURNIAUX, J.-M. and D. VAN DER MENSBRUGGHE (1991), *Trade Policies in a Global Context: Technical Specification of the Rural/Urban-North/South (RUNS) Applied General Equilibrium Model*, OECD Development Centre Technical Paper No. 48, Paris.

BURNIAUX, J.-M. and J. WAELBROECK (1985), "The Impact of CAP on Developing Countries: A General Equilibrium Analysis", in Stevens and Verloren van Themaat (eds), *Pressure Groups, Policies and Development, EEC and the Third World: A Survey 5*, Hodder and Stoughton, London.

BURNIAUX, J.-M. (1989), "Intersectoral Effects of CAP Trade Liberalization", in Tarditi *et al.*, (eds), *Agricultural Trade Liberalization and the European Community*, Clarendon Press, Oxford.

CARRIN, G., J. W. GUNNING and J. WAELBROECK (1983), "A General Equilibrium Model for the World Economy: Some Preliminary Results", in B. Hickman (ed.), *Global International Economic Models*, Norh Holland, Amsterdam.

CEPAL REVIEW (1987), Special Issue on Structural Adjustment and Agriculture in Latin America, No. 33, December.

CEPII (1988), "CHELEM-Banque de Données du CEPII", document de travail No. 88-14, Centre d'Etudes et d'Informations Internationales, décembre, Paris.

CHEETHAM, R., S. GUPTA and A. SCHWARTZ (1979), "The Global Framework", *World Bank Staff Working Paper* No. 355, September.

CHIPMAN, J. and J. MOORE (1980), "Compensating Variation, Consumer's Surplus and Welfare", *American Economic Review*, 70:933-49.

CORNIA, A.C., R. JOLLY and F. STEWART (eds) (1987), *Adjustment with a Human Face: Protecting the Vulnerable and Promoting Growth*, Oxford University Press, Oxford.

CONTRÉ, F. and I. GOLDIN (1990), *Agriculture and the Economic Cycle: An Economic and Econometric Analysis with Special Reference to Brazil*, OECD Development Centre Technical Paper No. 15, Paris.

CONTRÉ, F. and I. GOLDIN (1991), "L'Agriculture en période d'ajustement au Brésil", *Revue Tiers Monde*, 32, 126, avril-juin.

COWITT, P. (1991), *1988-1989 World Currency Yearbook*, International Currency Analysis, Brooklyn, NY.

DEATON, A. and J. MUELLBAUER (1980), *Economics and Consumer Behavior*, Cambridge University Press, Cambridge.

DELGADO, C. and T. TSHIBAKA (eds) (1990), *Structural Change in African Agriculture*, IFPRI, Washington, D.C.

DELORME, F. and D. VAN DER MENSBRUGGHE (1990), "Assessing the Role of Scale Economies and Imperfect Competition in the Context of Agricultural Trade Liberalisation: A Canadian Case Study", *OECD Economic Studies*, No. 13, pp. 205-36.

DERVIS, K., J. DE MELO and S. ROBINSON (1982), *General Equilibrium Models for Development Policy*, A World Bank Research Publication, Cambridge University Press, Cambridge.

DEVARAJAN, S. *et al.* (1991), "External Shocks, Purchasing Power Parity, and the Equilibrium Real Exchange Rate", Department of Agricultural and Resource Economics, *Working Paper* No. 611, University of California, Berkeley.

DIXON, P.B. (1975), *The Theory of Joint Maximization*, Norh Holland, Amsterdam.

DIXON, P.B., P. PARMENTER, J. SUTTON and D. VINCENT (1982), *ORANI: A Multisectoral Model of the Australian Economy*, Norh Holland, Amsterdam.

EDWARDS, S. (1989), *Real Exchange Rates, Devaluation, and Adjustment*, MIT Press, Cambridge.

ECHENIQUE, J. (1989), "Les deux faces du boom agricole", *Problèmes d'Amérique Latine*, 94, 4.

ECONOMIC COMMISSION FOR AFRICA (ECA) (1983), *Perspectives on the Decade*, United Nations, Addis Ababa.

ECONOMIC COMMISSION FOR AFRICA (ECA) (1990), *Statistics and Policies*, United Nations, Addis Ababa.

EC (1991), *The Agricultural Situation in the Community 1990*, EC Commission, Brussels.

EVANS, H.D. (1989a), *Comparative Advantage and Growth: Trade and Development in Theory and Practice*, Harvester-Wheatsheaf Press, Hemmel Hempstead.

EVANS, H.D. (1989b), "Alternative Perspectives on Trade and Development", Chapter 24, in the *Handbook of Development Economics*, Vol. II, edited by H. Chenery, and T.N. Srinivasan, Amsterdam.

EVANS, H.D. (1991), "Visible and Invisible Hands in Trade Policy Reform", in C. Colclough and J. Manor (eds), *States or Markets? Neo-liberalism and the Development Policy Debate*, Oxford University Press, Oxford.

EVANS, D., I. GOLDIN and D. VAN DER MENSBRUGGHE (1992), "Trade Reform and the Small Country Assumption", in Goldin and Winters, (eds), *Open Economies: Structural Adjustment and Agriculture*, Cambridge University Press, Cambridge.

FAINI, R., F. CLAVIJO and A. SENHADJI-SEMLALI (1990b), "The Fallacy of Composition Argument: Does Demand Matter for LDC's Manufacturing Exports?", mimeo.

FERRONI, M., and A. VALDÉS (1991), "Agriculture in the Latin American Open Economy", *Food Policy*, February.

FISCHER, G., K. FROHBERG, M.A. KEYZER and K.S. PARIKH (1988), *Linked National Models: A Tool for International Food Policy Analysis*, International Institute for Applied Systems Analysis (IIASA), Kluwer Academic Publishers, Dordrecht.

FONTAINE, J.-M. (1991), *Fertilizer Use and Structural Adjustment in Sub-Saharan Africa*, Technical Paper No. 49, OECD Development Centre, Paris.

FULGINITI, L.E. and R.K. PERRIN (1991), "Prices and Productivity in Agriculture", mimeo, Department of Economics, Iowa State University, October.

FULLERTON, D. (1991), "Reconciling Recent Estimates of the Marginal Welfare Cost of Taxation", *American Economic Review* 81(1), 302-9.

GALBRAITH, J. and J. BLACK (1938), "The Maintenance of Agricultural Production during a Depression: The Explanations Reviewed", *Journal of Political Economy*, 46, 3.

GENERAL AGREEMENT ON TARIFFS AND TRADE (1986-90), *International Trade Year Book*, GATT, Geneva.

GATT (1986), *Ministerial Declaration of the Uruguay Round*, Doc. 1396, GATT, Geneva.

GATT (1990), *International Trade 89-90*, GATT, Geneva.

GATT (1992a), *Annual Report 1991*, GATT, Geneva.

GATT (1992b), *International Trade 90-91*, GATT, Geneva.

GINSBURGH, V. and J. WAELBROECK (1975a), "A General Equilibrium Models of World Trade, Part 1: Full Format Computation of Economic Equilibria", *Cowles Foundation Discussion Paper* 412, Yale University.

GINSBURGH, V. and J. WAELBROECK (1975b), "A General Equilibrium Model of World Trade, Part 2: The Empirical Specification", *Cowles Foundation Working Paper* 413, Yale University.

GINSBURGH, V. and J. WAELBROECK (1976), "Computational Experience with a Large General Equilibrium Model", in J. and M. Los (eds), *Computing Equilibria: How and Why*, Norh Holland, Amsterdam.

GINSBURGH, V. and J. WAELBROECK (1979), "A Note on the Simultaneous Stability of Tâtonnement Processes for Computing Equilibria", *International Economic Review* 20, 376-380.

GINSBURGH, V. and J. WAELBROECK (1981), *Activity Analysis and General Equilibrium Modelling*,, Norh Holland, Amsterdam.

GODFREY, M. (1985), "Trade and Exchange Rate Policy", *IDS Bulletin*, July, pp. 31-38.

GOLDIN, I. and G. REZENDE (1990), *Agriculture and Economic Crisis: Lessons from Brazil*, OECD Development Centre Studies, Paris.

GOLDIN, I. and O. KNUDSEN (eds) (1990), *Agricultural Trade Liberalization: Implications for Developing Countries*, OECD, Paris and World Bank, Washington, D.C.

GOLDIN, I. and M. BROWN (1991), *The Future of Agriculture: Developing Country Concerns*, OECD Development Centre Studies, Paris.

GOLDIN, I. and D. VAN DER MENSBRUGGHE (1992), *Trade Liberalisation: What's at Stake?*, OECD Development Centre Technical Paper No. 5, Paris.

GOLDIN, I. and A. WINTERS (eds) (1992), *Open Economies: Structural Adjustment and Agriculture*, Cambridge University Press, Cambridge.

GOLDSTEIN, M. (1986), "The Global Effects of Fund-Supported Adjustment Programs", *IMF Occasional Paper* No. 42, IMF, Washington, D.C.

HARRIGAN, J. and P. MOSLEY (1991), "Evaluation of the Impact of World Bank Structural Adjustment Lending 1980-87", *Journal of Development Studies*, Vol. 27, No. 3, April.

HARRIS, J. and M. TODARO (1970), "Migration Unemployment and Development: A Two-Sector Analysis," *American Economic Review*, Vol. 60., pp. 126-42.

HAYAMI, Y. and V.W. RUTTAN (1971), *Agricultural Development: An International Perspective*, The Johns Hopkins University Press, Baltimore.

HAYAMI, Y. and V.W. RUTTAN (1985), *Agricultural Development: An International Perspective*, (revised edition), The Johns Hopkins University Press, Baltimore.

HELPMAN, E. (1978), "The Exact Measure of Welfare Losses which Results from Trade Taxes", *International Economic Review*, 19(1): 157-63.

HERTEL, T.W. (1990), "Agricultural Trade Liberalization and the Developing Countries: A Survey of the Models", in I. Goldin and O. Knudsen (eds), *Agricultural Trade Liberalization: Implications for Developing Countries*, OECD, Paris and World Bank, Washington, D.C.

HICKMAN, B.G. (1973), "A General Linear Model of World Trade", in R.J. Ball (ed.), *International Linkage of National Economic Models*, Norh Holland, Amsterdam.

HICKS, Norman L. (1976), "A Model of Trade and Growth for the Developing World", *European Economic Review*, 7, 239-265.

INTERNATIONAL MONETARY FUND, WORLD BANK, OECD, AND EUROPEAN BANK FOR RECONSTRUCTION AND DEVELOPMENT (1991), *A Study of the Soviet Economy, February*, Washington, D.C., London and Paris.

JANVRY, A. de (1973), "A Socioeconomic Model of Induced Innovations", *Quarterly Journal of Economics*, Vol. LXXXVII, No. 3, August.

JANVRY, A. de, *et al.* (1988), "Rural Development in Latin America", Semanario Internacional la Agricultura Latinoamericana, 1-4 September, Punta de Tralca.

JOHNSON, H.G. (1950-51) "Optimum Welfare and Maximum Revenue Tariffs", *Review of Economic Studies*, 19, 28-36.

KAMINSKY, M. (1988), *Las Agriculturas de los Paises de America Latina y el Caribe en la Crisis Actual*, San Jose, IICA.

KARUNASEKERA, M. (1984), "Export Taxes on Primary Products: A Policy Instrument in International Development", *Commonwealth Economic Papers* No. 19, Commonwealth Secretariat, London.

KING, B.B. (1985), "What is a SAM?", in Pyatt and Round (eds), *Social Accounting Matrices: A Basis for Planning*, World Bank, Washington, D.C.

KING, R. (1992), "Macroeconomic Simulation with the RUNS Model: A Case Study with Fiscal Shocks", mimeo Department of Economics, OECD, Paris.

KOESTER, U., H. SCHAFER and A. VALDÉS (1990), *Demand-Side Constraints and Structural Adjustment in Sub-Saharan African Countries*, IFPRI, Washington, D.C.

KOESTER, U., J.-P. LOY and K. HALLMANN (1992), "Consequences of CAP Reform for Relations with Eastern European Countries", draft paper, prepared for the Commission of the European Community, February, Brussels.

KRUEGER, A.O. (1961), "Export Prospects and Economic Growth", *Economic Journal*, June, pp. 436-42.

KRUEGER, A.O. (1978), *Foreign Trade Regimes and Economic Development: Liberalization Attempts and Consequences*, Ballinger Press/NBER, Cambridge.

KRUEGER, A., M. SCHIFF and A. VALDÉS (eds) (1990), *Economia Politica de las Intervenciones de Precios Agricolas en America Latina*, World Bank, Washington, D.C.

LELE, U. (1975), *The Design of Rural Development: Lessons from Africa*, World Bank, The Johns Hopkins University Press, Baltimore.

LEWIS, W.A. (1980), "The Slowing Down of the Engine of Growth", The Nobel Lecture, *American Economic Review*, Vol. 70, No. 4, pp. 555-564.

LIEFERT, W.M. (1991), "Trade According to Comparative Advantage and Budget Effects for a Traditional or Reforming Centrally Planned Economy: An Application to the USSR", mimeo, Centrally Planned Economies Branch, Economic Research Service, USDA, November, Washington, D.C.

LIEFERT, W.M., R. KOOPMAN and E. COOK (1991), "The Effect of Soviet Agricultural Trade Liberalization on the USSR", mimeo, Agriculture and Trade Analysis Division, Economic Research Service, USDA, November, Washington, D.C.

LINNEMAN, H., J. DE HOOGH, M.A. KEYZER and H.D.J. VAN HEEMST (1979), *Moira: A Model of International Relations in Agriculture*, Norh Holland, Amsterdam.

LIPTON, M. (1987), "Limits of Price Policy for Agriculture: Which Way for the World Bank?", *Development Policy Review*, 5, p. 197-215.

LLUCH, C. (1973), "The Extended Linear Expenditure System", *European Economic Review*, Vol. 4, pp. 21-32.

MABBS-ZENO, C. and B. KRISSOFF (1990), "Tropical Beverages in the GATT", in I. Goldin and O. Knudsen, (eds), *Agricultural Trade Liberalization: Implications for Developing Countries*, OECD, Paris and World Bank, Washington, D.C.

MARTIN, W. (1990), "Modelling the Post-Reform Chinese Economy", *China Working Paper* 90/1, National Centre for Development Studies, Australian National University.

MARTIN, W., O. KNUDSEN, M. TSIGAS and D. VAN DER MENSBRUGGHE (1992), "Implications of Partial Agricultural and Manufacturing Trade Liberalization: Welfare Effects", mimeo, World Bank, Washington, D.C.

MARTIN, W., O. KNUDSEN, M. TSIGAS and D. VAN DER MENSBRUGGHE (1992), "Welfare Implications of Partial Agricultural Liberalization in a Distorted World Economy", paper presented at a joint OECD Development Centre/World Bank Workshop, 5-7 February, Washington, D.C.

McNAMARA, R. (1990), *Africa's Development Crisis*, Africa Leadership Forum, Ottawa.

McKENZIE, G. and I. PEARCE (1976), "Exact Measures of Welfare and the Cost of Living", *Review of Economics and Statistics*, 43.

MELO, J. de and S. ROBINSON (1989), "Product Differentiation and the Treatment of Foreign Trade in Computable General Equilibrium Models of Small Economies", *Journal of International Economics*, Vol. 27, pp. 47-67.

MICHAELY, M. (1986), "The Timing and Sequencing of Trade Policy Reform", in A.M. Chokin and D. Papageorgiou (eds), *Economic Liberalization in Developing Countries*, Blackwell, Oxford.

MKANDAWIRE, T. (1990), *Structural Adjustment and Agrarian Crisis in Africa: A Research Agenda*, Codesria, Dakar.

MUNDLAK, Y. (1979), "Intersectoral Factor Mobility and Agricultural Growth," *IFPRI Research Report* No. 6.

MUNDLAK, Y. and R. HELLINGHAUSEN (1982), "The Intercountry Agricultural Production Function: Another View", *American Journal of Agricultural Economics,* Vol. 64, No. 4, pp. 664-72, November.

ORGANISATION FOR ECONOMIC CO-OPERATION AND DEVELOPMENT (OECD) (1987) *National Policies and Agricultural Trade*, Paris.

OECD (1989), *Agricultural Policies, Markets and Trade: Monitoring and Outlook, 1989*, Paris.

OECD (1990a), *Agricultural Policies, Markets and Trade: Monitoring and Outlook, 1990*, Paris.

OECD (1990b), *Special Issue: Modelling the Effects of Agricultural Policies*, OECD Economic Studies, No. 13, (Winter 1989-1990), Paris.

OECD (1990c), *Reforming Agricultural Policies: Direct Income Support*, Paris.

OECD (1991a), *Technology in a Changing World,* TEP, The Technology/Economy Programme, Paris.

OECD (1991b), *Tables of Producer Subsidy Equivalents and Consumer Subsidy Equivalents: 1979-1990*, Paris.

OECD (1991c), *The Soviet Agro-Food System and Agricultural Trade: Prospects for Reform*, Paris.

OECD (1991d), *Agricultural Policies, Markets and Trade: Monitoring and Outlook, 1991,* Paris.

PANAGARIYA, A. and M. SCHIFF (1990a), "Commodity Exports and Real Income in Africa: A Preliminary Analysis", paper prepared for the World Bank Africa Economic Issues Conference, 4-7 June, Nairobi.

PANAGARIYA, A. and M. SCHIFF (1990b),"Optimum and Revenue Maximising Trade Taxes in a Multicountry Framework", mimeo.

PANAGARIYA, A. and M. SCHIFF (1991), "Taxes Versus Quotas", *PRE Working Paper* No. 756, Country Economics Department, World Bank, August, Washington, D.C.

PAPAGEORGIOU, D., A. CHOKSI and M. MICHAELY (1990-1991), *Liberalizing Foreign Trade in Developing Countries* (7 Volumes), Blackwell, Oxford.

PREBISCH, R. (1950), *The Economic Development of Latin America and its Principle Problems*, United Nations, New York.

PREOBRAZHENSKI, E. (1956), T*he New Economics*, Clarendon Press, Oxford.

PYATT, G. and J.I. ROUND (1985), *Social Accounting Matrices: A Basis for Planning*, World Bank, Washington, D.C.

RIEDEL, J. (1984), "Trade as the Engine of Growth in Developing Countries", revisited, *Economic Journal*, No. 373, Vol. 94, March, pp. 56-73.

RIEDEL, J. (1988), "The Demand for LDC Exports of Manufacturers: Estimates from Hong Kong", *Economic Journal*, Vol. 98, No. 389, March, pp. 38-148.

RIVM (1991), *Sustainable Use of Groundwater: Problems and Threats in the European Community*, National Institute of Public Health and Environmental Protection, The Hague.

ROBINSON, S., M. KILKENNY and K. HANSON (1990), "The USDA/ERS Computable General Equilibrium (CGE) Model of the United States", Staff Report No. AGES9049, Economic Research Service, U.S. Department of Agriculture, Washington, D.C.

ROBINSON, S., M.J. SOULE and S. WEYERBROCK (1992), "Import Demand Functions, Trade Volumes, and Terms of Trade Effects in Multi-Country Trade Models", mimeo, Department of Agricultural and Resource Economics, University of California, Berkeley.

ROE, T.L. and P.G. PARDEY (1991), "Economic Policy and Investment in Rural Public Goods: A Political Economy Perspective", in P.G. Pardey, J. Roseboom and J.R. Anderson (eds), *Agricultural Research Policy: International Quantitative Perspective*, Cambridge University Press, Cambridge.

ROLAND-HOLST, D. W. (1991), *Estimates of Non-Agricultural Trade Control Measures for Applied General Equilibrium Analysis*, mimeo, Department of Economics, Mills College, Oakland, CA.

RUTTAN, V.W. (1982), *Agricultural Research Policy*, University of Minnesota Press, Minneapolis.

SALVATORE, D. and T. HATCHET (1991), "Inward and Outward Oriented Trade Strategies", *Journal of Development Studies*, Vol. 27, No. 3, pp. 1-25.

SCHIFF, M. and A. VALDÉS, *The Political Economy of Agricultural Price Interventions*, Vol. IV, The Johns Hopkins University Press, forthcoming, Baltimore.

SCHULTZ, T. (1945), *Agriculture in an Unstable Economy*, Praeger, New York.

SHONKWILER, J. (1985), "Consumer Surplus Revisited", *American Journal of Agriculture Economics,* 73:2, 410-14.

SHOVEN, J. B. and J. WHALLEY (1984), "Applied General-Equilibrium Models of Taxation and International Trade: An Introduction and Survey," *Journal of Economic Literature,* Vol. XXII(3), pp. 1007-51, September.

SIAMWALLA, A. (1990), "Agricultural Trade Reform, Price Stability, and the Impact on Developing Countries", in N. Islam and A. Valdés (eds), *The GATT Agriculture, and the Developing Countries*, International Food Policy Research Institute, Washington, D.C.

SICHRA, U. (1981), "The FAP Data Bank", in Parikh and Rabar (eds), *Food for All in a Sustainable World*, IIASA Food and Agriculture Program, Status Report Conference, February.

SINGER, H.W. (1950), "The Distribution of Gains between Investing and Borrowing Countries", *American Economic Review*, Vol. 40, No. 2, pp. 473-485.

STEWART, F. (1984), "Recent Theories of International Trade: Some Implications for the South", in H. Kierskowski (ed.), *Monopolistic Competition and International Trade*, Oxford University Press, Oxford.

SYRQUIN, M. and H.B. CHENERY (1989), "Patterns of Development 1950 to 1983", *Discussion Papers* No. 41, World Bank, Washington, D.C.

SUBRAMANIAN, S. (1992), "Trade Liberalisation and Indian Agriculture", in I. Goldin (ed.), *Economic Reform, Trade and Agricultural Development*, forthcoming, Macmillan, London.

THOMAS, V., K. MATIN and J. NASH (1990), "Lessons in Trade Policy Reform", *Policy and Research Series*, No. 10, World Bank, Washington, D.C.

THOMAS, V. and J. NASH (1990), "Trade Policy Reform: Recent Evidence from Theory and Practice", mimeo.

TIMMER, C P., W.P. FALCON and S.R. PEARSON (1983), *Food Policy Analysis*, A World Bank Publication, The Johns Hopkins University Press, Baltimore.

TOWER, E. (1977), "Ranking the Optimum Tariff and the Maximum Revenue Tariff", *Journal of International Economics*, 7, pp. 73-79.

TRELA, I. and J. WHALLEY (1990), "Internal Quota Allocation Schemes and the Costs of the MFA", mimeo, UNCTAD, September, Geneva.

TULUY, H. and B.L. SALINGER (1989), *Trade, Exchange Rate, and Agricultural Pricing Policies in Morocco*, World Bank, Washington, D.C.

TYERS, R. and K. ANDERSON (1989), "Price Elasticities in International Food Trade: Synthetic Estimates from a Global Model," *Journal of Policy Modeling*, 11(3), pp. 345-59.

UNCTAD (1989, 1990), *Trade and Development Report*, United Nations, Geneva.

UNITED NATIONS (1990), *Africa's Commodity Problems: Towards a Solution*, UNCTAD, Geneva.

VALDÉS, A. (1986), *Impact of Trade and Macroeconomic Policies on Agricultural Growth: The South American Experience*, IFPRI, Washington, D.C.

VALDÉS, A. and J. ZIETZ (1980), *Agricultural Protection in OECD Countries: Its Costs to Less-Developed Countries*, Research Report No. 21, IFPRI, Washington, D.C.

VAN DER MENSBRUGGHE, D., J. MARTIN and J.-M. BURNIAUX (1990), "How Robust are WALRAS Results?", *OECD Economic Studies*, No. 13, pp. 173-204.

VARTIA, Y. (1983), "Efficient Methods of Measuring Welfare Change and Compensated Income in Terms of Ordinary Demand Functions", *Econometrica*, 51:1, 79-98.

WAELBROECK, J. and S. GUPTA (1984), "World Bank Modelling, a Survey of Developments", in E. Gahan (ed.), *Proceedings of the Fourth Input Output Conference*, UNIDO, Vienna.

WEBB, S.H. (1991), "China's Agricultural Commodity Policies in the 1980's", *Agriculture and Trade Report: China*, pp. 38-45, RS-91-3, ERS, USDA, July, Washington, D.C.

WEBB, A.J., M. LOPEZ and R. PENN (1990), "Estimates of Producer and Consumer Subsidy Equivalents", *Statistical Bulletin*, No. 803, ERS, USDA, April, Washington, D.C.

WHITBY, M. (1991), "The CAP and the Countryside", in C. Ritson and D. Harvey (eds), *The Common Agricultural Policy and the World Economy*, CAB, Oxford.

WILLIG, R. (1976), "Consumer's Surplus Without Apology", *American Economic Review*, 66: 589-97, 1976.

WORLD BANK (1987), *World Bank Development Report, 1987: World Economic Recession and Prospects for Recovery*, Oxford University Press, Oxford.

WORLD BANK (1988), "Adjustment Lending: An Evaluation of Ten Years Experience", *Policy and Research Series*, No. 1, World Bank, Washington, D.C.

WORLD BANK (1989), *Africa's Adjustment and Growth in the 1980s*, World Bank and UNDP, Washington, D.C.

WORLD BANK (1990a), *The Long-Term Perspective Study of Sub-Saharan Africa*, World Bank, Washington, D.C.

WORLD BANK (1990b), *Brazilian Agricultural Sector Review: Policies and Prospects*, World Bank, July, Washington, D.C.

WORLD BANK (1990c), "Adjustment Lending Policies for Sustainable Growth", *Policy Research Series*, No. 14, World Bank, Washington, D.C.

ZIETZ, J. and A. VALDÉS (1989), "Agriculture in the GATT: An Analysis of Alternative Approaches to Reform", International Food Policy Research Institute (IFPRI), *Research Report* No. 70, November.

MAIN SALES OUTLETS OF OECD PUBLICATIONS
PRINCIPAUX POINTS DE VENTE DES PUBLICATIONS DE L'OCDE

ARGENTINA – ARGENTINE
Carlos Hirsch S.R.L.
Galería Güemes, Florida 165, 4° Piso
1333 Buenos Aires Tel. (1) 331.1787 y 331.2391
Telefax: (1) 331.1787

AUSTRALIA – AUSTRALIE
D.A. Information Services
648 Whitehorse Road, P.O.B 163
Mitcham, Victoria 3132 Tel. (03) 873.4411
Telefax: (03) 873.5679

AUSTRIA – AUTRICHE
Gerold & Co.
Graben 31
Wien I Tel. (0222) 533.50.14

BELGIUM – BELGIQUE
Jean De Lannoy
Avenue du Roi 202
B-1060 Bruxelles Tel. (02) 538.51.69/538.08.41
Telefax: (02) 538.08.41

CANADA
Renouf Publishing Company Ltd.
1294 Algoma Road
Ottawa, ON K1B 3W8 Tel. (613) 741.4333
Telefax: (613) 741.5439

Stores:
61 Sparks Street
Ottawa, ON K1P 5R1 Tel. (613) 238.8985
211 Yonge Street
Toronto, ON M5B 1M4 Tel. (416) 363.3171
Telefax: (416)363.59.63

Les Éditions La Liberté Inc.
3020 Chemin Sainte-Foy
Sainte-Foy, PQ G1X 3V6 Tel. (418) 658.3763
Telefax: (418) 658.3763

Federal Publications Inc.
Suite 103, 388 King Street W
Toronto, ON M5V 1K2 Tel. (416) 581.1552
Telefax: (416) 581.1743

Les Publications Fédérales
1185 Université
Montréal, QC H3B 3A7 Tel. (514) 954.1633
Telefax : (514) 954.1635

CHINA – CHINE
China National Publications Import
Export Corporation (CNPIEC)
16 Gongti E. Road, Chaoyang District
P.O. Box 88 or 50
Beijing 100704 PR Tel. (01) 506.6688
Telefax: (01) 506.3101

DENMARK – DANEMARK
Munksgaard Export and Subscription Service
35, Nørre Søgade, P.O. Box 2148
DK-1016 København K Tel. (33) 12.85.70
Telefax: (33) 12.93.87

FINLAND – FINLANDE
Akateeminen Kirjakauppa
Keskuskatu 1, P.O. Box 128
00100 Helsinki

Subscription Services/Agence d'abonnements :
P.O. Box 23
00371 Helsinki Tel. (358 0) 12141
Telefax: (358 0) 121.4450

FRANCE
OECD/OCDE
Mail Orders/Commandes par correspondance:
2, rue André-Pascal
75775 Paris Cedex 16 Tel. (33-1) 45.24.82.00
Telefax: (33-1) 45.24.81.76 or (33-1) 45.24.85.00
Telex: 640048 OCDE

OECD Bookshop/Librairie de l'OCDE :
33, rue Octave-Feuillet
75016 Paris Tel. (33-1) 45.24.81.67
(33-1) 45.24.81.81

Documentation Française
29, quai Voltaire
75007 Paris Tel. 40.15.70.00

Gibert Jeune (Droit-Économie)
6, place Saint-Michel
75006 Paris Tel. 43.25.91.19

Librairie du Commerce International
10, avenue d'Iéna
75016 Paris Tel. 40.73.34.60

Librairie Dunod
Université Paris-Dauphine
Place du Maréchal de Lattre de Tassigny
75016 Paris Tel. (1) 44.05.40.13

Librairie Lavoisier
11, rue Lavoisier
75008 Paris Tel. 42.65.39.95

Librairie L.G.D.J. - Montchrestien
20, rue Soufflot
75005 Paris Tel. 46.33.89.85

Librairie des Sciences Politiques
30, rue Saint-Guillaume
75007 Paris Tel. 45.48.36.02

P.U.F.
49, boulevard Saint-Michel
75005 Paris Tel. 43.25.83.40

Librairie de l'Université
12a, rue Nazareth
13100 Aix-en-Provence Tel. (16) 42.26.18.08

Documentation Française
165, rue Garibaldi
69003 Lyon Tel. (16) 78.63.32.23

Librairie Decitre
29, place Bellecour
69002 Lyon Tel. (16) 72.40.54.54

GERMANY – ALLEMAGNE
OECD Publications and Information Centre
August-Bebel-Allee 6
D-53175 Bonn 2 Tel. (0228) 959.120
Telefax: (0228) 959.12.17

GREECE – GRÈCE
Librairie Kauffmann
Mavrokordatou 9
106 78 Athens Tel. (01) 32.55.321
Telefax: (01) 36.33.967

HONG-KONG
Swindon Book Co. Ltd.
13–15 Lock Road
Kowloon, Hong Kong Tel. 366.80.31
Telefax: 739.49.75

HUNGARY – HONGRIE
Euro Info Service
POB 1271
1464 Budapest Tel. (1) 111.62.16
Telefax : (1) 111.60.61

ICELAND – ISLANDE
Mál Mog Menning
Laugavegi 18, Pósthólf 392
121 Reykjavik Tel. 162.35.23

INDIA – INDE
Oxford Book and Stationery Co.
Scindia House
New Delhi 110001 Tel.(11) 331.5896/5308
Telefax: (11) 332.5993

17 Park Street
Calcutta 700016 Tel. 240832

INDONESIA – INDONÉSIE
Pdii-Lipi
P.O. Box 269/JKSMG/88
Jakarta 12790 Tel. 583467
Telex: 62 875

IRELAND – IRLANDE
TDC Publishers – Library Suppliers
12 North Frederick Street
Dublin 1 Tel. (01) 874.48.35
Telefax: (01) 874.84.16

ISRAEL
Electronic Publications only
Publications électroniques seulement
Sophist Systems Ltd.
71 Allenby Street
Tel-Aviv 65134 Tel. 3-29.00.21
Telefax: 3-29.92.39

ITALY – ITALIE
Libreria Commissionaria Sansoni
Via Duca di Calabria 1/1
50125 Firenze Tel. (055) 64.54.15
Telefax: (055) 64.12.57

Via Bartolini 29
20155 Milano Tel. (02) 36.50.83

Editrice e Libreria Herder
Piazza Montecitorio 120
00186 Roma Tel. 679.46.28
Telefax: 678.47.51

Libreria Hoepli
Via Hoepli 5
20121 Milano Tel. (02) 86.54.46
Telefax: (02) 805.28.86

Libreria Scientifica
Dott. Lucio de Biasio 'Aeiou'
Via Coronelli, 6
20146 Milano Tel. (02) 48.95.45.52
Telefax: (02) 48.95.45.48

JAPAN – JAPON
OECD Publications and Information Centre
Landic Akasaka Building
2-3-4 Akasaka, Minato-ku
Tokyo 107 Tel. (81.3) 3586.2016
Telefax: (81.3) 3584.7929

KOREA – CORÉE
Kyobo Book Centre Co. Ltd.
P.O. Box 1658, Kwang Hwa Moon
Seoul Tel. 730.78.91
Telefax: 735.00.30

MALAYSIA – MALAISIE
Co-operative Bookshop Ltd.
University of Malaya
P.O. Box 1127, Jalan Pantai Baru
59700 Kuala Lumpur
Malaysia Tel. 756.5000/756.5425
Telefax: 757.3661

MEXICO – MEXIQUE
Revistas y Periodicos Internacionales S.A. de C.V.
Florencia 57 - 1004
Mexico, D.F. 06600 Tel. 207.81.00
Telefax : 208.39.79

NETHERLANDS – PAYS-BAS
SDU Uitgeverij
Christoffel Plantijnstraat 2
Postbus 20014
2500 EA's-Gravenhage Tel. (070 3) 78.99.11
Voor bestellingen: Tel. (070 3) 78.98.80
Telefax: (070 3) 47.63.51

**NEW ZEALAND
NOUVELLE-ZÉLANDE**
Legislation Services
P.O. Box 12418
Thorndon, Wellington Tel. (04) 496.5652
Telefax: (04) 496.5698

NORWAY – NORVÈGE
Narvesen Info Center – NIC
Bertrand Narvesens vei 2
P.O. Box 6125 Etterstad
0602 Oslo 6 Tel. (022) 57.33.00
Telefax: (022) 68.19.01

PAKISTAN
Mirza Book Agency
65 Shahrah Quaid-E-Azam
Lahore 54000 Tel. (42) 353.601
Telefax: (42) 231.730

PHILIPPINE – PHILIPPINES
International Book Center
5th Floor, Filipinas Life Bldg.
Ayala Avenue
Metro Manila Tel. 81.96.76
Telex 23312 RHP PH

PORTUGAL
Livraria Portugal
Rua do Carmo 70-74
Apart. 2681
1200 Lisboa Tel.: (01) 347.49.82/5
Telefax: (01) 347.02.64

SINGAPORE – SINGAPOUR
Information Publications Pte. Ltd.
41, Kallang Pudding, No. 04-03
Singapore 1334 Tel. 741.5166
Telefax: 742.9356

SPAIN – ESPAGNE
Mundi-Prensa Libros S.A.
Castelló 37, Apartado 1223
Madrid 28001 Tel. (91) 431.33.99
Telefax: (91) 575.39.98

Libreria Internacional AEDOS
Consejo de Ciento 391
08009 – Barcelona Tel. (93) 488.30.09
Telefax: (93) 487.76.59

Llibreria de la Generalitat
Palau Moja
Rambla dels Estudis, 118
08002 – Barcelona
(Subscripcions) Tel. (93) 318.80.12
(Publicacions) Tel. (93) 302.67.23
Telefax: (93) 412.18.54

SRI LANKA
Centre for Policy Research
c/o Colombo Agencies Ltd.
No. 300-304, Galle Road
Colombo 3 Tel. (1) 574240, 573551-2
Telefax: (1) 575394, 510711

SWEDEN – SUÈDE
Fritzes Information Center
Box 16356
Regeringsgatan 12
106 47 Stockholm Tel. (08) 690.90.90
Telefax: (08) 20.50.21

Subscription Agency/Agence d'abonnements :
Wennergren-Williams Info AB
P.O. Box 1305
171 25 Solna Tel. (08) 705.97.50
Téléfax : (08) 27.00.71

SWITZERLAND – SUISSE
Maditec S.A. (Books and Periodicals - Livres et périodiques)
Chemin des Palettes 4
Case postale 266
1020 Renens Tel. (021) 635.08.65
Telefax: (021) 635.07.80

Librairie Payot S.A.
4, place Pépinet
CP 3212
1002 Lausanne Tel. (021) 341.33.48
Telefax: (021) 341.33.45

Librairie Unilivres
6, rue de Candolle
1205 Genève Tel. (022) 320.26.23
Telefax: (022) 329.73.18

Subscription Agency/Agence d'abonnements :
Dynapresse Marketing S.A.
38 avenue Vibert
1227 Carouge Tel.: (022) 308.07.89
Telefax : (022) 308.07.99

See also – Voir aussi :
OECD Publications and Information Centre
August-Bebel-Allee 6
D-53175 Bonn 2 (Germany) Tel. (0228) 959.120
Telefax: (0228) 959.12.17

TAIWAN – FORMOSE
Good Faith Worldwide Int'l. Co. Ltd.
9th Floor, No. 118, Sec. 2
Chung Hsiao E. Road
Taipei Tel. (02) 391.7396/391.7397
Telefax: (02) 394.9176

THAILAND – THAÏLANDE
Suksit Siam Co. Ltd.
113, 115 Fuang Nakhon Rd.
Opp. Wat Rajbopith
Bangkok 10200 Tel. (662) 225.9531/2
Telefax: (662) 222.5188

TURKEY – TURQUIE
Kültür Yayinlari Is-Türk Ltd. Sti.
Atatürk Bulvari No. 191/Kat 13
Kavaklidere/Ankara Tel. 428.11.40 Ext. 2458
Dolmabahce Cad. No. 29
Besiktas/Istanbul Tel. 260.71.88
Telex: 43482B

UNITED KINGDOM – ROYAUME-UNI
HMSO
Gen. enquiries Tel. (071) 873 0011
Postal orders only:
P.O. Box 276, London SW8 5DT
Personal Callers HMSO Bookshop
49 High Holborn, London WC1V 6HB
Telefax: (071) 873 8200
Branches at: Belfast, Birmingham, Bristol, Edinburgh, Manchester

UNITED STATES – ÉTATS-UNIS
OECD Publications and Information Centre
2001 L Street N.W., Suite 700
Washington, D.C. 20036-4910 Tel. (202) 785.6323
Telefax: (202) 785.0350

VENEZUELA
Libreria del Este
Avda F. Miranda 52, Aptdo. 60337
Edificio Galipán
Caracas 106 Tel. 951.1705/951.2307/951.1297
Telegram: Libreste Caracas

Subscription to OECD periodicals may also be placed through main subscription agencies.

Les abonnements aux publications périodiques de l'OCDE peuvent être souscrits auprès des principales agences d'abonnement.

Orders and inquiries from countries where Distributors have not yet been appointed should be sent to: OECD Publications Service, 2 rue André-Pascal, 75775 Paris Cedex 16, France.

Les commandes provenant de pays où l'OCDE n'a pas encore désigné de distributeur devraient être adressées à : OCDE, Service des Publications, 2, rue André-Pascal, 75775 Paris Cedex 16, France.

07-1993

Printed on behalf of the
Organisation for Economic Co-operation and Development
and the World Bank by
OECD PUBLICATIONS, 2 rue André-Pascal, 75775 PARIS CEDEX 16
PRINTED IN FRANCE
(41 93 10 1) ISBN 92-64-13962-1 - No. 46647 1993
ISBN 0-8213-2633-3